ACTS OF THE APOSTLES

Tom O'Reilly ssc

ACTS OF THE APOSTLES

A READING FOR MISSION TODAY

VERITAS

First published 2021 by
Veritas Publications
7–8 Lower Abbey Street
Dublin 1
Ireland
publications@veritas.ie
www.veritas.ie

ISBN 978 1 84730 980 8

Copyright © Tom O'Reilly ssc, 2021

10 9 8 7 6 5 4 3 2 1

*The material in this publication is protected by copyright law. Except as
may be permitted by law, no part of the material may be reproduced
(including by storage in a retrieval system) or transmitted in any form or
by any means, adapted, rented or lent without the written permission of
the copyright owners. Applications for permissions should be addressed to
the publisher.*

A catalogue record for this book is available from the British Library.

Cover design by Colette Dower, Veritas Publications
Printed in the Republic of Ireland by SPRINT-print, Dublin

*Veritas books are printed on paper made from the wood pulp of managed
forests. For every tree felled, at least one tree is planted, thereby renewing
natural resources.*

In gratitude to my family for their loving support, and my Columban colleagues for their unfailing companionship in walking the missionary path together.

CONTENTS

Preface 13

Introduction 15

CHAPTER I: LUKE AND HIS WRITINGS 25
Luke's Two-Volume Work 25
Luke and his Communities 27
Luke, a Biblical Historian 31
Luke, a Literary Artist 34
Reflection 44

CHAPTER 2: LAUNCHING THE MISSION
(ACTS 1:1–2:41) 51
Building a Bridge (Acts 1:1-11) 52
The Expectant Disciples (Acts 1:12-14) 55
Restoration of the Twelve (Acts 1:15-26) 56
The Pentecost Experience (Acts 2:1-41) 57
        Pentecost Event (Acts 2:1-13) 58
        Peter's Pentecost Speech (Acts 2:14-41) 61
Reflection on Acts 1:1–2:41 65

CHAPTER 3: MISSION AND COMMUNITY IN JERUSALEM
(ACTS 2:42–8:3) 71

Overview 71
First Major Summary (Acts 2:42-47) 73
Cure of the Lame Man (Acts 3:1-26) 74
Arrest and Trial of Peter and John (Acts 4:1-22) 77
Discerning Prayer of the Community (Acts 4:23-31) 79
Second Major Summary (Acts 4:32-35) 81
Stories of Barnabas, Ananias and Sapphira
    (Acts 4:36–5:11) 82
Third Major Summary (Acts 5:12-16) 83
Arrest and Trial of all the Apostles (Acts 5:17-42) 83
Appointment of the Seven (Acts 6:1-7) 86
Stephen's Mission, Arrest, Trial and Death (Acts 6:8–8:3) . .89
    Stephen's Mission, Arrest and Trial (Acts 6:8-15) . . .89
    Stephen's Speech (Acts 7:1-53) 90
    Stephen's Martyrdom (Acts 7:54–8:3) 96
Reflection on Acts 2:42–8:3 97

CHAPTER 4: MISSION IN JUDEA AND SAMARIA
(ACTS 8:4–11:18) 105

Philip's Mission in Samaria and Judea (Acts 8:4-40) 105
    Philip's Mission in Samaria (Acts 8:4-25) 106
    Conversion of the Ethiopian Eunuch
    (Acts 8:26-40) 110
Saul's Conversion, Initial Preaching and Contact
    with the Apostles (Acts 9:1-31) 112
    Saul's Conversion (Acts 9:1-19a) 113
    Saul's Initial Mission in Damascus (Acts 9:19b-25) . .117
    Saul's Visit to Jerusalem (Acts 9:26-31) 118
Peter's Judean Mission and the Conversion of Cornelius'
    Household (Acts 9:32–11:18) 119
    Peter's Mission in the Coastal Area of Judea
    (Acts 9:32-43) 120
    The Cornelius Episode (Acts 10:1–11:18) 121
Reflection on Acts 8:4–11:18 131

CHAPTER 5: LAUNCH OF THE GENTILE MISSION
(ACTS 11:19–15:35) 141

Overview 141
Foundation of the Church in Antioch (Acts 11:19-30) . .142
Peter's Escape from Prison and Herod's Death
    (Acts 12:1-25) 145
Mission from Antioch to Cyprus and Asia Minor
    (Acts 13:1–14:28) 150
    Commissioning of Barnabas and Saul (Acts 13:1-3) . .150
    Mission in Cyprus (Acts 13:4-12) 151
    Mission in Antioch of Pisidia (Acts 13:13-52) 153
    Mission in Iconium, Lystra and Derbe (Acts 14:1-20) . .159
    Return to Antioch in Syria (Acts 14:21-28) 161
The Council of Jerusalem (Acts 15:1-35) 163
    Historical Note on Acts 15:1-35 163
    Luke's Message in Acts 15:1-35 165
Reflection on Acts 11:19–15:35 171

CHAPTER 6: MAJOR MISSIONS OF PAUL (1)
(ACTS 15:36–18:22) 181

Mission in Macedonia (Acts 15:36–17:15) 182
    On the Way to Macedonia (Acts 15:36–16:10) 182
    Mission in Philippi (Acts 16:11-40) 184
    Mission in Thessalonica (Acts 17:1-9) 188
    Mission in Beroea (Acts 17:10-15) 189
Mission in Achaia (Acts 17:16–18:17) 189
    Mission in Athens (Acts 17:16-34) 190
    Mission in Corinth (Acts 18:1-17) 198
Paul's Visit to Antioch via Jerusalem (Acts 18:18-22) . . .201
Reflection on Acts 15:36–18:22 202

CHAPTER 7: MAJOR MISSIONS OF PAUL (2)
(ACTS 18:24–21:16) 211

Mission in Ephesus (Acts 18:24–19:41) 211
    Mission of Apollos (Acts 18:24-28) 212
    Meeting with Baptist's Disciples (Acts 19:1-7) 213
    Success of Mission to Jews and Greeks
        in Ephesus (Acts 19:8-20) 214
    Paul's Future Plans (Acts 19:21-22) 216
    Riot of the Silversmiths in Ephesus (Acts 19:23-41) . .216
Paul's Farewell Journey and Orientation towards
    Jerusalem (Acts 20:1–21:16) .218
    From Ephesus to Macedonia and on to Troas
        (Acts 20:1-6) 219
    Farewell Visit to Troas (Acts 20:7-12) 220
    From Troas to Miletus (Acts 20:13-16) 221
    Farewell Discourse to Ephesian Elders
        (Acts 20:17-38) 221
    From Miletus to Jerusalem (Acts 21:1-16) 226
Reflection on Acts 18:24–21:16 228

CHAPTER 8: WITNESS IN JERUSALEM
(ACTS 21:17–23:35) 235

Overview 235
Paul's Reception by the Jerusalem Church
    (Acts 21:17-26) 237
Paul's Arrest in the Temple (Acts 21:27-39) 239
Paul's Speech in the Temple (Acts 21:40–22:29) 241
Paul before the Sanhedrin (Acts 22:30–23:11) 246
Paul's Transfer to Caesarea (Acts 23:12-35) 249
Reflection on Acts 21:17–23:35 251

CHAPTER 9: WITNESS IN CAESAREA
(ACTS 24:1–26:32) 257

Paul before Felix (Acts 24:1-27) 258
Paul before Festus (Acts 25:1-12) 262
Paul before Herod Agrippa II and Festus
    (Acts 25:13–26:32) 264
    Prelude to the Hearing (Acts 25:13-22) 264
    Proceedings at the Hearing (Acts 25:23–26:29) 265
    Result of the Hearing (Acts 26:30-32) 271
Reflection on Acts 24:1–26:32 271

CHAPTER 10: TOWARDS ROME
(ACTS 27:1–28:31) 277

Paul's Journey to Rome (Acts 27:1–28:16) 278
    Paul's Sea Voyage and Shipwreck (Acts 27:1-44) . . .278
    Paul in Malta (Acts 28:1-10) 285
    Paul's Arrival in Rome (Acts 28:11-16) 286
Paul's Witness in Rome (Acts 28:17-31) 288
    First Meeting with Jews in Rome (Acts 28:17-22) . .288
    Second Meeting with Jews in Rome (Acts 28:23-28) . .289
    Paul's Witness to All Comers in Rome
    (Acts 28:30-31) 291
Reflection on Acts 27:1–28:31 293

Further Reading 301

PREFACE

The Acts of the Apostles was the first book of the Bible that I ever read. It featured in the Christian doctrine course in the secondary school that I attended. It was presented as a history of the early Church and we were expected to memorise names, places, events and dates. I was impressed by the exploits of courageous missionaries who covered a lot of ground and endured much hardship in spreading the message of Jesus Christ. I like to think that, at least subconsciously, the story of those missionaries influenced my decision at the end of my secondary education to become a missionary priest.

This present work presupposes that the reader is going through the text of Acts and reflecting on what it might be saying to us today. There is no substitute for personal reading of the biblical text, and an initial reading of Acts from start to finish is recommended to get some sense of the developing story before one looks more closely at individual passages. We each bring our own prior understandings and experiences to this reading, which influence what we look for and what we see in the text. Remember that the text, as the word of God, is also searching us, encouraging us and leading us to a deeper faith commitment as missionary disciples of Jesus Christ. My hope is that my commentary and reflections will facilitate your own engagement with Acts.

I wrote this book during periods of lockdown in 2020 due to the Covid-19 pandemic. Since then, we are realising more and more that our way of life is being turned upside down by this horrific crisis. While acknowledging the tragic effects of the Covid-19 crisis, Pope Francis is also seeing it as a call to re-assess our individual and communal lives. The pandemic has made us more aware of great fault lines in a world driven by individualism, consumerism, exclusion, excessive nationalism, manipulative populism and disregard for the environment. However, throughout the pandemic we are also seeing the great witness of many people spending themselves selflessly in solidarity with suffering humanity. At a time when the human family is experiencing painful fragility and vulnerability, we are being called to actively seek a new way of living together which is focused on the common good, respect for the basic human dignity of each person, care for the most vulnerable, inclusion and participation of all, and protection of the Earth which is our common home. And the Church needs to be to the fore in this, as a sign and instrument of the communion which is God's dream for our world. Pope Francis' vision for the life and mission of the Church today is, in many respects, similar to the vision that the author of the Acts of the Apostles held up for the Christian communities of his day.

I wish to acknowledge my debt to the work of many scholars on Acts, particularly Luke Timothy Johnson, Joseph Fitzmyer, and Robert Tannehill. I'm also most grateful to my Columban colleagues from whom I learned so much about the meaning and practice of mission today. A special word of thanks to Mauricio Silva, whose invitation to give a series of talks in Birmingham at the end of 2019 rekindled my interest in Acts, and to Maurice Hogan who read the manuscript closely and gave me much encouragement and valuable suggestions. Finally, I would like to sincerely thank Colette Dower and others in Veritas who were most kind and helpful in getting the manuscript ready for publication.

Tom O'Reilly ssc
St Columban's, Dalgan Park, Navan
March 2021

INTRODUCTION

For more than fifty years as a Columban missionary, two questions have really engaged me – the meaning of the Bible and the meaning of contemporary mission. Preoccupation with the immediate job in hand often led me to focus on just one of these questions, while giving little attention to the other. However, living through major changes in mission, and learning of new approaches to the interpretation of the Bible, made me realise that my two questions needed to be addressed simultaneously. Bringing questions about mission today to the Bible helped me to see new meaning in the text. At the same time, the text challenged me to respond to the missionary call in a rapidly changing situation, becoming a source of enlightenment and encouragement.

Mission Today

How are we to understand and practise mission today? I joined the Columban missionaries just before the Second Vatican Council (1962-65) when most were saying that mission is about implanting the Church in places where it is not well established for the purpose of saving souls. This Council was the watershed for the development of a new understanding of Catholic mission which was greatly influenced by the experience from 'mission areas'. The years after the Council were both exciting and confusing for missionaries, as they went through a lot of questioning and soul-searching in a time of great transition. Gradually a new model of mission began to emerge.[1] At the risk of oversimplification, we can outline some major elements of this model.

Firstly, there is now a fuller understanding that the salvation proclaimed by Jesus involves more than saving souls for the hereafter. Salvation includes a liberation and transformation in the here and now, affecting not only individuals, but also social structures, cultures, religious traditions and indeed the whole of creation. The Church has a prophetic role to play in our world, standing in solidarity with the poor, the excluded and the exploited earth.

Secondly, the Christian faith has to find expression in the lived experience of every culture, not just Western culture. God's Spirit is already present in peoples' cultures and religious traditions, long before missionaries arrive on the scene. So, along with witnessing to one's own faith in Christ, mission becomes a search for the signs of the Spirit's activity in the situation to which one is sent. Missionaries are learners, called to cooperate with what God is doing, particularly among the poor and the excluded of our world.

Thirdly, the essential missionary nature of the Church means that each local church, no matter how needy, is called to be a sending and receiving church in the service of mission. Mission is no longer a one-way flow from mother churches to daughter churches, but a mutually enriching exchange between sister churches.

Fourthly, the missionary vocation is now seen to be rooted, not in priestly ordination or religious profession, but in our common baptism. Every baptised Christian is a missionary disciple of Jesus Christ, called to live out one's own missionary vocation, along with supporting the missionary vocation of others. Mission needs a partnership of ordained, religious and lay members of the Church, a partnership of equals in which each brings their own distinctive and necessary contribution.

Reflecting on my own grappling with missionary questions over the years, I think of three moments. The first was my experience of mission in Pakistan where I went in 1979 as a member of a small team to open a new Columban mission. It was the first time Columbans were sent on mission to a predominantly Muslim country, so we had few precedents to guide us. We were convinced that we weren't going to Pakistan to convert Muslims to Christianity. But we weren't sure what mission in such a situation might entail. And what would it mean to be on mission among the small pockets of Pakistani Christians who were very poor, uneducated and often marginalised in a Muslim country? Surely, it wasn't a matter of telling them to accept their present lot in the hope of a better life in the hereafter. The second moment was the time I spent as a member of the Columban central leadership team. Visiting Columban missionaries in many different countries was a most enriching experience. And, taking part in countless discussions on mission, I learned to be less dogmatic about the meaning of mission, seeing how one's understanding and practice of mission is very much shaped by one's local situation. The third moment was my experience of being on Columban mission in Ireland and Britain. Previously, Columban operations in these places were aimed at providing personnel and finances for the 'real missions' overseas. But we came to realise that these places were also a locus for our mission and we continually discerned what the shape of that mission might be. Working with Columban lay missionaries and co-workers at this time convinced me of the vital importance of genuine partnership in mission.

Approaches to Biblical Interpretation

How are we to approach the Bible in seeking some answers to the many missionary questions we have today? In the early 1970s, I did post-graduate studies in Scripture at the Pontifical Biblical Institute in Rome, followed by five years teaching in a major seminary. The Second Vatican Council had recently highlighted the vital importance of the word of God for the life and mission of the Church. Catholic exegetes were encouraged to use more critical methods to uncover the life-giving meaning of the sacred text for us. The dominant approach to the study of Scripture at that time was the historical critical method. The focus was put on the *world behind the text*, the historical situations in which the faith traditions developed and were eventually written down. It was assumed that the more one knows about the historical background of the text the more one understands what it really means. The aim was to discover the intention of the original author, though it was recognised that this could not always be done with certainty.

I had a long break from formal study of the Bible during my time in Pakistan and my time on our central leadership team. In 1995, however, I was invited to teach Scripture in the Kimmage Mission Institute, Dublin, which meant a return to the books for me. I was surprised to discover that approaches to the interpretation of the Bible had changed quite a lot from the time I taught in the seminary some seventeen years previously. The historical critical method was still seen as valid and necessary, if we are to avoid fundamentalism and wildly subjective interpretations. However, attention had shifted more and more from *what the text meant* in the past to *what the text means* in the present. The *world before the text*, the world of the contemporary reader's experiences, presuppositions and questions, was seen as a key component in the process of discovering the meaning of the text for today. And the *world of the text*, the way the text was composed and shaped to influence the reader, was also receiving more attention. Whether we realise it or not, in the reading process the text is working on us, drawing us in, and leading us to adopt its vision and values. The text, then, is not just a *window* through which we look to gain information about the past, but it is also a *mirror* which reflects who we are as disciples of Jesus Christ and seeks to bring about our transformation in the present. Though at times I was somewhat confused by the multiplicity of approaches to the text, I came to see them as complementing one another, each contributing valid insights and meaning. It has been said that different methodological approaches could be likened to a set of keys on a ring. The more keys one has the more doors one can open to discover the rich treasury which is the word of God.

Engagement with the Acts of the Apostles

The Kimmage Mission Institute was a consortium set up by missionary groups in Ireland for theological education in the context of contemporary mission. One of my regular courses there was on the Acts of the Apostles, perhaps the most overtly missionary book in the New Testament. In exploring the meaning of Acts, I was struck by the many points of intersection between its story of early Christian mission and the story of mission today. There is much in Acts that reflects and clarifies our missionary experience. Putting our missionary questions to the text and being open to its challenge can enlighten and encourage us in responding to our missionary call.

The main purpose of this present book is to provide a guide for reading the Acts of the Apostles in the context of mission today. I pay little attention to the more academic and historical questions, and focus mainly on insights relevant for contemporary mission. In sharing my own understanding of the text, I am aware that people approaching the text with experiences and questions different from mine will see layers of valid meaning and relevance that I have missed. If that happens, I'm happy that my purpose in writing this book is being fulfilled. My hope is that readers, searching together in the faith community, will find meaning for their own situation and not just be satisfied with my insights. Of course, we must never lose sight of the historical perspective. An effort should be made to discover the meaning of the text in its original setting, which acts as a guide for new meanings when read in different settings. Acts was written in a world which was very different from ours and we can't expect it to provide ready-made answers to all our missionary questions today. But it can stimulate us to search for these answers and often point us in the right direction.

Readers in Mind

For many years I had some involvement in renewal courses at the IMU (Irish Missionary Union) Institute at Dalgan Park, Navan. It was my privilege to reflect on the Scriptures with missionaries on sabbatical and to learn from their rich missionary experience. Perhaps this book can be of some help for people like them. However, I have in mind not only 'professional' missionaries seeking meaning in their changing missionary situation. From Easter to Pentecost each year we hear a reading from the Acts of the Apostles in the celebration of the Eucharist each day. That can be a reminder that all baptised Christians are called to be missionary disciples of the risen Lord in their own situations. And the Scriptures must be at the centre of our common mission. As Pope Francis says,

> The study of the sacred Scriptures must be a door opened to every believer. It is essential that the revealed word radically enrich our catechesis and all efforts to pass on the faith. Evangelisation demands familiarity with God's word, which calls for dioceses, parishes and Catholic associations to provide for a serious ongoing study of the Bible, while encouraging its prayerful individual and communal reading.[2]

From May 2019 to January 2020, Pope Francis gave a series of twenty catecheses on the Acts of the Apostles during his weekly general audiences because of its relevance for the renewal of Church life and mission today. During the Extraordinary Month of Mission (October 2019), intended by Pope Francis to be an occasion for biblical and theological reflection on the Church's mission, I met with a group of mainly lay people in the multicultural city of Birmingham to reflect together on the Acts of the Apostles and its relevance for their various ministries and parish life. Their positive and enthusiastic response, as well as their rich insights, has encouraged me to write this book. My hope is that it may prove useful for such groups coming together to reflect on their mission in the light of the word of God.

Proposed Outline

In reading Acts, I will focus on the developing storyline, having my missionary antennae extended in the hope of tuning into meanings which are relevant for mission today. While the general movement of the story is clear, we should not look for water-tight divisions in Acts. Luke, the good storyteller, interlocks the various parts of his story with great skill. In dealing with one stage of the story, he has the habit of announcing the next stage well in advance.

Chapter 1 sees the Acts of the Apostles as the second part of a two-volume work of Luke and puts it in the wider context of this evangelist's writings. We ask what we can know about Luke and the communities for which he wrote. We look at the kind of history Luke wrote and how he shaped his work as a unified continuous story in a way that draws the readers into it and moves them to play their part in the ongoing mission of Jesus. The main subject of *Chapter 2* is the launch of the missionary Church at Pentecost. This includes a consideration of the way Luke prepares for the Pentecost event by linking the life and mission of Jesus with the life and mission of his Church. *Chapter 3* tells the story of mission in Jerusalem, the centre of the Jewish world. We see how the Spirit is creating a sharing, praying and discerning community. The same Spirit is also empowering the community's bold mission to others in the face of mounting opposition which reaches a climax in the execution of Stephen. *Chapter 4* takes the story of Christian mission beyond Jerusalem to Judea and Samaria. But here we also see how Luke's mind is racing ahead and preparing the ground for the spread of the word of God even further afield to the wider Greco-Roman world. He tells of the conversion of Saul, who is to be the 'vessel of election' to carry the saving word of God not only to Jews, but also to Gentiles. We also hear of the conversion of Cornelius, the event in which God signals and sanctions the Gentile mission.

In *Chapter 5* we treat the launch of the Gentile mission from Antioch, which replaces Jerusalem as the main centre for missionary outreach. The first missionary journey of Paul and Barnabas leads to a major influx of Gentiles into what was a predominantly Jewish Christian Church. This challenges the Church to face basic questions about identity, core beliefs, conditions for entry into the Church and intercultural living. After much disagreement and debate, the Council of Jerusalem, under the guidance of the Spirit, reaches decisions which will have a profound effect on the Church's self-understanding and mission. *Chapters 6 and 7* are about the major missions of Paul, who after the Council of Jerusalem takes centre stage in Luke's ongoing story of Christian mission. Though there were many missionaries in the early Church, Luke focuses almost exclusively on Paul as the one who best exemplifies the Christian call to reach out to the whole world with the Good News of Jesus Christ. *Chapters 8 and 9* focus on Paul the prisoner who is on trial, first in Jerusalem and then in Caesarea. However, his mission continues as his imprisonment and trials become occasions for bold witness to Jesus Christ. Finally, *Chapter 10*, entitled 'Towards Rome,' deals with the climax of Luke's narrative. In fulfilment of his promise and in the face of seemingly insurmountable difficulties, God brings Paul the prisoner to Rome. For Luke, Paul's bold and unhindered preaching at the heart of the known world is a powerful demonstration of God's plan of salvation for all.

Each chapter of this book ends with a reflection which tries to bring together in a mutually enriching way the experience of mission today and the word of God revealed in the Acts of the Apostles. When the early Church was facing fundamental questions at a time of great transition in mission, James, the leader of the Jerusalem community, showed how the Scriptures throw light on the meaning of mission and how the experiences of mission open up new understandings of the Scriptures (see Acts 15:13-18). The same can happen as we reflect on transitions in mission today.[3]

NOTES

[1] Developments in the understanding and practice of mission in the Catholic Church have to be seen in the context of reflections on mission in all Christian churches. See David J. Bosch, *Transforming Mission. Paradigm Shifts in the Theology of Mission,* American Society of Missiology Series (New York: Orbis Books, 1991), which is widely regarded as a classic in mission studies today.

[2] *Evangelii Gaudium. The Joy of the Gospel* (London: Catholic Truth Society, 2013), no. 175.

[3] In the opening chapters of Pope Francis' latest encyclical (*Fratelli Tutti. On Fraternity and Social Friendship* [Dublin: Veritas, 2020]), we find the interplay between the experience of contemporary reality (the signs of the times) and the reading of Scripture. In chapter 1, the Pope gives an overview of the trends in today's closed world which are hindering universal fraternity. Then, in chapter 2, he brings that to a reading of the Lukan Good Samaritan parable, which provides the vision and inspiration for his teaching in the remainder of the encyclical about an open, fraternal world.

CHAPTER 1

LUKE AND HIS WRITINGS

Luke's Two-Volume Work

The Acts of the Apostles, the story of early Christian mission, opens with these words: 'In the first book, Theophilus, I wrote about all that Jesus began to do and teach until the day when he was taken up to heaven, after giving instructions through the Holy Spirit to the apostles whom he had chosen' (Acts 1:1-2).[1] The author tells us that he has already written a book about the mission of Jesus up to the time of his ascension, a mission which began at a particular time but is still unfinished. Even in the opening sentence of Acts we are getting a strong hint that the Spirit-filled Jesus will continue on mission in and through the mission of his followers. The addressee of the present work is Theophilus whose name means 'lover of God'. Some say the author is using a symbolic name and has in mind every Christian disciple to whom his work is addressed. While the message is intended for a wide audience, it is better to see Theophilus as a real person. He may well have been the author's well-to-do patron who facilitated the circulation of his work among Christian communities.

It is not difficult to discover the 'first book' the author is speaking about. The arguments are very strong for saying it is the Gospel of Luke. In the prologue of this Gospel (Lk 1:1-4) Theophilus is again the addressee. There are many words, phrases and stylistic features which occur in the New Testament only in Luke's Gospel and Acts. Some information about Jesus, which is found only in Luke, is found also in

Acts. For instance, only from the third Gospel and Acts do we learn that Jesus was brought before Herod during his passion (Lk 23:7-12; Acts 4:27). The ascension of Jesus is narrated only in these books (Lk 24:50-53; Acts 1:6-11). Furthermore, one finds an obvious parallelism between events in Luke's Gospel and events in Acts, about which we will have more to say below. Finally, there is a basic theological unity between the third Gospel and Acts. Many would say that one overarching theme unifies both books. Again, we will look more closely at this below.

The close relationship between Luke's Gospel and Acts means they are to be read as two parts of one continuous story. Luke intended those who read Acts to have already acquainted themselves with the story in his Gospel. At the end of the Gospel, Jesus tells his disciples to wait for something marvellous to happen, to expect to be clothed with power from on high (Lk 24:49). We are left in a state of suspense and expectation, anxious to know how the story is going to unfold. Most say that Luke wrote a single two-volume work and the two parts were later separated in the order of New Testament writings. Some think Luke wrote Acts as a sequel sometime after he wrote his Gospel. Be that as it may, each one of these books cannot be adequately studied and understood without reference to the other. As John J. Kilgallen puts it,

> The Gospel and Acts complement each other; neither can be fully understood without the other. Luke wrote so that each work needed the other, because his understanding of reality was just like that: the life of Jesus was fully intelligible only by reading about the spread of God's word to the ends of the earth, and what was happening at the ends of the earth was intelligible only when one has read the life of Jesus of Nazareth.[2]

It has been said that to commence reading Acts with little or no knowledge of the Gospel of Luke is like arriving to see the second part of a drama after the intermission. In such a situation, it would help if, during the intermission, one could come across a friend who has been watching the drama from the beginning and can answer a few questions. 'What can you tell me about the identity and background of the playwright? What's the drama all about? What has been happening in the first part of the drama and where are we now in the unfolding plot? Who are the main characters in the drama?' It is to questions like these that we now turn our attention before we immerse ourselves in the drama of Acts itself. Some, who adopt a literary approach to Acts, prefer to leave aside historical questions. However, knowing something about the historical background of the author and original readers can deepen our understanding and appreciation of the work and help us see its relevance for mission today.

Luke and his Communities

Neither the third Gospel nor Acts gives us the name of the author of the two-volume work. Early Church tradition tells us it was Luke. Eusebius, Bishop of Caesarea, (AD 264-349) sums up the tradition about Luke at the end of the third century: Luke was a physician from Antioch in Syria, a companion of Paul, and the writer of a Gospel and the Acts of the Apostles. What Eusebius says about Luke's profession is most probably based on Col 4:14 which speaks of 'Luke, the beloved physician'. Attempts to confirm this by seeking medical language in Luke's writings have met with little success. There is little reason to question Antioch as the place of Luke's origin. The author of Acts certainly has a very good acquaintance with Antioch as an important centre of Christian missionary activity (Acts 11:19-20; 13:1-4; 14:26-28; 15:1-3, 13-40; 18:22-23). The question about Luke being a companion of Paul is debated.

The majority say that Luke was a travelling companion of Paul, for some time at least. Evidence for this is found in the Pauline letters. Along with what Col 4:14 says, Phm 24 numbers Luke among Paul's fellow-workers and in 2 Tm 4:11 we hear the plaintive cry 'Only Luke is with me'. The fact that Luke gives almost exclusive attention to Paul in the second part of Acts is also seen as evidence that he was well acquainted with Paul. In certain passages in the second part of Acts, the author uses the pronoun 'we' in a way that implies he was a companion of Paul on the occasions in question (Acts 16:10-17; 20:5-15; 21:1-8; 27:1–28:16).

Though the arguments for saying that Luke was a companion of Paul are quite compelling, some are not convinced. They see significant discrepancies between the portrayal of Paul in Acts and the image of Paul derived from the latter's own writings, as well as differences between Paul's theology in Acts and his theology in the letters. For instance, the Paul of Acts is a great orator who never writes a letter, who has a much more positive attitude to the law and the Gentiles, and who prefers to focus more on the significance of Jesus' resurrection rather than the saving effects of his death. They regard the 'we' passages in Acts as either the travel diary of someone other than Luke or a literary device to make the narrative more vivid and create a sense of participation for the reader. In response to the arguments put forward by those who deny that Luke was a companion of Paul, it can be said they overlook the many points of convergence between the Paul of Acts and the Paul of the letters. Luke was presenting his own theological vision, rather than reproducing the theology of Paul's letters. Furthermore, if the 'we' passages were taken from the travel diary of someone other than Luke, one would expect them to have a style different from Luke's usual style, which is not the case. So, we can conclude that Luke was an occasional, rather than inseparable, companion of Paul.

Whatever one might say about Luke being a physician, he was certainly an educated person, well versed in the traditions of Israel and in Hellenistic culture. He could write the Greek language very well, at times adapting his style to suit the occasion, and he was quite familiar with Greek literary genres and philosophies. He also had a good knowledge of the Scriptures of Israel, which he quotes in their Greek version (the Septuagint, abbreviated as LXX). As a native Syrian, Luke's own cultural background was Semitic. Most would say he was a Gentile, rather than a Jew. Before he became a Christian disciple he may well have been one of those 'God-fearers' mentioned regularly in the Acts of the Apostles (see, for instance, Acts 10:2; 13:16; 16:14; 17:4, 17; 18:7). These were Gentiles who attached themselves in varying degrees to Judaism, frequented the synagogue, but did not convert fully to Jewish religious practices. When Paul preached the Christian message in synagogues, God-fearers were often the ones who were most responsive.

Luke's Christian community of origin was in Antioch. This great cosmopolitan city ranked third among the cities of the Roman world because of its size and prosperity. It had a mixed population of native Syrians and settlers (for instance, Macedonians, Cretans, Cypriotes, Argives and Jews). So Luke lived in a multi-cultural environment, which would have posed for him the challenges of cross-cultural Christian living and mission.

What can be said of the Christian communities for which Luke wrote? In answering this question we are often at the level of probability and educated guesswork, rather than certainty. With regard to their composition, it is generally agreed that these communities were predominantly Gentile churches with some Jewish members. While there were some well-to-do people in them, the majority belonged to the poorer classes. In writing for these communities in the mid-eighties of the first century, it seems Luke was not addressing local and momentary issues, as was the case when Paul wrote to the individual communities he had evangelised. One view is that Luke was addressing communities which were going through a profound and extended transition after some decades of missionary outreach.[3] They were experiencing a lack of enthusiasm from within and some hostility from without. They were faced with three interrelated crises.

Firstly, they were dealing with a *crisis of identity*. What began as a renewal movement within Judaism was now in the process of breaking away from its Jewish moorings, a process very much accelerated by the increasing number of Gentiles joining the movement. Some Jews were reporting the movement to the authorities as an illegitimate offshoot of the Judaism which lived under the protective umbrella of the Roman Empire. In becoming Christians, the Gentile members had in many respects cut themselves off from their Gentile past and may well have been experiencing strained relations with former friends and acquaintances. And the cross-cultural living in mixed communities of Gentiles and Jews gave rise to internal tensions and questions about cultural identity. Residing in Asia Minor and Greece in the mid-eighties, these communities also felt distant in time and space from their origins in the mission of Jesus and the Jerusalem-based mission of the early Church. So, on the whole, they did not have a strong sense of identity. They did not feel anchored; rather, they felt they were drifting at sea wondering who they were and in what direction they were going.

Secondly, Luke's communities were going through a time of stagnation in mission and were experiencing a *crisis of missionary motivation*, which to some extent came from a weak sense of identity and inner security. They owed their origin to the missionary work of people like Paul and they themselves had reached out in mission to those around them with significant success. Now they were experiencing a lack of response and increasing opposition, particularly on the part of some Jews. Should they give up on mission because it was just too difficult and was yielding meagre returns? Thirdly, they were experiencing a *crisis of faith* because things were not working out as they had hoped or expected. They had questions about God's fidelity. 'Is the failure of many Jews to accept God's Messiah a sign that God did not bring about the fulfilment of his promises to Israel and even allowed their Temple in Jerusalem to be destroyed? Can God be trusted? Will God be faithful to us as we live in a difficult present and face an uncertain future?'

Luke, a Biblical Historian

We usually think of Luke as the Church's first historian. The Acts of the Apostles is seen to provide the historical framework for Paul's letters and indeed other parts of the New Testament. Some have spoken of Luke as a Hellenistic novelist who wrote to entertain his readers. Others have numbered him among the Hellenistic biographers who wrote lives of the founders of philosophical schools and their followers. Still others regard Luke as an apologist who wrote to defend Christians before Roman authorities or to defend Paul and his teaching which was still treated with suspicion in some Jewish-Christian circles. However, it is best to see Luke as a biblical historian who used the genre of Hellenistic historiography in telling the story of Jesus and the early Church.

Luke himself considered his work to be a history. The prologue in Lk 1:1-4 is meant to introduce his whole two-volume work. He wants to write an 'orderly account' of the ministry of Jesus and its fulfilment in the lives of his Christian communities. In doing this he has carefully examined what has been handed on by 'eyewitnesses and servants of the word'. Luke did rely on sources, though his writings are shaped quite a lot by his own free composition. In writing his Gospel, we know he borrowed heavily from Mark's Gospel and he also drew from a source with sayings of Jesus (commonly called Q – from the German word *quelle*, meaning 'source'), a source he shared with the evangelist Matthew. Luke may well have used sources for writing the Acts of the Apostles – for instance, the 'we' passages mentioned above – but he has re-written his sources for Acts so thoroughly that it is impossible to identify them with any degree of certainty. We know how important sources are for historians. The function of historians is not just to collate information about names, dates and events. They have to interpret their sources, prioritise key events and people, indicate the forces and ideas influencing people and giving direction to events, and point out the significance of past events for the present.

When Luke speaks of 'eyewitnesses and servants of the word,' he most probably means 'eyewitnesses who became servants of the word'. Their role was not just to give an eyewitness account of what happened; more importantly, they had to discern the word of God in what happened. While Luke was not an eyewitness to many of the events he relates, he would have understood himself as a servant of the word. As a biblical historian, he wants to discern and highlight the presence and activity of God in what happened, to point out the significance of events for our lives, and to elicit a faith response from us. Luke is not giving information in any take-it-or-leave-it fashion. He is more interested in the transformation of his readers and the strengthening of their faith. He wants Theophilus 'to know the truth (*asphaleia*) concerning the things about which you have been instructed' (Lk 1:4). The truth in question is not intellectual or scientific truth. The Greek word has the connotation of assurance, confidence and security. Luke is writing so that his communities will be able to stand on the solid ground of faith in God.

As a biblical historian highlighting the presence of the God who makes and fulfils promises, Luke understands history as linear rather than cyclic. This linear history, in which the faithful God is continuously active, can be depicted as follows:[4]

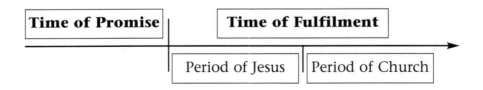

History can be divided into two major parts, the 'Time of Promise (prophecy)' and the 'Time of Fulfilment'. In Luke's mind, the Time of Promise began with creation and the Time of Fulfilment is still continuing today. Both the Period of Jesus and the Period of the Church fall within the Time of Fulfilment. Luke emphasises continuity between the Time of Promise and Time of Fulfilment, and between the Period of Jesus and the Period of the Church. The break between the Period of Jesus and the Period of the Church is not a major break; the more decisive demarcation occurs between the Time of Promise and the Time of Fulfilment. With the advent of Jesus, the Time of Fulfilment begins and is carried over into the Period of the Church. While the earthly life and mission of Jesus have a unique and unrepeatable character, which makes it legitimate to speak of the 'Period of Jesus,' the risen Christ continues to act in the Period of the Church. We will have more to say below about Luke's theology of promise and fulfilment, his understanding of God's purpose and plan, and the role of Jesus Christ in the working out of that plan.

In assessing the historical reliability of Luke's entire work, as well as any individual episode he narrates, one must never overlook Luke's theological purpose. Furthermore, he is not to be judged by the standards of modern history writing. Firstly, Luke is a historian of his own day, very much influenced by the standards and conventions of Hellenistic historiography. We can learn of these in the works of historians like Dionysius of Halicarnassus (circa 30 BC), Lucian of Samosate (circa AD 160) and the Jewish historian Flavius Josephus (AD 37-100). Among the criteria for good historiography were: apt subject; omission of what is not essential; vividness; commitment to telling the truth. And historians used such conventions as: prologue to state the purpose of the work; focus on dramatic events; speeches which give insight into the significance of the events related.

Secondly, in writing his own work, Luke was influenced by biblical paradigms and frameworks.[5] Thirdly, unlike many of the historians of his time, Luke does not confine his interest to the most prominent and influential people in society. True, he situates his story in the context of world history to emphasise its universal significance (Lk 1:5; 2:1-2; 3:1-2), but it's a story about ordinary people who were taken up into the unfolding of God's plan – people like Peter and John (fishermen from Galilee), Paul (a tentmaker from Tarsus), Cornelius (a relatively low-ranking Roman soldier), Lydia (a small-business woman, though of some means).

Finally, Luke is selective. He does not set out to tell us the whole story of the early expansion of Christianity. For instance, we hear nothing about the foundation of the Church in places like Galilee, Damascus, Alexandria and Rome. In the second part of Acts, Luke focuses almost exclusively on the missionary activity of Paul and gives little information about the activity of other Christian missionaries. Luke is focusing on people and events which best serve his theological purpose, that is, to show the unfolding of God's plan of salvation for all. In our reading of the Acts of the Apostles we will touch on questions of factual history only when they might help us to understand better what Luke is saying to us.

Luke, a Literary Artist

Luke is a compelling and gifted storyteller. Only in Luke's Gospel do we find the memorable and vivid parables of the good Samaritan (Lk 10:30-35), the rich fool (Lk 12:16-21), the lost son (Lk 15:11-32), the shrewd manager (Lk 16:1-8), and the rich man and Lazarus (Lk 16:19-21). Much of the final shape of these parables is probably due to Luke himself. One also thinks of the dramatic episodes in Luke's infancy narratives and the stories about Zacchaeus (Lk 19:1-10) and the two disciples on the road to Emmaus (Lk 24:13-35) which are found only in Luke's Gospel. The Acts of the Apostles also has stories which are very well told; for instance, the stories of Ananias and Sapphira (Acts 5:1-11), Peter's release from prison (Acts 12:6-17) and Paul's shipwreck (Acts 27:1-44). In fact the whole of Acts is a quite gripping story.

Luke is not only a writer of good short stories. From all the material at his disposal he was able to forge a single narrative with great coherence, continuity and movement. The single story of Luke-Acts stretches over fifty-two chapters which amount to one quarter of the entire New Testament! Mark was the first to present the Good News in the form of a continuous narrative of Jesus' life, death and resurrection, but Luke gives us a story wider in scope than anything previously attempted. He continues the story of Jesus and his mission into the ongoing story of the Church and its mission. Or, more correctly, the Period of Jesus and the Period of the Church fuse into one continuous narrative. Luke Timothy Johnson points to the importance of reading Luke-Acts as a single story:

> To regard Luke-Acts as a *story* means, at the least, that we do not read it as a systematic treatise. Rather, we must see Luke's meaning through the movement of the story. It is of primary importance to locate where something occurs in Luke's narrative. The connection between individual vignettes is as important as their respective contents. The sequence itself provides the larger meaning.[6]

As intimated above, Luke-Acts is a single story. It has one major *unifying plot*, one overarching theme that permeates the entire work. In short, we can say that Luke's story is about the stage-by-stage unfolding of God's plan of salvation for all in and through Jesus Christ and with the guidance and power of the Spirit.[7] This theme of universal salvation is made explicit at the beginning of Luke's work. Both Mary and Zechariah see the coming of Jesus as the fulfilment of God's promise to Abraham that all the families of the earth will be blessed in him (Lk 1:55, 73). Simeon takes the child Jesus in his arms and speaks of him as 'a light for revelation to the Gentiles and for glory to your people Israel' (Lk 2:32). John the Baptist announces the time when 'all flesh shall see the salvation of God' (Lk 3:6). Jesus' ancestors are traced back to Adam, the father of the whole human race (Lk 3:23-38).

In beginning his ministry in the synagogue of Nazareth, Jesus insists that his Spirit-filled mission to the poor is universal in scope (Lk 4:16-30). It's clear that God's salvation is for all nations, cultures and classes; no one is to be excluded. On almost every page of Luke's Gospel we find Jesus reaching out to the poor and excluded ones of society. He has a positive attitude to Samaritans (Lk 9:52-55; 10:30-37; 17:11-19) and Gentiles (Lk 7:1-10; 8:26-39; 13:29). With the exception of Jesus' visit to the country of the Gerasenes (Lk 8:26-29), however, there is little evidence that he engaged directly in mission to non-Jews. The outreach beyond Israel has hardly got off the ground in the third Gospel, but at the end of the Gospel the risen Jesus says the time has come for repentance and the forgiveness of sins to be proclaimed in his name to all nations, beginning in Jerusalem (Lk 24:47). Acts tells how the Good News of universal salvation spreads out from Jerusalem in many directions on its journey to the ends of the earth (Acts 1:8).

What can we learn from Luke's story about the kind of salvation God is offering to all? Luke is the only Synoptic evangelist to use the title 'Saviour' (*Sōtēr*) for Jesus (see Lk 1:69; 2:11; Acts 5:31; 13:23). John uses it just once (Jn 4:42). Luke is the only evangelist to use the noun 'salvation' (*sōtērion* and *sōtēria*) in connection with Jesus' ministry. Like the other evangelists, he uses the verb 'to save' (*sōzein*). So Luke's terminology shows his interest in Jesus as Saviour and what salvation means. For Luke, the salvation Jesus brings is an integral salvation which affects the whole person (body and soul), all dimensions of life (the physical and spiritual, the individual and social), and all our relationships.[8] Salvation is both a liberation and transformation, with the main emphasis on liberation. It implies release, deliverance and freedom from whatever holds us in bondage. Jesus says that he is sent 'to proclaim release to the captives' (Lk 4:18). The word 'release' (*aphesis*) was a socio-economic term referring to release of prisoners, release from debt, or release from oppression. It can also be used in a religious sense – release from the bondage of sin and from the legacy that human sinfulness has left the world: sickness, pain, alienation, exclusion, oppressive relationships and structures, etc. In the biblical view these various disorders came into the world through human sinfulness (see, for instance, Gn 3). The same word *aphesis* is used in Luke's writings for the forgiveness of sins. Release from the bondage of sin and the forgiveness of sin go hand in hand. Jesus' ministry is a ministry of forgiveness of sins (see Lk 5:17-26; 7:36-50; 15:1-32). His healings can be seen as a rescue operation which entails confrontation between the power of the kingdom of God, which sets people free, and the power of evil (Satan) which keeps people in bondage (see Lk 13:10-17).

As mentioned above, the content of the message to be proclaimed to all nations is 'repentance and the forgiveness of sins' (Lk 24:47). In the Acts of the Apostles we see the early Christian community constantly preaching repentance and forgiveness (see Acts 2:38; 3:19, 26; 8:22; 10:43; 13:38; 17:30; 20:21; 26:18, 20). Along with an experience of liberation, salvation is also understood as an experience of transformation in Luke's writings. It is a restoration to a state of wholeness and integrity. Jesus' healing ministry not only released people from bondage, but also restored them to health, well-being and community. The Gerasene demoniac (Lk 8:26-39), for instance, experienced both release and restoration.

A favourite word of Luke to speak of the wholeness which salvation brings is 'peace' (*eirēnē*) (see Lk 1:79; 2:14, 29; 19:41; 24:36; Acts 10:36). Peace is more than the absence of war. It means a state of well-being, wholeness, harmony and concord in relationships, security and health. What Luke says about Jesus bringing peace is to be understood against the claim that the Roman emperor brings peace – *pax Romana* – which was often enforced and maintained by military power. In the biblical view, peace is God's gift. The salvation (liberation and transformation) which Jesus brings is not just a gift to be experienced in the future. While it certainly has a future dimension, it must also be experienced in the here and now: '*Today* salvation has come to this house' (Lk 19:9; see also 2:11; 4:21; 23:43). Salvation is an ongoing process with past, present and future dimensions. In Acts 2:47 Luke refers to new converts as 'those who were being saved'. We have already indicated that what is required on the human side to appropriate salvation is 'repentance' (*metanoia*, literally 'a change of mind') (Lk 24:47). This word is closely related to 'conversion' (*epitrophē*, literally 'a turning around'). The two cognate verbs for these nouns are found side by side in Acts 3:19. So, what is needed from us is a change of mind and direction, a turning to God in faith in order to experience his salvation. Three times in the Gospel of Luke Jesus says to a person, 'Your faith has saved you' (Lk 7:50; 8:48; 17:19). Faith amounts to trust in a saving God. In Luke's Gospel we notice that the 'outsider' often responds more readily than the 'insider' to what God is doing in and through the mission of Jesus.[9]

In Acts, baptism in the name of Jesus is also mentioned as part of the human response to the saving God (see Acts 2:38; 8:16; 10:48; 19:5). Baptism, the rite of initiation into the community of Jesus, is probably seen as the public expression of faith and repentance. Finally, what must be excluded on the part of humans seeking God's salvation are the spirit of vengeance and the use of violence. Jesus' way is the way of love and non-violent resistance (see, for instance, how Jesus, in giving the programme for his mission in Lk 4:18-19, omits the reference to vengeance in quoting the text from Is 61).

Every good storyteller develops the *characters* with consistency and purpose, showing what role they are playing in the unfolding plot of the story. Who are the main actors in Luke's story and how does Luke characterise them? The main actor is God who is continually present and at work in what is happening. Some say the Acts of the Apostles should really be called the Acts of God. For Luke, the God 'who made the heaven and the earth, the sea and everything in them' (Acts 4:24; 14:15; 17:24) is also the powerful Lord of history who guides the course of history according to the divine plan of salvation for all (for references to this 'plan' [boulē], see Lk 7:30; Acts 2:23; 4:28; 20:27). To remind us that events have to unfold according to God's plan, Luke often uses the Greek term meaning 'it is (was) necessary' (dei, edei) (see Lk 2:49; 4:43; 9:22; 24:26; Acts 1:21; 19:21). Nothing will thwart the unfolding of God's plan. God is also a compassionate God who reaches out to all, especially the poor, the outcasts, the excluded and the lost – all who were seen as unworthy to draw near to God. Nowhere is this image of the compassionate God seen more clearly than in the parables of Lk 15.

Furthermore, God is the faithful God who makes and keeps promises. For instance, in the infancy narratives (Lk 1–2), Luke shows how prophecies made in the Time of Promise are being fulfilled. Promises made in the Period of Jesus (for instance, the promise of the Spirit in Lk 24:49) are fulfilled in the succeeding Period of the Church. Luke's characterisation of God as the compassionate and faithful God who is Lord of history would have meant a lot to the communities experiencing crises of identity, missionary motivation and faith. They are not adrift without purpose or direction, but are firmly situated in the flow of God's unfolding plan. Their mission must continue because it is a participation in the compassionate mission of God which does not cease. They can trust the faithful God who will be there for them in their difficulties and uncertainties.

On very rare occasions, the voice of God is heard in the narrative (see Lk 3:22; 9:35) and at times God acts through an angel (see, for instance, Lk 1:11, 26; 2:9; Acts 5:19; 8:26; 10:3; 12:7; 27:23). But God's main agent in the unfolding of the divine plan of salvation for all is Jesus. God was behind everything that happened in Jesus' life and mission (see especially the summary of Jesus' life and mission in Acts

10:37-43). How does Luke characterise Jesus? The portrait of Jesus drawn in the third Gospel is that of the Spirit-filled saviour and prophet with a strong and urgent sense of mission, wanting to bring all to an experience of God's salvation (compassion, acceptance, release, forgiveness, life, peace), having a special concern for those who are excluded and to whom life is most denied, finding direction and energy for his mission in prayerful union with God, remaining faithful to God's mission and trusting in God's fidelity to him, despite opposition, rejection and death on a cross. As the many meal scenes in Luke's Gospel suggest, Jesus is the messenger of a hospitable God who invites all, without exception, to sit at his table. Jesus is on-stage for the first part of Luke's story. Though it could be said he is off-stage during the second part of the story, the risen Jesus remains present and active in his followers who engage in mission in his name and in his way.

The ascension, which Luke alone narrates (Lk 24:50-53; Acts 1:6-11), does not imply his absence, but his ongoing presence in a new way. The risen Jesus appears to key figures to guide and strengthen them and to direct events: Paul (Acts 9:1-19; 18:9; 22:18-23; 23:11); Stephen (Acts 7:56); Ananias (Acts 9:10-16). Signs and wonders are worked 'in Jesus' name' (Acts 4:7, 9, 12), that is, through the powerful presence of Jesus. Peter says to the paralytic Aeneas, 'Jesus Christ heals you' (Acts 9:34). Paul speaks of the risen Jesus as one who continues to 'proclaim light both to our people and to the Gentiles' (Acts 26:23). The main way the risen Jesus guides and empowers his missionaries is through his Spirit. The Spirit is the 'Spirit of Jesus' (Acts 16:7). The Spirit, who initiated, guided and empowered the mission of the earthly Jesus is the same Spirit who initiates, guides and empowers the mission of his followers which is a participation in the ongoing mission of the risen Jesus (see Acts 1:8). They too are characterised as Spirit-filled prophets (see, for instance, Acts 4:8; 5:32; 6:3; 7:55; 11:24; 13:9). Among these Spirit-filled prophets, Peter is to the fore in the first part of Acts and Paul takes centre stage in the second part. On the other hand, those who oppose God's plan are characterised as stiff-necked people who oppose the Holy Spirit (see Acts 7:51). In Paul's letters, the Spirit is seen mainly as the Spirit of sanctification. For Luke, however, the Spirit is always the Spirit of mission. While Matthew's Gospel ends with a missionary *mandate* to make disciples of all nations (Mt 28:16-20), Luke's Gospel ends with a missionary *promise*, the promise to send the Spirit (Lk 24:29). The Spirit of mission looms so large in the story of Acts that some have referred to it as the Gospel of the Holy Spirit.[10]

Luke employs a number of *literary devices* to hold his story together, to give it movement forward, and to engage the reader in the story. These techniques were in common use in Hellenistic historiography and Luke uses them for his own purposes. Being aware of Luke's literary devises helps us to understand how Luke is communicating his message and how he is drawing us into the story. Luke is moving us to identify with those who accept and promote God's plan and to distance ourselves from those who oppose it. He wants us to open ourselves to the guidance and power of Spirit, so that we can imitate the God who continually reaches out in compassion (see Lk 6:36) and journey with Jesus on mission. Here are the main literary devices Luke uses to achieve his aims:

> *Journey*: Luke's whole story is cast in the form of a journey from Galilee to Jerusalem in the person of Jesus (see especially Lk 9:51–19:28) and from Jerusalem to the ends of the earth (in the persons of Jesus' followers, particularly Paul). It is really the story of the journey of God's saving word reaching out to all. To emphasise the journey motif, Luke has important episodes taking place on a journey (see, for instance, the stories of the two disciples on the road to Emmaus [Lk 24:13-35], the Ethiopian eunuch on the road to Gaza [Acts 8:26-40] and Paul on the road to Damascus [Acts 9:1-9]). Placing

his story in the context of a journey gives us the sense that things are moving forward in a definite direction and with purpose. We are also reminded that Christian discipleship and mission involve being on a journey. Luke speaks of the Christian movement as 'the Way' (Acts 9:2; 19:9, 23; 22:4; 24:14, 22).

Dramatic Episodes: Like a good Hellenistic historiographer, Luke concentrates on vivid, dramatic episodes which arrest the attention of the reader. We have mentioned some of these episodes above – stories which are found only in Luke's Gospel, as well memorable stories in the Acts of the Apostles. The dramatic episodes in Acts are presented as striking examples of the Church's internal life and external mission. Some of these episodes also mark significant turning points in the story (for instance, Stephen's martyrdom [Acts 6:8–8:1]; Paul's call [Acts 9:1-9]; Cornelius' conversion [Acts 10:1–11:18]).

Summaries: In his Gospel, Luke takes over summaries from Mark and increases their number (Lk 1:80; 2:52; 4:14-15; 7:21-22; 8:1-3; 13:22; 19:47; 21:37). He gives us major summaries in the early part of Acts, probably because he had less narrative material available to him (Acts 2:42-47; 4:32-35; 5:12-16). Smaller summaries are used throughout Acts to fill in the gaps in the narrative, mark transitions, reinforce the impression of repeated or frequent action, and convince us that God's word is progressing on its journey (see, for instance, Acts 5:42; 6:7; 9:31; 12:24; 19:20). They also help us to keep in view the bigger picture and avoid getting lost in the details of the narrative.

Speeches: An important narrative device in Acts is the use of speeches. The canticles in the infancy narrative of Luke (Lk 1:46-55, 68-97; 2:29-32) function like speeches by key people in the story. In the first eight chapters of Acts there are nine speeches of greater or lesser length (Acts 1:4-8; 1:16-22; 2:14-36; 3:12-26; 4:8-12; 4:24-30; 5:35-39; 6:2-4; 7:2-53), which account for half the narrative up to that point. Indeed, speeches in Acts represent one-third of the whole work. No one provided Luke with transcripts of the missionary and defence speeches in Acts. These speeches are compositions of Luke himself, though he is very conscious of the speaker's character, the occasion, the topic addressed and the audience. The speeches are addressed principally to his readers. Putting a speech on the lips of someone in order to explain to the reader the meaning and significance of what was happening was a common practice in Hellenistic historiography. However, it should be noted that the missionary speeches in Acts display some insights and patterns which may well go back to the primitive apostolic preaching (for instance, the understanding that Jesus became the Messiah at his resurrection [Acts 2:36] and the recurring refrain about the way God reversed what people did to Jesus [Acts 2:23-24; 3:13; 4:10; 13:27-30]).

Parallelism: Luke is very fond of the literary device of parallelism. He matches persons and events in different parts of his narrative as a way of holding his story together and interpreting it for the reader. The parallels between events in the Gospel and events in Acts are perhaps the most striking. Note, for instance, the parallels between the descent of the Spirit on Jesus at the beginning of his mission and the descent of the same Spirit on the disciples before they embark on mission (Lk 3:21-22; Acts 2:1-13), between the death of Jesus and the death of Stephen (Lk 23:34, 46; Acts 7:59-60), and between the trial of Jesus and the trial of Paul (Lk 23:1-25; Acts 25-26). The parallels between the healing ministry of Peter and that of Paul are also obvious (compare, for instance, Acts 3:1-10 with 14:8-11, and 9:36-42 with 20:7-12). These healings are similar to those worked by Jesus (see Lk 5:17-26; 8:40-56). By his use of parallelism, then, Luke is saying that Jesus continues on mission in the mission of his followers. He is thus prompting his readers to seek parallels between their experience of mission and the mission of Jesus, so that they too can be convinced that Jesus is on mission through them also.

Reflection

As I mentioned in the introduction, over the last fifty years we have been going through a time of great transition in mission, a paradigm shift in the way we understand and practise mission. A new model of mission has been emerging, as we attempt to respond to the 'signs of the times' in a changing world and a changing Church. I have already outlined very briefly some elements of this model. Because the Church must continually respond to the signs of the times, its understanding and practice of mission needs continual assessment. Listening to the Scriptures, which draw our attention to the presence and activity of God among us, is indispensable in any assessment of the Church's mission. The story of mission in the early Church, as recounted in the Acts of the Apostles, helped Luke's communities as they went through significant transition in their internal life and external mission. Here I mention just a few insights from what we have considered above, which I think are fundamental for the understanding and practice of mission today.

Luke is asking us to focus on the deepest foundation of our mission. Our mission is rooted in the Mission of God, who continually reaches out in love and compassion to a broken world. Luke is moving and inspiring us to participate in the Mission of God and allow ourselves to be drawn into the working out of God's plan for the salvation of all, particularly those who are most excluded from the life God wishes for all his children. And Luke clearly reminds us that God is faithful and can be trusted to fulfil his promises and plans. To put it in another way, our mission is a sharing in the ongoing mission of Jesus Christ, the one who plays the key role in God's unfolding plan. We engage in mission in the way of Jesus and in the power of his Spirit. Luke is setting before us the primary motivation for our mission. In the midst of rapidly changing times, and despite the experience of failure and loss of credibility, the Church must always continue on mission because the compassionate and faithful God is a missionary God and the risen Jesus is calling us to join him in his ongoing mission today. The Church is not a club for the benefit of the members, but a community on mission reaching out to the world.

The plan of God has to do with salvation, which is the goal of mission. Luke helps us to see that the salvation in question cannot be reduced to the salvation of one's soul in the afterlife. In our world today, people can easily be marginalised and excluded from full participation in society on the basis of race, colour, culture, religion, social and economic status, gender and sexual orientation. Cultural and religious conflicts, as well as economic hardships and ecological devastation, have led to mass migration and displacement of peoples who can rarely find places of acceptance, welcome and hospitality. Salvation in Luke's Gospel is described in the imagery of a banquet prepared by a hospitable God to which all are invited and from which no one is to be excluded (see, for instance, Lk 14:15-24). The Lukan Jesus' practice of table fellowship and his many references to food are to be seen in that light. The world today badly needs to hear the good news of God's all-inclusive hospitality which is central to Luke's understanding of mission.

The positive assessment of the outsiders' response in Luke's Gospel can remind us that strangers can often be our evangelisers. The Spirit of Jesus is present and active in our world bringing about the universal communion desired by God. This universal communion involves right relationships with God, with one another, and with all creation. The present emphasis on right relationship with creation as an integral part of the missionary challenge today would not be foreign to Luke's missionary vision. The God of Luke is the one who created the world and everything in it and gave it order and harmony (Acts 17:24-26; see also Acts 4:24; 14:15). Luke traces Jesus' ancestry back to Adam (Lk 3:23-38), to a time when Adam lived in harmony with all creation. Adam's fall disrupted that harmony and integral salvation must include its restoration. I think what Paul says in Rm 8:19-23 about the whole creation groaning for an experience of salvation would win approval from Luke the universalist. The missionary call for the Church today is to be a sign and instrument of universal communion in a conflictual, divided, broken and exploited world. While communion is meant to be a present reality, we are always moving towards the fullness of communion in the future, which ultimately is communion with the Triune God. Luke's vision of universal salvation and communion is remarkably similar to the vision that underpins everything Pope Francis says in his 2020 encyclical on fraternity and social friendship, *Fratelli Tutti*, which is not surprising as the vision of the encyclical is inspired mainly by the Lukan parable of the Good Samaritan (Lk 10:25-37).[11]

The fact that Luke has placed his story of mission in the context of a journey says something important about the model for mission today. As Jesus set his face to go to Jerusalem, he invited his followers to go with him on a journey that would call for great commitment and single-mindedness (Lk 9:51-62). At the beginning of Acts, he invites them to continue with him on the journey towards the ends of the earth (Acts 1:8). To be on mission is to embark on an ongoing journey, not settling down like people who have arrived at their destination. We are not given a detailed roadmap for this journey. What we have is the compass of the Spirit of Jesus who guides us on the way and strengthens us to keep going when we feel we can't go any further. Mission today needs people who are companions on the journey, search together for the way forward, can live with uncertainty and insecurity, and stay with the questions when the answers are far from clear. Ultimately we are searching for the footprints of the risen Jesus who leads the way and for signs of the movement of his Spirit in our situation. There is a greater realisation today that we need a discerning and contemplative approach in our mission.

If we read the Acts of the Apostles just to get accurate historical information about persons, events and dates we may well be disappointed. This 'second book' does not tell us everything about the story of early Christian mission and often leaves us unclear about what actually happened. At best, we will end up glorifying heroes in the dim and distant past. If, on the other hand, we seek inspiration for our mission today, we will find much that reflects and clarifies our experience in mission. Acts will not give us answers to all our missionary questions, but it will point us in the right direction. And, like the two disciples on the road to Emmaus (Lk 24:13-35), we too will feel our hearts burning to share with all, and especially the poor and marginalised, the Good News of the risen Jesus whom we have met on the road.[12]

NOTES

[1] Quotations from the text of Acts are from the New Revised Standard Version, unless stated otherwise. In this case, the translation of the Greek text of Acts 1:1-2 is slightly different from the NRSV text.

[2] *A Brief Commentary on the Gospel of Luke* (New York: Paulist Press, 1988), 1-2.

[3] On Luke's communities as missionary communities in transition, see Bosch, *Transforming Mission*, 84-88; Donald Senior and Carroll Stuhlmueller, *The Biblical Foundations for Mission*, (New York: Orbis Books, 1983), 256; Robert J. Karris, 'Missionary Communities: A New Paradigm for the Study of Luke-Acts,' *Catholic Biblical Quarterly* 41 (1979), 80-97.

[4] The division of history into three stages is often associated with the insights of Hans Conzelmann, who wrote a book in the early 1950s (English translation: *The Theology of St Luke* [New York: Harper,

1960]) which became very influential in Lukan studies. The linear history diagram we give is a refinement of Conzelmann's three stages. However, his view that Luke wanted Christians to forget about the second coming of Jesus and focus only on the present challenges was not so widely accepted.

5 For instance, Luke Timothy Johnson (*The Gospel of Luke*, Sacra Pagina series, Vol. 3 [Collegeville: Glazier, 1991], 17-21) argues that the story of Moses and the exodus provided the narrative structure for Luke-Acts. Others highlight the influence of the Elijah and Elisha cycles in 1-2 Kings, or the narration of a promised new exodus in Isaiah 40-45.

6 Johnson, *ibid.*, 4.

7 For Robert O'Toole (*The Unity of Luke's Theology: An Analysis of Luke-Acts*, GNS 9 [Wilmington: Glazier, 1984]), the unifying theme of Luke's writings is that God, who brought salvation to Israel, continues to bring salvation to his people in Israel, who are now the Christians. For Joel B. Green, 'Luke's agenda is... to write the story of the continuation and fulfilment of God's project' (*The Theology of the Gospel of Luke* [Cambridge: Cambridge University Press, 1995], 47).

8 '"Salvation" in Luke's Gospel has many aspects: reconciliation with God, physical healing, freedom from dehumanising constraints and controls, being brought from the margins of society to a central and honoured place within the community (hospitality), rescue from persecution and from the troubles associated with the end of the age, eternal life in the finally established kingdom of God' (Brendan Byrne, *The Hospitality of God. A Reading of Luke's Gospel* [Collegeville: The Liturgical Press, 2000], 195).

9 'So the faith of the centurion (Lk 7:1-10) is greater than that found in Israel. The sinful woman "loves much", far more than the Pharisee Simon (Lk 7:42-50). The towns of Tyre and Sidon are declared more likely to reform than the cities of Galilee (Lk 10:13-15). The queen of the south and the citizens of Nineveh responded better to the wisdom of Solomon and the preaching of Jonah than "this generation" does to the "something greater" proclaimed by Jesus (Lk 11:29-32). The Samaritan leper knows how to give thanks (Lk 17:11-19) and a Samaritan turns out to be a faithful keeper of the love command, the essence of the law (Lk 10:29-37). The poor man Lazarus (Lk 16:19-31) and the repentant publican (Lk 18:9-14) are heard by God, while the rich man and the proud Pharisee fail. The offering of the poor widow is worth more than the mighty gifts of the rich (Lk 21:1-4)' (Senior and Stuhlmueller, *The Biblical Foundations for Mission*, 265).

10 In his 1990 encyclical letter *Redemptoris Missio*, Pope John Paul II devoted a chapter to the Holy Spirit as the Principal Agent of Mission (see *Mission of the Redeemer* [Boston: Paulist Press & Media, 1992], nos 21-30).

11 'It is my desire that, in this our time, by acknowledging the dignity of each human person, we can contribute to the rebirth of a universal aspiration to fraternity. Fraternity between all men and women... Let us dream, then, as a single human family, as fellow travellers sharing the same flesh, as children of the same earth which is our common home, each of us bringing the richness of his or her beliefs and convictions, each of us with his or her own voice, brothers and sisters all' (*Fratelli Tutti*, no. 8). On the theme of universal communion in the context of care for the earth, see Pope Francis' *Laudato Si'. On Care for our Common Home* (London: Catholic Truth Society, 2015), nos 89-92.

12 Senior and Stuhlmueller (*The Biblical Foundations for Mission, 277*) conclude their consideration of mission in Luke-Acts with these words: 'Luke-Acts provides a theological basis for the community's mission, and wise instruction for those involved in witnessing to it.' Speaking of the importance of the study of Acts for mission today, William Kurz (*Acts of the Apostles*, [Grand Rapids: Baker Academic, 2013], 20) comments: 'Studying this inspired account of the earliest years of the Church increases our faith in the power of God, raises our expectations of what God can do in and through us, and helps us understand how the Spirit and his gifts can operate in the lives of all who commit themselves to the Church's mission of evangelisation.'

CHAPTER 2

LAUNCHING THE MISSION
(ACTS 1:1–2:41)

In Acts 1:1–8:3 the locale for Luke's continuing story is Jerusalem. The movement of the story in Luke's Gospel has been towards Jerusalem. Luke presents Jesus on a journey to his destiny in the centre of Jewish religion. The artificially constructed travel narrative (Lk 9:51–19:28) begins with the words: 'When the days drew near for him to be received up, he set his face to go to Jerusalem' (see also Lk 13:33). In a number of ways throughout the Gospel, Luke keeps our focus on Jerusalem: the Gospel begins and ends in the Temple in Jerusalem; in the infancy narratives (Lk 1-2), Luke has three journeys to Jerusalem; in Lk 4:1-13 the sequence of Jesus' temptations is changed so that the climactic one takes place in Jerusalem; in Lk 24 (unlike Mk 16, Mt 28 and Jn 21), there are no references to resurrection appearances outside Jerusalem and its environs. In relating Jesus' mission, Luke does all he can to ensure that the focus on Jerusalem is not lost. He often eliminates geographical references from his sources that might distract from Jesus' resolute and single-minded journey to Jerusalem. One might ask: 'Why this focus on Jerusalem?' Jerusalem, for Luke, is the city of Jesus' destiny. The events of Jesus' death, resurrection and ascension which took place in Jerusalem are the pivotal centre for the whole story in Luke-Acts. These events are described as Jesus' 'exodus' (*exodos*) which he was to accomplish at Jerusalem (Lk 9:31) or his 'being taken up' (*analēmpsis*) (Lk 9:51). Jerusalem, the place towards which the mission of the earthly Jesus was moving, will now become the place from which the mission of the risen Jesus in his followers will move out to the ends of the earth. To put it in another way, mission in Jerusalem will be the first stage in the continuing universal mission of Jesus through his followers (see Acts 1:8). Acts' account of Christian life and mission in Jerusalem (Acts 1:1–8:3) could be subdivided in a number of ways. In this chapter we look at what is happening in Acts 1:1–2:41. Firstly, Luke is building a solid bridge between the mission of Jesus he has described in the Gospel and the ongoing mission he is about to relate in Acts. Secondly, he is showing the group of Jesus' followers waiting for the fulfilment of Jesus' promise of the Spirit to empower them for mission. Thirdly, he narrates the descent of the Spirit on that group, transforming them into a community on mission. Having seen how the mission is launched in this chapter, we will focus in our next chapter on how the Jerusalem community's internal life and external mission develop in Acts 2:42–8:3.

Building a Bridge (Acts 1:1-11)[1]

In the infancy narratives at the beginning of his Gospel, Luke is looking backwards and forwards. He is forging a strong link between the Time of Promise and the Time of Fulfilment by recalling figures and promises in the Old Testament. And he is also announcing the major themes in the story of the fulfilment of God's plan of universal salvation which he is about to relate. In Acts 1 Luke is doing something similar. He looks back to what happened in the Period of Jesus and looks forward to what will happen in the Period of the Church. Thus he is building a bridge between these two periods. Acts 1:1-11 repeats a lot of what we find at the end of the Gospel in Lk 24. Both Acts 1:1-11 and Lk 24 refer to the suffering of Jesus (Acts 1:3; Lk 24:25-27), the resurrection appearances (Acts 1:3; Lk 24:15-16, 30-31, 36), the instruction of the disciples by the risen Jesus (Acts 1:3; Lk 24:27, 45-47), the commissioning of the disciples as witnesses (Acts 1:2; 1:8; Lk 24:48); the indication that the risen Jesus eats with the disciples (Acts 1:4; Lk 24:41-43), the command to remain in Jerusalem (Acts 1:4; Lk 24:49), the promise of the Spirit (Acts 1:4-5, 8; Lk 24:49), and the ascension (Acts 1:9-11; Lk 24:50-51).

Jesus' ministry is characterised in a general way as a ministry in word and deed (Acts 1:1). Of all that Jesus did during his ministry, Luke focuses on the choice and commissioning of the apostles which happened under the direction of the Spirit (Acts 1:2).[2] The role of the risen Jesus as teacher of the disciples is emphasised. Jesus, who had instructed the disciples on the way to Jerusalem, now continues teaching them about the kingdom of God during a forty-day period before his ascension (Acts 1:3). The kingdom of God will be central to the apostles' mission (see, for instance, Acts 8:12; 19:8; 20:25; 28:31), as it was for the mission of Jesus. By mentioning the period of forty days, Luke may be paralleling the apostles' preparation with Jesus' preparation for his Spirit-filled mission in Lk 4:1-2, and he may also be alluding to incidents in the life of Moses and Elijah (see Ex 34:28; Deut 8:2; Ps 90:10 [LXX]; 1 Kgs 19:8).

As in Lk 24, the reality of Jesus' resurrection is stressed, probably because in Luke's mind the primary function of an apostle/missionary is to bear witness to the resurrection (see Acts 1:22). The apostles received many convincing proofs that Jesus is alive (Acts 1:3). The fact that the risen Jesus eats with the disciples could also serve to remind us of the many meals the Lukan Jesus shared with people to symbolise the gift of God's all-inclusive salvation.

Jesus not only enlightens the disciples' minds through teaching, but also directs their attention to the coming gift of the Spirit, who is called the 'promise of the Father' (Acts 1:4; 2:33; Lk 24:29). This will be an experience of immersion in the power of the Spirit (Acts 1:5; Lk 24:49). In Acts 1:8, as in Lk 24:48-49, it is clearly said that this empowerment is for missionary witness. The commissioning of the disciples by Jesus underlines the universal scope of the mission: 'You will be my witnesses in Jerusalem, in all Judea and Samaria, and to the ends of the earth.' These words indicate the programme and movement for the story of mission in Acts.[3] The disciples can set out on that mission only if they are moved and energised by the Spirit. Luke shows them in Acts 1:6-11 still locked in old ways of thinking, hesitant, and almost incapable of moving on to their future mission. They need to divert their attention away from any thoughts of political messianism (Acts 1:6-7) and from an exclusive emphasis on the second coming of Jesus (Acts 1:11a) in order to focus on their immediate task as Jesus' witnesses in the world (Acts 1:7-8). The second coming is by no means denied (Acts 1:11b).

Acts 1:9-11 gives Luke's second account of the ascension (see Lk 24:50-52). For Luke, the ascension, which focuses attention on Jesus as the exalted Lord, is an important hinge event, joining the two parts of his story.[4] The movement in the Gospel is towards Jesus' ascension (see Lk 9:51; Acts 1:2) and the event in Lk 24:52 is seen as the end of Jesus' earthly ministry. The atmosphere in Lk 24:50-52 is liturgical. Jesus is surrounded by his worshipping disciples and he blesses them as he withdraws from them. The account of the ascension in Acts 1:6-11, on the other hand, is described in terms of the beginning of a new stage. Attention is directed to the future mission of the disciples before Jesus' final victory. Notice all the words in Acts 1:9-11 which refer to the disciples' seeing, watching and looking – Luke has in mind Elijah's promise to Elisha that the latter will inherit the prophetic spirit of Elijah if he 'sees' Elijah ascending into heaven (2 Kgs 2:10, 12). The cloud, the sign and veil of God's presence (Ex 19:16-20; 24:15-18), and the interpreting messengers were common symbols used in apocalyptic literature to describe God's presence and saving action. We recall that Moses ascended Mount Sinai into a cloud and received the Law to give to the people. Jesus ascends into a cloud to receive the Spirit to pass on to his followers. Jesus will return 'in the same way' as he went. Could that be an allusion to 'one like a son of man' coming in the clouds (Dn 7:13-14; see Lk 21:27)?

The Expectant Disciples (Acts 1:12-14)

In Acts 1:12-14 we see the group of Jesus' followers waiting to become a Spirit-filled community. Luke picks up on what he said in Lk 24:52-53 about the disciples' return from Olivet to Jerusalem, which is important in Luke's geographical scheme. Olivet is significant because it was the place from which the glory of the Lord left Jerusalem (Ez 11:23) and to which it will return in the last times (Zec 14:4 LXX). The list of apostles is the same as that in Lk 6:14-16, with the omission of Judas Iscariot and a change in order (note how John, who is to feature alongside Peter in the early chapters of Acts, is now placed alongside Peter in the list). The atmosphere in the group is one of harmony and continuous prayer in preparation for the coming of the Spirit. The disciples are gathered 'with one accord' (*homothymadon*).[5] Luke is the only evangelist to tell us that Jesus was at prayer before the Spirit of mission came on him (Lk 3:21-22). The Jesus of Luke is a person who prays at all the critical moments of his ministry (see Lk 6:12; 9:18, 28-29; 11:2; 22:41; 23:46). In teaching his disciples to pray, he reminds them that the Spirit is the gift of prayer (Lk 11:13).

As the story of Acts progresses, Luke will remind us from time to time of the importance of discerning prayer in Christian mission (see Acts 1:24; 6:6; 9:11; 10:2-4, 9, 30; 11:5; 13:3; 14:23; 20:36). The mention of Mary and the women disciples may well reinforce this picture of a listening, discerning, receptive and attentive group.[6] In Luke's infancy narrative, Mary, who conceived through the power of the Spirit (Lk 1:35), is portrayed as one who waits with a contemplative attitude, reflecting on what she was experiencing (Lk 2:19, 51). Mary is the model disciple who receives the word in faith and acts on it (see Lk 1:45; 8:19-21; 11:27-28; see also Lk 8:15 which could be taken as a description of what is involved in faith). The 'brothers' of Jesus (Acts 1:14) refers to his relatives, one of whom, James, will assume a leading role in the Jerusalem church (see Acts 12:17; 15:13). So, in Acts 1:12-14, Luke calls to mind some of the actors in the first part of the story (particularly the apostles), with a view to their continuing role as the story progresses.

Restoration of the Twelve (Acts 1:15-26)

Before telling us about the coming of the Spirit, Luke pauses to deal with one outstanding issue, which concerns the question of continuity in the movement of his story. With the defection of Judas, the Twelve have become eleven and as such the symbolic integrity of the group has been shattered. That symbolic integrity of the Twelve needs to be restored, so that it can be clearly seen that the community which is formed at Pentecost is the restored Israel (not an illegitimate growth from Judaism, as some Jews claimed), and that what is happening in their lives is in continuity with God's dealings with Israel of old.[7] The number 120 (Acts 1:15) may also be intended to underline the link with Israel and the symbolism of the Twelve – it was the minimum number for a legitimate synagogue community, the officers of which number one tenth of its numerical strength. Peter takes the initiative (Lk 22:32) and his speech (Acts 1:16-25) interprets for the readers the significance of what is happening. He stresses that both the tragedy of Judas' apostasy and the election of his successor fall within God's plan, which can be discerned in the Scriptures (note the Lukan 'must'/necessity [*dei, edei*] in Acts 1:16, 21). God has not lost the plot and human failure will not hinder the working out of God's plan. Peter would have come to realise this through his own experience of failure.

In Acts 1:16-20a we have the Lukan version of the fate of Judas, which is not quite the same as the end of Judas described in Mt 27:3-10. The two accounts have in common the name of the place (Field of Blood) and the conviction that Judas' violent death fulfilled the Scriptures. But the differences are quite notable. Acts appeals to Ps 69:25 (68:26 LXX) with some slight modifications, while Matthew appeals to Zec 11:12-13 (+ Jer 32:6-15). In Acts the field is called

Hakeldama because of *Judas'* (bloody) death there; in Matthew it receives the name because blood money (money for *Jesus'* blood) was used to purchase it. In Acts Judas buys the field; in Matthew the leaders of the Jews buy it. The manner of death differs in both accounts. This is one instance where we see Luke's interest in theological significance rather than accuracy in historical details.

The Scripture quotation in Acts 1:20b which grounds the selection of Matthias in God's plan is Ps 109:8 (108:8 LXX). The occasion gives Luke the opportunity to define his understanding of an apostle (Acts 1:21-22). For him, the apostle is one who bears witness to the resurrection and, from the personal experience of being with Jesus during his ministry, can testify that this risen Jesus is the same Jesus who walked the roads of Palestine with his disciples. The apostle for Luke is a vital link between the time of Jesus and the time of the Church. Again the note of continuity is sounded. The group presents two candidates to fill the vacancy left by Judas (Acts 1:23). The more specific information about Joseph Barsabbas, and the hint that he was a man of great integrity, tricks the reader into expecting his selection. One has to be open to the surprises of God! The prayer before the selection, composed of established formulae (Acts 1:24-25), parallels the prayer of Jesus before he chose the Twelve (Lk 6:12-14). It is a prayer addressed to the risen Jesus in the understanding that he is the one who chooses. The casting of lots (Acts 1:26) also emphasises that full play is left to the divine initiative in this important decision for the group about to become a missionary Church through the coming of the Spirit at Pentecost. We don't hear of Matthias again. He comes into the story to 'make up the numbers' which in this case is an important function.

The Pentecost Experience (Acts 2:1-41)

The Church's Pentecost experience is seen by Luke as the fulfilment of Jesus' promise of the Holy Spirit (Lk 24:49; Acts 1:4–5:8) and of God's promises to Israel through the prophet

Joel (Acts 2:17-21). This experience again underlines the continuity between the time of Israel, the time of Jesus and the time of the Church. As Luke is accustomed to do, he first narrates the event (Acts 2:1-13) and then gives us a discourse (Acts 2:14-41), which interprets the event and sets the missionary programme for the rest of the narrative. He is also constructing a parallel between the experience of the disciples and the experience of Jesus. Jesus' mission began when the Spirit descended on him at the Jordan (Lk 3:21-22) and in the programmatic discourse in the synagogue at Nazareth (Lk 4:16-30) he interprets what the descent of the Spirit on him means.

Pentecost Event (Acts 2:1-13)

The context and background for the descent of the Spirit is the Jewish feast of Pentecost (Ex 34:22; Lev 23:15).[8] Originally, it was an agricultural feast to give thanks for the wheat harvest, but the Israelites made it a thanksgiving celebration for something that happened in their history. It was to thank God for the gift of the land (compare Deut 26:1-11), as well as to commemorate and renew the making of the covenant on Mount Sinai and to give thanks for the gift of the Law. At Sinai they were given the Law (Torah) to indicate how they should live in their special relationship with God (see, for instance, Ps 119:105). The literal translation of Acts 2:1a is 'When the day of Pentecost was fulfilled'. 'What Luke points to is the birth of the people of Yahweh of the new covenant, the fulfilment of which is proclaimed to people of all nations so that "the day of Pentecost was fulfilled".'[9]

Acts 2:4a gives the core meaning of the Pentecost event and experience: 'All of them were filled with the Holy Spirit.' It was a deep religious experience and Luke uses audio-visual symbols in an attempt to say something about it. Note that Luke is speaking analogously: 'a sound *like* the rush of a violent wind', 'tongues *as of* fire'. Wind and fire were traditional images to speak of the presence and activity of God (Ex 19:18; 24:17; Ez 1:4-12). What is the symbolism in the 'tongues as of fire'? *Glōssa* can mean 'language' as well as 'tongue'. In saying that divided languages/tongues appeared among the disciples and rested on each one of them (Acts 2:3), Luke may well be hinting at the universal dimension of what is happening and emphasising that the Spirit makes possible the preaching of the Good News to all peoples. According to a Jewish tradition, the voice of God proclaiming the Law on Mount Sinai split into seventy tongues so that every nation could hear the law in its own language.[10] In fact, Luke says that under the influence of the Holy Spirit the disciples began to speak in different languages (Acts 2:4) and what they were saying was received and understood in the various languages of the recipients (Acts 2:6-8). The Pentecost event inaugurates a universal mission leading to the creation of a universal community.

The focus shifts to the audience in Acts 2:5, which is made up of 'devout Jews' from the Diaspora. Some may have retired back permanently to Jerusalem and some may have been temporary residents who came on pilgrimage for Pentecost. Having an audience of Jews makes it possible for Luke to present the descent of the Spirit in terms of the restoration of Israel around the nucleus of the Twelve.[11] By pointing out that this Jewish audience comes from many different nations (Acts 2:5, 9-11), Luke is able to highlight the universal significance of what is happening and foreshadow the preaching about 'God's deeds of power' (Acts 2:11) to the ends of the earth. The list of nations in Acts 2:9-11 is probably to be seen as a broad sweep from East to West, from the extremities of the Roman Empire (Parthians, Medes and Elamites) to Rome itself. Luke points out the strong reaction of the audience: they were 'bewildered' (Acts 2:6), 'amazed and astonished' (Acts 2:7), 'amazed and perplexed' (Acts 2:12). But they were also divided. While some are asking questions which indicate that they want to know the meaning of what is going on (Acts 2:12), others are sneering at the disciples, saying that they are drunk (Acts 2:13). The division which the Good News provokes is a constant theme in Luke-Acts (see, for instance, Lk 2:34-35; Acts 28:24).

The action of the Spirit is bringing people into communion with one another. The new community of God's covenant people is being formed. Whereas at Sinai an external law was given as the community's rule of life, now the Spirit is given as the principle of the community's inner life and relationships, as well as the driving force in the community's mission. The community formed at Pentecost transcends barriers of race and language. The Spirit binds people together, making authentic relationship and communication possible. Some suggest that Luke sees the Pentecost event as a reversal of the Tower of Babel incident (Gn 11:1-9). Sin leads to the fragmentation of community and a breakdown in relationships and communication. The Spirit at Pentecost, on the other hand, gathers a crowd and transforms it into a community in which there is mutual understanding and communication (the ability to speak each other's 'language').

What can be said about the historicity of the Pentecost event as recorded in Acts 2:1-13? Here again Luke is not interested merely in giving the details of the historical event, but wants rather to highlight the theological significance of what is happening. In John's Gospel, the Spirit was given on Easter Sunday (Jn 20:22). The miracle of speaking foreign languages intelligibly is not attested by any other New Testament author. Onlookers would hardly conclude that the disciples speaking foreign languages they did not previously know were drunk. Many hold that Luke had in the tradition he received a story of a charismatic manifestation of the Spirit through 'speaking in tongues' (*glōssolalia*) (see 1 Cor 14) and, in the interest of his universalist mission theology, he transformed it into a story of speaking in intelligible foreign languages (*xenolalia*) under the inspiration of the Spirit. There is a very close connection between the resurrection experience and the Pentecost experience. They are in effect two aspects of the one experience. In the Pentecost experience the emphasis is not on what happened to Jesus, but on what happened to the disciples because of

Jesus' resurrection. Luke does not mean to imply that the Holy Spirit did not descend before Pentecost or will not descend after Pentecost. In fact he will relate other remarkable comings of the Spirit as his story in Acts unfolds (Acts 4:31; 8:17; 10:44; 19:6).[12]

Peter's Pentecost Speech (Acts 2:14-41)

This discourse is a Lukan composition addressed to the readers to interpret what is happening. It is not a verbatim report, nor even a synopsis, of a speech made by Peter on this occasion. We are not saying that the speech does not contain elements of the early Christian preaching. Luke may well be using sources here, but it is difficult to isolate those sources. Scholars detect the following pattern or common elements in the missionary speeches of Acts: introduction relating the discourse to the narrative framework; the Jesus-kerygma, that is, the proclamation of the earthly ministry (briefly), death and resurrection of Jesus; proof from Scriptures; appeal for conversion. The elements do not necessarily appear in this order.

Acts 2:14-15 could be taken as the introduction relating the speech to its narrative framework. Peter, in the company of the other apostles, corrects the misunderstanding in Acts 2:13 and gives the real meaning of the Pentecost event, thus inaugurating the Church's Spirit-filled mission. We can divide the body of the speech into three parts: the prophecy of Joel (Acts 2:16-21); the Jesus kerygma (Acts 2:22-36); appeal for conversion (Acts 2:37-41).

Peter, first of all, points out in Acts 2:16-21 that the Pentecost event is the fulfilment of the prophecy of Joel (circa 400 BC). Luke is using the version of the prophecy from the Greek text of the Old Testament (LXX). It is highly unlikely that Peter was speaking Greek on the day of Pentecost or quoting from the Greek Old Testament. Luke even introduces some changes in the quotation to give a better connection with the Pentecost situation.[13] This prophecy speaks of God's promise to pour out his Spirit on all humankind (all flesh), both men and women, which will lead to the re-appearance of prophetic activity on a grand scale. Prophecy is understood as Spirit-filled preaching (see Acts 19:6; 21:9; 1 Cor 14:1). Luke probably sees a connection between the cosmic disturbances attending the Day of the Lord (Acts 2:19-20) and the noise and fire mentioned in Acts 2:2. Conventional cosmic imagery underlines the universal, earth-shaking significance of what is happening. 'Portents' and 'signs' (Acts 2:19) are what give a prophet credibility. Moses (Ex 4:8, 9, 17; Deut 34:10-12) and Jesus (Acts 2:22) worked signs and wonders, and in the subsequent narrative of Acts we will hear of the signs and wonders which the disciples, in the power of the Spirit, work in Jesus' name (see, for instance, Acts 2:43; 5:12). For Peter, the 'Lord' in Acts 2:21, on whose name one calls for salvation, is Jesus.

The mention of the 'Lord' in Acts 2:21 leads Peter to focus his attention on Jesus, who is Lord and Messiah (Acts 2:36), in the central part of the discourse which we can call the Jesus-kerygma (Acts 2:22-36). In this Jesus-kerygma, God is seen as the hidden character behind what happens to Jesus. In Acts 2:23-24 we have the antithesis or contrast which is frequent in the Jesus-kerygma of Acts (see also Acts 2:36): 'You crucified and killed Jesus (by the hands of those outside the law – Romans?), but God raised him up.' The guilt of the hearers provides the preacher with the basis for the call to conversion in Acts 2:38. We see this same pattern in other missionary discourses in Acts: guilt and responsibility for what happened to Jesus (Acts 3:13b-15a; 4:10-11; 5:30; 10:39-40; 13:27-30) as a basis for the call to repentance (Acts 3:19; 5:31). Yet Jesus' death and crucifixion happened according to the plan (*boulē*) and foreknowledge (*prōgnosis*) of God (Acts 2:23) – this is an important Lukan emphasis (see Lk 7:30; Acts 2:23; 4:28; 20:27). God reversed the human verdict on Jesus by raising him up and releasing him for the 'pangs of death'.

Peter now shows that all of this happened according to the 'plan and foreknowledge of God' by appealing to the Scriptures in which the will of God is expressed. The text he first chooses is Ps 16:8-11 (LXX). Originally, this psalm was a prayer of thanksgiving for recovery from a serious illness, but in the LXX translation it becomes a prayer expressing the hope of living with God even after the experience of death. An important assumption by Peter and his hearers is that David wrote the psalms and David was a prophet. Behind Acts 2:29-31 is the question: Who is David talking about in this psalm? He can't be talking about himself because he died, was buried and his tomb is still there to be seen as a proof that he experienced corruption. David must have been speaking about the Messiah who was to be his descendant (see, for instance, 2 Sm 7; Ps 132:11-12).

Acts 2:32-36 takes up again the kerygmatic statement of Acts 2:24 ('this Jesus God raised up') and goes on to show the connection between the resurrection of Jesus and the outpouring of the Spirit at Pentecost. The resurrection meant that Jesus was exalted to a position of sovereignty and power at God's right hand, and as such becomes the Giver of the Spirit. To 'prove' that Jesus' exaltation was within the scope of God's plan and foreknowledge, Peter again appeals to Scripture, this time to Ps 109:1 (LXX). Originally, this was an oracle addressed by a court prophet to the Israelite king on the day of his coronation to emphasise that he was God's chosen one. However, on the assumption that David himself wrote those words, the question arises: Who is David addressing as 'his Lord?' David cannot be talking about himself, because he never ascended into heaven (Acts 2:34). Peter's answer is that David is speaking about the Messiah who is exalted to God's right hand and that person is Jesus of Nazareth, who through his resurrection ascended to God. So what the audience see and hear is in fact the manifestation of the outpouring of the Spirit by the exalted Lord (Acts 2:33). The disciples are but witnessing to the fact that God raised Jesus up (Acts 2:32; see Acts 3:15; 5:32). Peter confidently reaches the climax of his argument in Acts 2:36, which repeats the antithesis of Acts 2:23-24.[14] This verse represents both the climax of the preceding argument and the beginning of the appeal for conversion with which the discourse ends. Presenting Jesus as Lord and Messiah is already an appeal to change one's present attitude to him and accept him.

In Acts 2:37-41 we have the direct appeal for conversion which is implicit in Acts 2:36. In Luke's Gospel the crowds are generally well disposed to Jesus and what he has to say. So we should not be too surprised to hear that they were deeply affected ('cut to the heart') by the manifestation of the Spirit and the words of Peter. The people respond, asking Peter and the other apostles what they should do (Acts 2:37), the same question put to John the Baptist by the crowd after his preaching (Lk 3:10). Peter's reply in Acts 2:38 explains what is involved in an authentic response. It calls for repentance *(metanoia)*, turning away from one's besetting sin, which in this case is the rejection of the Messiah. It involves being baptised 'in the name of Jesus Christ'. Repentance and baptism result in the forgiveness of sins and the gift of the Holy Spirit. Baptism here is the rite of immersion in the Spirit (Acts 1:5), as distinct from John's baptism which was a 'baptism of repentance' (13:24) in preparation for the in-breaking of the kingdom of God.

Peter is telling his hearers that they too can experience the power of the Spirit in their lives; they too can have their Pentecost experience.[15] Notice how Peter reminds people who are asking 'what should *we* do' that it is the *Lord* who takes the initiative in calling people to himself and that call is addressed to both Jews (the hearers and their children) and Gentiles (those who are far off) (Acts 2:39). Thus Peter's speech gives the programme for the mission of the disciples in Acts, as Jesus' speech in the synagogue at Nazareth in Lk 4 gave the programme for his mission. Acts 2:40 strikes again the note of division as a result of the preaching of the word; the restored Israel is separated from 'this corrupt generation'. The number 3,000 (Acts 2:41) may be a round figure dramatising the extraordinary success at the launch of the Spirit-filled Pentecost mission.

Reflection on Acts 1:1–2:41

Being involved in Christian mission today often means facing seemingly insurmountable challenges. A lot of time can be spent on deciding what to do and how best to do it. But do we give sufficient time to reflecting on why we are involved in mission in the first place and where we get the proper perspective and energy to engage in mission? At the beginning of Acts Luke is telling us where we find ultimate meaning, motivation and empowerment for our mission. He is at pains to ground the life and mission of the emerging Church in the life and mission of Jesus, and particularly in the pivotal events which took place in Jerusalem – Jesus' death, resurrection, ascension and the giving of the Spirit. In Lk 24:46-49 Jesus tells his disciples that they are to be his witnesses. This is the only time that the word 'witness' occurs in the Gospel, but it becomes a key term for Christian mission in Acts, where it occurs thirteen times. Before his ascension Jesus continued teaching his disciples about the kingdom of God (Acts 1:3) which will be central to their missionary witness. In Luke's mind, the essence of God's kingdom is God's acceptance, welcome, all-inclusive hospitality, compassion and forgiveness. Because Jesus played the decisive role in the in-breaking of God's kingdom, his person and mission become the focus for Christian mission. In particular, Christian missionaries in Acts are to be witnesses to the resurrection (Acts 1:22) which is the high point of God's saving activity in and through Jesus. The resurrection is also a reminder that the Christ who proclaimed the kingdom of God is not just a figure of the past, but one who is alive and active in the present, continuing to reach out to all with the offer of God's salvation. Throughout the story of mission in Acts we will hear how the disciples of Jesus bore witness to the kingdom of God and the resurrection of Jesus. Acts closes with Paul in Rome 'proclaiming the kingdom of God and teaching about the Lord Jesus Christ with all boldness and without hindrance' (Acts 28:31). It is not enough to understand what our mission is all about. Like the early missionaries, we have to be empowered to engage in mission in the way of Jesus (see Lk 24:49; Acts 1:8). The Spirit who descended at Pentecost is the Spirit of mission and throughout the Acts of the Apostles we see how the Spirit initiates, guides and empowers mission. If we are to respond faithfully to our missionary call today, we too have to open ourselves continually to the action of the Spirit of mission.

Mission in Luke-Acts has a strong community dimension. Mission is undertaken by a community bound together by the Spirit and is not just a matter for individual enterprise. In Acts 1-2 we hear how the Spirit transformed the band of Jesus' followers into a community on mission. Their mission brings people of different linguistic and cultural backgrounds into communion. At Pentecost the missionary Church, the renewed Israel, was born. The Church does not become missionary after a period of consolidation. It is missionary from the moment of its birth. Even young, underdeveloped churches are called to be missionary. Furthermore, the call to missionary witness is not just for some in the Church. The missionary Spirit descends on all.[16]

Pope Francis has reminded us that all baptised Christians are called to be missionary disciples.[17] Though people are called to missionary witness in different ways, there is need for partnerships in which different experiences and gifts are complementary in responding to our common call. Without these partnerships the Church's missionary witness is poorer. In recent years Pope Francis has been calling for a Church which is more 'synodal' in its life and mission. The theme chosen by him for the Synod of Bishops in Rome in October 2022 is: 'For a Synodal Church: communion, participation and mission.'[18] 'Synodality' literally means 'journeying together'. While respecting the legitimate teaching role of the Pope and bishops, a synodal Church is a Church where there is mutual listening and in which everyone has something to learn. Ultimately, it's about listening together to hear the voice of the guiding and empowering Spirit.

Perhaps we get an initial glimpse of this in the group waiting 'with one accord' (*homothymadon*) for the Spirit in Acts 1:12-14. As the story develops, we will hear of the disciples adopting a discerning approach when faced with issues in Church life and mission (see, for instance, Acts 4:23-31; 6:1-6; 15:1-35). The group in Acts 1 is by no means perfect. It still has its sights set on earthly glory (Acts 1:6). It is coping with the experience of failure in discipleship (Acts 1:15-20). Out of his own experience of failure and repentance, Peter tells them that human failure will not frustrate God's saving purpose. The scandals in the Church in recent years have led to low morale and loss of missionary nerve. Along with those who heard Peter's Pentecost speech, the Church today needs to ask what it should do and heed the call to conversion (Acts 2:37-38). Conversion will involve becoming a more humble, listening, learning and discerning Church in need of forgiveness. It will also mean opening ourselves in our failures to the Spirit who enlightens and empowers.

NOTES

[1] The prologue in Lk 1:1-4 introduces both parts of Luke's work. The purpose of the second prologue in Acts 1:1-11 is to give a brief summary of the first part and state the purpose of the second part.

[2] Johnson (*The Acts of the Apostles*, 24) thinks that Luke here has in mind the Spirit's role in both the apostles' initial selection by Jesus and their post-resurrection commissioning.

[3] The story of mission in Acts ends in Rome (Acts 28). In Luke's mind, when the Good News arrives in Rome, it has reached the centre of the known world and its universal dynamism and scope have been clearly demonstrated. Some think Luke saw Rome as 'the ends of the earth'. It is perhaps better to take 'the ends of the earth' as a phrase that does not refer to a geographical location but is a reminder of the universal and unlimited scope of Christian mission. In Is 49:6 the Servant of the Lord is appointed as a light to the nations to bring God's salvation to 'the ends of the earth'. Jesus is that Servant (see Lk 2:30-32) and his missionaries share in his Servant role (see Acts 13:47).

[4] 'In his storyline the author is using the single resurrection-ascension complex as a hinge. From God's viewpoint the ascension

of the risen Jesus after death is timeless, but there is a sequence from the viewpoint of those whose lives it touched. For the Gospel the ascension visibly terminates the activity of Jesus on earth; for Acts it will prepare the apostles to be witnesses to him to the ends of the earth' (Raymond E. Brown, *An Introduction to the New Testament* [New York: Doubleday, 1997], 281). On the historicity of the ascension, see Joseph A. Fitzmyer, *A Christological Catechism* (New York: Paulist Press, 1982), 81-82.

5   In Acts 1:14 the NRSV translates the Greek adverb *homothymadon* as 'constantly'. The New American Bible (NAB) translation 'with one accord' is better. 'The expression "with one accord" (*homothymadon*) is frequent in Acts, describing the community's united prayer before Pentecost (1:14), their communal gatherings in the Temple after Pentecost (2:46), their prayer for boldness (4:24), their togetherness in Solomon's portico (5:12), the united attention of the Samaritans to Philip (8:6), and the unity at the Council of Jerusalem (15:12). In Romans 15:6 Paul prays "that with one accord (*homothymadon*) you may with one voice glorify the God and Father of our Lord Jesus Christ". The unity of Christians, especially in prayer and fellowship, builds the faith of members and attracts new believers, whereas disunity repels them' (Kurz, *Acts of the Apostles*, 86).

6   Luke goes out of this way to highlight the presence and role of women in the life and ministry of Jesus. Women are prominent in the Infancy narratives (Mary, Elizabeth, Anna). Luke often matches an incident about a man with an incident about a woman (for instance, the cure of a man in a synagogue [Lk 6:6-11] and the healing of a woman in a synagogue [Lk 13:10-17]; the man who lost a sheep and the woman who lost a coin [Lk 15:3-10]; the raising of a widow's only son [Lk 7:11-17] and the raising of a man's only daughter [Lk 8:42, 49-56]; the list of male disciples [Lk 6:12-16] and list of female disciples [Lk 8:1-3]). Widows, who are vulnerable, are singled out for special attention (see Lk 7:15; 18:1-8; 21:1-4). In the Lukan passion and resurrection narratives, women are portrayed in a better light than men. All of this has to be seen against the background of a patriarchal society which marginalised women.

7   'The Twelve are reconstituted so that they confront Israel assembled in Jerusalem on the first great feast day following Passover, the feast of Assembly or (in Greek) Pentecost. What Peter and the other eleven will proclaim at that important assembly is the first instance of testimony given by the apostles to the Twelve Tribes of God's people: despite the death of God's anointed one,

God still addresses the message of salvation first to the children of Abraham, to the Twelve Tribes of Israel' (Joseph A. Fitzmyer, *The Acts of the Apostles*, The Anchor Bible 31 [New York: Doubleday, 1998], 221).

8   On the Jewish feast of Pentecost, see Fitzmyer, *The Acts of the Apostles*, 233-235.

9   Jerome Crowe, *The Acts*, New Testament Message 8 (Dublin: Veritas, 1979), 10.

10 See George T. Montague, *The Holy Spirit: Growth of a Biblical Tradition* (New York: Paulist Press, 1976), 277-279.

11 We often speak of the birth of the Church at Pentecost. In doing this we must not forget that for Luke the Church is the restored Israel. There is not a complete break with Israel of old, as we mentioned in dealing with Luke's understanding of the history of salvation. Continuity is always important for Luke. It is more correct to speak of the Church as the renewed Israel, rather than as the new Israel.

12 For a treatment of the recurring descent of the Spirit in Luke's writings, see Earl Richard, 'Pentecost as a Recurrent Theme in Luke-Acts,' in E. Richard, ed., *New Views on Luke and Acts* (Collegeville: Liturgical Press, 1990), 133-149.

13 Luke makes the following changes in the Greek text of Joel: 'In the last days' (Acts 2:17) replaces the simple 'afterwards' to bring out more strongly the eschatological dimension in what is happening; 'And they shall prophesy' (Acts 2:18) is added by Luke to underline that the powerful action of the Spirit is manifested in the preaching of the Church's missionaries; 'I will show portents in the heavens and on the earth' is changed in Acts 2:19 to 'I will show portents in the heaven *above* and *signs* on the earth *below*' – this change may have been made to bring out more clearly the connection between what is happening on the heavenly level (the ascended Lord pouring out the Spirit) and what is happening on the earthly level (the prophesying of the Spirit-filled disciples), as well as to refer to *signs*, which form a pair with *wonders* in the subsequent narrative (see Acts 2:22; 2:43; 5:12).

14 It has been suggested that Acts 2:36 is a fragment of a primitive confession of faith which says that Jesus became Lord and Messiah at the moment of his resurrection. Luke's own tendency is to attribute these titles to Jesus even *before* the resurrection (see Lk 2:11, 26; 4:41; 5:8, 12; 7:13, 19; 10:1-2; 11:1; 13:23; 19:8). What this verse may mean in the context of Luke's whole work is that Jesus, through his resurrection/ascension, was manifested and enthroned as Messiah with sovereign lordship.

ACTS OF THE APOSTLES

[15] 'Peter and his companions have received the Holy Spirit and now they promise that the same Holy Spirit will be given to all believers. In terms of the fundamentals of the Christian life there will be no second-class citizens, and the same equality in receiving the gift of the Spirit will prove true when the first Gentiles are baptized (Acts 10:44-48)' (Brown, *An Introduction to the New Testament*, 286).

[16] The 'they' in Acts 2:1 most probably refers to the whole group of Jesus' disciples and not just the twelve apostles. The eleven apostles are found in prayer among a wider group of women and men in Acts 1:12-14. We are told that before Pentecost the disciples numbered one hundred and twenty people (Acts 1:15). The prophecy of Joel, which is fulfilled at Pentecost, speaks of the outpouring of the Spirit on women and men, young and old. The grouping of Peter with the eleven (Acts 2:14) is best taken as a reminder again that the whole community is the restored Israel.

[17] *Evangelii Gaudium*, no. 120.

[18] In March 2018, the Church's International Theological Commission published a document on 'Synodality in the Life and Mission of the Church' (this can be downloaded from the Vatican website – www.vatican.va).

CHAPTER 3

MISSION AND COMMUNITY IN JERUSALEM
(ACTS 2:42–8:3)

Overview

The Church's mission in Jerusalem has already got under way with the Pentecost speech of Peter. From now till Acts 8:3, Luke will keep the main focus on what is happening in Jerusalem. He will show us the powerful action of the Spirit, both in the internal life of the community and its external mission to others. The Spirit is creating a prayerful, discerning community, open to what God is doing in its midst. It is a community in which there is a marvellous spirit of unity and sharing, a community taking care of those who are needy and in want. The Spirit is also maintaining the community's urgent sense of mission to others and giving success to that mission. We get a number of indications of the steady growth of the young Spirit-filled community. The people are positively disposed to the words and actions of the missionaries. Yet, the picture is not altogether rosy. There are counter-spirits at work both inside and outside the community which are trying to obstruct and frustrate the work of the Spirit. We get glimpses of people within the community who are moved by a spirit contrary to the unifying action of the Spirit – the spirit of collusion, deceit, hypocrisy, possessiveness, factionalism and division.

The opposition from outside, trying to halt the mission, comes mainly from the Jewish leaders who see the twelve apostles usurping their role as the authoritative teachers of the people. Jesus had promised the Twelve that they will exercise a leadership role in the restored Israel (Lk 22:30). The opposition gradually mounts and reaches a climax in the execution of Stephen. But we are left in no doubt that the Spirit creating community is more powerful than the spirits trying to break up the community. The same Spirit continues to energise the community in its bold mission. Nothing can halt the spread of the Good News! Acts 2:42–8:3 can be divided as follows:

1. Acts 2:42-47: First major summary – internal life of the community
2. Acts 3:1-26: Cure of the lame man
3. Acts 4:1-22: Arrest and trial of Peter and John
4. Acts 4:23-31: Discerning prayer of the community
5. Acts 4:32-35: Second major summary – internal life of the community
6. Acts 4:36–5:11: Stories of Barnabas, Ananias and Sapphira
7. Acts 5:12-16: Third major summary – external mission
8. Acts 5:17-42: Arrest and trial of all the apostles
9. Acts 6:1-7: Appointment of the Seven
10. Acts 6:8–8:3: Stephen's mission, arrest, trial and death

Luke has combined and shaped different types of material into a unified narrative which serves his theological purpose, the unfolding of God's plan of salvation under the direction and power of the Spirit. We see most of Luke's literary devices operating in this part of Acts. *Dramatic episodes* give us vivid snapshots of community life and mission – cure of the lame man, Ananias and Sapphira, community tensions, arrests and trials, escape from prison, execution. *Speeches* by key characters bring out the meaning of what is going on. There are six speeches in these chapters of Acts. *Summaries* give concise reports of what is happening within the community and in the community's mission. The three major summaries of Acts all occur in the first five chapters, where Luke's information was probably most fragmentary. *Parallelism* between the experience of Jesus and the experience of the early Christian community is evident, especially in the story of Stephen's arrest, trial and execution. When we look at Acts 2:42–8:3 as a whole, we also notice the interweaving of material about the community's internal life with material about its external mission. This is Luke's way of reminding us of the close connection between community and mission.

1. First Major Summary (Acts 2:42-47)

This summary focuses primarily on the internal life of the community, though the external mission is not forgotten. Acts 2:42 lists four essential features of community life which are the characteristic marks of its unity: 'They devoted themselves to the apostles' teaching and fellowship, to the breaking of bread and the prayers.' The *teaching (didache) of the apostles* continued the teaching of Jesus and witnessed to his risen presence in the community (Acts 1:22). A prominent theme in this teaching was an emphasis on Jesus as the fulfilment of God's promises in the scriptures of Israel. The focus on the continuity with Jesus and Israel would have strengthened the community's sense of identity and rootedness in the ongoing history of God's people. Notice how the apostles' teaching is accompanied by 'wonders and signs' as in the case of Jesus (Acts 2:22, 43). The Greek term *koinonia (fellowship),* used only here in Luke's writings, probably refers both to the spirit that binds people together (communion) and the group itself which is animated by that spirit. It involved a common faith and experience of salvation. Luke understands this salvation as a continuing process, rather than a once-off experience (Acts 2:47b). What Luke will emphasise in Acts is the fellowship expressed by a sharing of goods or holding things in common (Acts 2:44-45). We will look at this more closely in considering the second summary on the internal life of the community (Acts 4:32-35) where this emphasis is developed.

Acts 2:46 speaks of *breaking of bread* in the homes with glad and generous hearts. Originally the breaking of bread was the ritual opening of a festive Jewish meal. By Luke's day, the 'breaking of bread' had become for Christians a technical term for the Eucharist (see Acts 20:7, 11). 1 Cor 11:23-26 gives us some idea of how the Eucharist was understood in the early community – a memorial (re-presentation) of Christ's death and resurrection, celebrated in the sure hope that Christ will come again. It also recalls Jesus' all-inclusive table fellowship which is highlighted in Luke's Gospel as the sign of the all-inclusive hospitality of the compassionate God who invites all to sit at his table. One also thinks of the breaking of bread in the Emmaus story which was the moment of recognition of the risen Jesus (Lk 24:35). As *prayer* was central in the life of the Lukan Jesus (Lk 6:12; 9:18, 28-29; 11:2; 22:41; 23:46), so it was central in the life of his followers. 'With one accord' (*homothymadon*) the early Christians went regularly to the Temple to praise God (Acts 2:46-47), another reminder of the continuity between the faith of Israel and faith in Jesus Christ. The Gospel of Luke opens and closes in a context of prayer in the Temple (Lk 1:8-23; 24:53). Finally, we are reminded of the community's popularity with the people and the daily increase of new adherents (Acts 2:47).[1]

2. Cure of the Lame Man (Acts 3:1-26)

The cure of the cripple is a striking example of the Church's Spirit-driven mission. It also illustrates a number of points in the summary we have just read – apostles frequenting the Temple, having no personal financial resources, working wonders and signs, and being acclaimed by the people. The Temple is the missionary forum for the Christian community in Jerusalem. In Luke's Gospel, Jesus ended his ministry in the Temple (Lk 20-21). So, the mission of the Church takes up where Jesus left off. A parallel is being drawn between this cure, Jesus' cure of the paralytic in Lk 5:17-26 and Paul's cure of the cripple in Acts 14:8-13. Peter and John work as a team, just like Paul and Barnabas later in the story of Acts.

The man crippled from birth would be considered an outcast in Jewish society, not permitted to participate fully in the life and worship of the community, because of his 'blemish' (just as a blemished animal could not be used for sacrifice). So the healing of this man involves his restoration to community life. The fact that he sits begging at the gate of the Temple is symbolic of his pitiable state and his exclusion from the community. The emphasis on mutual looking and attention in Acts 3:4-5 takes the encounter to a deep personal level. In Acts 3:6-7 we have the healing through the word and gesture of Peter. The cripple is made whole 'in the name of Jesus of Nazareth,' that is, by the authority of Jesus or in the power of Jesus who is still present and active in the mission of his followers. This healing is a remarkable symbol of salvation through the name of the Lord, in fulfilment of the scriptural promise quoted in Acts 2:21. Being saved in the name of Jesus becomes the central point in Peter's Temple discourse following the cure and in Acts 4 when Peter and John are on trial. In Acts 3:8 we have the demonstration of the cure and the completeness of the healing, described in terms taken from Is 35:6 (a prophecy of the blessings of the age to come). The man goes into the Temple with the apostles – he who was excluded by reason of his 'blemish' is now restored to his rightful position in the worshipping community. The outsider becomes an insider. The strengthening of the man's ankles and feet (Acts 3:7) may suggest that one who was utterly dependent on others can now 'stand on his own feet'.[2] The bystanders who witnessed the cure react with wonder, amazement and astonishment (Acts 3:9-11), which is the typical response of the crowd to Jesus in his ministry (see especially Lk 5:26).

The astonished crowds gather around Peter in the Temple area called Solomon's Portico (Acts 3:11; see 5:12). Teaching in the Temple was reserved for the Jewish religious leaders and they would certainly not want anyone usurping their role. The discourse of Peter (Acts 3:12-26), which is typical of the preaching to Israel in Acts, is similar in pattern to his

Pentecost discourse. Its purpose is to interpret what has just happened in the cure of the cripple. It starts by correcting a misunderstanding – the cure is not due to any power or piety of Peter or John (Acts 3:12). The man's cure comes about through faith in the name of Jesus (Acts 3:16). Faith was not mentioned in the account of the cure. It is highlighted now because Peter is looking for a faith response from his audience, through which they open themselves to experience the salvation symbolised by the cure. Peter presents the Jesus-kerygma to which the apostles witness (Acts 3:13-16). The one whom the people rejected and put to death was raised up by God. Notice how the God who raised Jesus is called 'the God of Abraham, the God of Isaac, and the God of Jacob, the God of our ancestors' – the God revealed to Moses (see Ex 3:6, 15). The note of continuity with the history of God's people is again sounded. The unbelievable aspects of what the people did to Jesus are described in stark terms. They rejected God's Servant (see Is 52:13), the Holy One (see Lk 4:34; Lev 11:45; Ps 16:3), the Righteous One (see Lk 23:47; Acts 7:52) and the Author of Life, while asking for a murderer to be released.

The proclamation about Jesus is followed in Acts 3:17-26 by an appeal for repentance (change of heart and mind) and conversion (turning to God). Peter gives a number of motives for repentance/conversion. There were mitigating circumstances in the first rejection of the Messiah by the people, but now the people can no longer hide behind ignorance (Acts 3:17-18). Repentance is called for in view of the second coming of Jesus understood as 'the time of universal restoration' (Acts 3:20-21).[3] The 'times of refreshing' is best understood as a period of respite now offered before the onset of Jesus' second coming, a time to start afresh. Those who rejected Jesus are now being given a second chance. As further motivation for repentance, Peter tells his hearers that they are in danger of being cut off from the people if they reject Jesus again, the prophet like Moses whom God has now raised up. The quotation in Acts 3:22-23 is a combination of Deut 18:15-16a and Lev 23:29. They will also miss out on the blessings promised to Israel, especially the blessings promised through Abraham, in whose progeny all the families of the earth will be blessed (see Gn 12:3).[4] Notice again the appeal to the Scriptures (here combined with the call for conversion), which features in the missionary discourses in Acts. Besides recalling the promise of a prophet like Moses and the promise to Abraham, Luke has three general references to the prophets who foretold how the faithful God will fulfil his promises through Jesus (Acts 3:18, 21, 24). In Acts 3:26 Peter enunciates a principle that Luke will continue to advocate in Acts: the word of God has to be preached first of all to Jews. While Israel may have precedence in receiving the Good News, it has no monopoly on salvation in Jesus Christ, which is meant for 'all the families of the earth'. As we begin the next part of the story, we are told that the preaching of Peter in the Temple was very successful. Those who believed in the word numbered about five thousand (Acts 4:4).

3. Arrest and Trial of Peter and John (Acts 4:1-22)

We now hear of the community's first experience of opposition to the new message. The tide of opposition will culminate in Acts 8:1 with the severe persecution of the Church in Jerusalem and the scattering of the community. This 'setback' will lead to the spread of the word farther afield. The pattern we saw in the Gospel of Luke is now repeated in Acts: while the people in general are favourable to the message, the leaders are opposed to it. Jesus had told his disciples that persecutions and trials would come their way. These persecutions and trials are to be seen as opportunities for bearing witness to him in the power of the Spirit (see Lk 12:8-12; 21:12-19).

Opposition came from the official circles in charge of the Temple where the apostles have been preaching the word. By teaching in the Temple Peter and John have assumed a leadership role among God's people which the authorities find greatly annoying (Acts 4:2). They are also upset that the apostles are talking about resurrection in Jesus. The Sadducees, a party made up for the most part of priests and aristocrats, are to the fore in opposing the apostles (Acts 4:1; 5:17).[5] They did not believe in resurrection, angels or demons and they recognised only the written Law of Moses (Pentateuch). Like Jesus, the apostles are held overnight for trial on the following day.[6] Before Luke gets on with telling us about the trial, he reminds us that the setback of the apostles' arrest will not disrupt the increasing success of the word (Acts 4:4).

The substance of Acts 4:5-12 is Peter's 'apologia' before a court in which members of the high priestly family were prominent. Peter is not defending himself and John; he is bearing witness to the Good News of Jesus' resurrection. The question put to Peter and John in Acts 4:7 recalls the question put to Jesus in the Temple: 'Tell us by what authority are you doing these things? Who is it who gave you this authority?' (Lk 20:2). Notice how the reasons for the arrest in Acts 4:2 have faded into the background and the focus goes immediately on the power working in the name (of Jesus), which is the constant refrain in Acts 3-5. Peter, filled with the Holy Spirit (Acts 4:8; see Lk 12:12), points out that the crippled man was healed in Jesus' name, that is, by Jesus' salvific presence, and goes on to state the universal principle that salvation can be experienced only in the name of Jesus (Acts 4:12).[7] This is an implicit appeal for conversion addressed to the authorities who are listening to Peter. Again we get the kerygmatic formula, stated very briefly: you crucified Jesus, but God raised him from the dead (Acts 4:10). As in all Peter's speeches to date, we have the quotation from Scripture (Ps 118:22) to show that what happened to Jesus was within the sphere of God's plan and control (Acts 4:11). Jesus, rejected in his passion and death, has become, by reason of his resurrection, the key figure in God's new building which is the reconstituted Israel.

In Acts 4:13-22 we have the deliberation of the authorities and the outcome of this first trial. This part is skilfully constructed to bring out the contrast between the leaders of official Judaism and the leaders of the restored Israel. The authorities are amazed, at a loss what to do, and fearful of the reaction of the people if they move against the apostles. The apostles, on the other hand, are bold (courageous, outspoken, free), confident that they are doing what God wants them to do, and they enjoy the support of the people. 'Boldness' (*parrēsia*, Acts 4:13) is a favourite word in Acts to describe the frankness and self-assurance of the Christian missionaries (see also Acts 4:29, 31; 9:27-28; 13:46; 28:31). In private deliberation the Sanhedrin consider their options (Acts 4:15-17). They are dumbfounded before the companions of Jesus, 'uneducated and ordinary men' who are speaking so boldly. The cure itself cannot be denied as the cured cripple is standing with the apostles. Fearing a popular reaction if they move against the apostles, the authorities decide to issue a (legal?) warning to the apostles to prevent the further spread of their teaching in the name of Jesus. We see the boldness of Peter and John in reply to this warning (Acts 4:19-20). They speak as men who experience the necessity of speaking about what they have experienced, what they have seen and heard. To obey/listen to this inner conviction is more important than obeying an external command of the authorities. Like the Lukan Jesus, his disciples have an urgent sense of mission.

4. Discerning Prayer of the Community (Acts 4:23-31)

After the trial the focus switches back to the inner life of the community. We have here a beautiful example of discerning prayer, in which the missionaries are enlightened and further empowered to continue their mission, even in the face of opposition. We are told that Peter and John after their release return to 'their own' (Acts 4:23). They belong to a community and in their mission they have acted as God's agents on behalf of this community. In response to the first experience of persecution, the group 'with one accord' (*homothymadon*) now turns to God in prayer, as Jesus did at key moments in his mission. They are following the advice of Jesus to pay at the time of testing (Lk 22:39-46). The prayer (Acts 4:24-30), which may be typical of early Christian prayers, is constructed on the model of Old Testament prayers, especially that of Hezekiah in 2 Kgs 19:15-19 (and Is 37:15-20).

In their prayer they first call to mind the sovereignty of God, the one who made heaven and earth and is really in control (Acts 4:24). The prayer then quotes Ps 2:1-2 which is regarded as the word of David uttered under the inspiration of the Spirit. Ps 2, originally addressed to the Israelite king, was seen by the early Church as an important messianic text (see Acts 13:33; Heb 1:5; 5:5). Acts 4:27 gives a Christian application of the psalm: Herod (= kings); Pilate (= rulers); gentiles (= Romans); peoples (= people of Israel). Only Luke's passion narrative tells us about the role of Herod and his subsequent friendship with Pilate (Lk 23:6-12). 'Servant' (Acts 4:27) echoes the prophetic Christology of Acts 3. The anointing of Jesus probably refers to his prophetic anointing with the Spirit at the Jordan, an event which has Ps 2 (and Is 42:1) in mind (Lk 3:22; see Lk 4:18; Acts 10:38).

The point of quoting Ps 2 appears in Acts 4:28. The enemies of God and his Anointed were in fact accomplishing the divine plan (*boulē*), which in this instance is revealed in Ps 2. By recalling the suffering and opposition which Jesus himself experienced, the community, in its own experience of opposition, is identifying with him, with the intention and desire to respond as he responded. They pray, not to be spared from persecution, but for boldness (*parrēsia*) in speaking the word and they ask that God will accompany their bold witness with signs and wonders performed in the name of his Servant Jesus. In Acts 4:31 we have the answer to the prayer: the house was shaken (earthquake is often used as a symbol for God's powerful presence – see Ex 19:18; Is 6:1) and they were filled with the Spirit. This is sometimes called 'Little Pentecost'. We are reminded once again that in Luke-Acts the Spirit is the fruit of prayer (Lk 11:13) and the effect of the coming of the Spirit is mission. In Acts 5:12-42 we will find the apostles again speaking boldly and working signs and wonders.

5. Second Major Summary (Acts 4:32-35)

In Acts 4:32-35 we have the second major summary where the focus remains on the internal life of the Christian community, although Acts 4:33 ensures that we do not forget the external mission with the grace of God. This summary takes up what had been said about community of goods in the first major summary (Acts 2:42-47) and develops it further as a striking sign of unity and harmony in the Church. This second summary also leads into the episodes of Barnabas (Acts 4:36-37) and Ananias and Sapphira (Acts 5:1-11) which immediately follow.

It is commonly held that Luke here is not telling us how exactly things were with regard to the possession of property; he is, rather, holding up an ideal for the inspiration of the Christian Church in his day. Not everyone in the community who had property sold it and put the proceeds at the disposal of the apostles. Barnabas' action of selling his land (Acts 4:36) would probably not have been remembered unless it was exceptional. In Acts 5:4 Peter says to Ananias that he did not have to sell his land, nor did he have to give the proceeds to the apostles. So, it seems that Luke is generalising from individual acts of striking generosity (like that of Barnabas) for the purpose of edification and inspiration. The ideal which Luke holds up combines the ideal for common life in Hellenistic society of his day ('friends are one heart and one soul' and 'the possessions of friends are common property') and the ideal of the covenant community in the Old Testament (see, for instance, Deut 15:4 – 'there will be no poor among you'). What is said in this summary is very much in line with the Lukan Jesus' concern for the poor (see Lk 4:18-19; 6:20-26; 7:18-23), warnings about the danger of riches (see Lk 12:13-21; 16:1-13, 19-31; 18:18-30; 19:1-10) and emphasis on almsgiving (see Lk 12:33-34).[8] Laying the proceeds at the apostles' feet is probably to be understood in terms of the community's recognition of the apostles' authority.

6. Stories of Barnabas, Ananias and Sapphira (Acts 4:36–5:11)

Luke meant the story of Barnabas and the story of Ananias and Sapphira to be taken together as positive and negative examples of the ideal that he has just stated in the second major summary. The positive example of Barnabas (Acts 4:36-37) made a lasting impression on the tradition. These two verses also serve to introduce Barnabas who will play a very important role in the unfolding story in Acts as one who encourages and is a mediator between the apostles in Jerusalem and Paul, the missionary to the Gentiles (see Acts 9:27; 11:22-23, 25-26). He is Paul's companion on mission (see Acts 13:1–14:28). He certainly lived up to his new name.

The good example of Barnabas leads on, by way of contrast, to the story of Ananias and Sapphira in Acts 5:1-11. The sin of the couple was clearly one of deceit, pretending to give the entire proceeds to the apostles, while in fact retaining a certain portion. It is seen as a lie to the Holy Spirit who directs the community (Acts 5:3, 4), a denial of the Spirit's work in the community. Satan is at work in the heart of community members, trying to negate the work of the Spirit bringing people into sincere unity and harmony.[9] The fact that Ananias and Sapphira colluded in this sin (Acts 5:1, 9) means that we have here the beginnings of a 'shadow counter-community of avarice, over against the spirit-community that shares its possessions'.[10] But Satan is no match for the Spirit. The Spirit-filled apostles, and Peter in particular, can detect this 'cancer' in the community and eradicate it. As Peter exposes the truth, Ananias drops dead and is carried out and buried by the young men (Acts 5:5-6). Three hours later, Sapphira arrives on the scene, ignorant of what has happened, and we get a repeat performance of the fate of Ananias.

While this story may have some basis in fact, it seems it has been embellished by popular imagination. Luke may be drawing a comparison between Ananias and the avaricious Judas who also had a field and met a tragic end. One can detect an allusion to the story of Achan (Jos 2:1-26), who kept back what should have been consecrated to the Lord – this story may have provided Luke with a rough model for his story.[11] The whole episode had a profound effect on the group of believers who are called 'church' for the first time in Acts (Acts 5:11).

7. Third Major Summary (Acts 5:12-16)

Acts 5:12-16 is another description of the Church in capsule form. Here the main emphasis is on the 'signs and wonders' which are evident in the Church's external mission (see Acts 2:43). The apostles are 'with one accord' (*homothymadon*) in their mission. The overall effect of the summary is to demonstrate the fulfilment of the community's prayer in Acts 4:30. They had asked God to accompany their bold preaching with signs and wonders. The increasing number of believers and the high esteem in which the apostles are held are again highlighted. The summary certainly intends to extol the position of Peter in the community (Acts 5:15-16). His healing work is to be seen as a continuation of Jesus' healing work (compare Mk 6:55-56) and Luke will present Paul in a similar way in Acts 19:11-12. Notice that the towns around Jerusalem are beginning to be affected by the apostolic preaching – perhaps a hint that the Good News is straining to go farther afield (Acts 5:16).

8. Arrest and Trial of all the Apostles (Acts 5:17-42)

The third major summary (Acts 5:12-16) has extolled the power at work in the new leaders of the restored Israel. In the Lukan narrative, this leads to another confrontation between them and the leaders of official Judaism. There are obvious similarities between the confrontation in Acts 4:1-22 and that in Acts 5:17-42. Similar wording is used in Acts 4:1-3 and

5:17-18 to introduce the two episodes; we have the same sequence of events (arrest, appearance before the Sanhedrin during which the apostles witness to Jesus, deliberation by the Sanhedrin without the apostles present, release of the apostles with a command not to speak in Jesus' name); the insistence by the apostles that they must obey God rather than the Sanhedrin (Acts 4:19-20; 5:29). However, in the second case there is development and intensification of the conflict: here we have an arrest and trial of all the apostles and not just Peter and John (Acts 5:18); the hostility of the Sadducees has hardened and increased (Acts 5:17); in place of a relatively mild enquiry issuing in a warning, we now have an angry court wanting to kill the apostles (Acts 5:33) and actually sentencing them to be flogged (Acts 5:40); the part God is playing in the story is also heightened. God intervenes by engineering the escape of the apostles from prison (Acts 5:19-20) and what Gamaliel says highlights the question of God's presence in the apostles' mission (Acts 5:34-39).

In Acts 5:19-20 we have the first of three miraculous releases from prison in Acts (see also 12:6-11; 16:26-27). Angels, as agents of God's will, appear quite frequently in Luke-Acts (see Lk 1:11, 26; 2:9, 13; 22:43; 24:23; Acts 8:26; 10:3, 7, 22; 11:13; 12:7-15, 23; 27:23). It is strange that this extraordinary release has little influence on what follows in the trial. It could well be a literary device to emphasise the fact that God is operative in the apostles' life and mission. Acts 5:21b-26 tells how the full Sanhedrin is convened, the escape is discovered, and the apostles are re-arrested in the Temple area, but without violence because of their great popularity with the people. The leaders' fear of the people parallels Lk 20:19 and 22:2.

The accusation of the high priest (Acts 5:28) again draws attention to the issue of teaching in the name of Jesus. He adds the accusation that the apostles are blaming the authorities for Jesus' death. In reply 'Peter and the apostles' (Acts 5:29) again announce the Jesus-kerygma (Acts 5:30-32), saying that they feel the urgency to obey God rather than human authority. They are picking up where Peter left off at the previous trial (Acts 4:19). The kerygmatic contrast between what God did and the leaders did is stated briefly. 'Hanging on a tree,' which heightens the shameful aspect of death on a cross, is probably an allusion to Deut 21:22 which belonged to the early Christian homiletic tradition about Jesus' death (see Acts 10:39; Gal 3:13; 1 Pt 2:24). Acts 5:31 gives us two titles for the exalted Jesus: *Leader* (see Acts 7:35; Heb 2:10; 12:2) and *Saviour* (see Lk 2:11; Acts 13:23). Note that repentance leading to the forgiveness of sins is God's gift to us (Acts 5:31; see 11:18). The missionaries and the Spirit are co-witnesses (Acts 5:32). Jesus' promise of the Spirit at the time of trials is fulfilled (Lk 12:12).

The intervention of Gamaliel the Pharisee (Acts 5:34-39) is best understood as a wise and sincere observation which underlines Luke's oft-repeated position that God is active in the Christian movement and consequently it will succeed despite hostile opposition. Nothing can stop the spread of the Good News. Gamaliel recalls two messianic frauds. According to the Jewish historian Josephus, Theudas led a revolt in AD 45-46. He proposed to emulate Joshua and lead an army of followers dry-shod across the Jordan. The Roman procurator Fadus suppressed the uprising. Note that this revolt took place *after* Gamaliel's speech (dated roughly AD 37). Judas the Galilean led a revolt in AD 6 when the first census was held and Judea was set up as a district of the Roman province of Syria (Quirinius was governor of Syria at the time). Luke says that Judas (AD 6) came *after* Theudas (AD 45). Again we see that Luke's main interest is in highlighting the presence and activity of God in events, rather than giving exact historical information.

Acts 5:40-42 gives us the outcome of the second trial. The apostles are beaten, again ordered not to preach in the name of Jesus and then released. Their reaction is one of joy that they were counted worthy to suffer 'for the sake of the name'. They are responding as Jesus had told them in Lk 6:22-23. The punishment and second warning not to speak in Jesus' name have absolutely no effect on the apostles. Every day, in the Temple and their homes, they are proclaiming Jesus as Messiah. The mission continues in Jerusalem, but the opposition which has been building up will now explode in violent persecution which will scatter many in the Jerusalem Church (but not the apostles! – see Acts 8:1).

9. Appointment of the Seven (Acts 6:1-7)

Acts 6:1–8:3, which is concerned almost exclusively with the mission and death of Stephen, could be seen as a bridge between the mission in Jerusalem and the mission farther afield. Stephen's violent death in Jerusalem was the culmination of the growing opposition to the Church which we saw in Acts 2–5. On the other hand, his mission and death is the occasion for a severe persecution of (Hellenistic) Christians, which drives them out of Jerusalem and thus initiates mission in Samaria and Judea (see Acts 8:1).

Both the internal life of the community and its external mission are in view in Acts 6:1-7. Luke's main concern is probably to introduce Stephen and Philip, who are now about to play important roles in his story, and to show how their mission has the approval of the Twelve and is in continuity with the mission of the apostles in Acts 2–5. Continuity is always important for Luke. But these verses also give us a further insight into the internal life of the community which is developing its organisation and structure in response to changing circumstances. The dominant picture of the community in Acts 1–5 is one of unity, harmony, mutual care and dependence – a community expressing its fellowship (*koinōnia*) in such exemplary ways as the sharing of goods. However, there were hints of tension within the community (see Acts 5:1-11). Now we see some of that tension surfacing again and leading to the Seven's appointment to ministry.

The Hellenists in particular are not happy because their widows are being neglected in the daily distribution of food.

In Acts 4:34-35 we heard about the practice of taking care of the needy in the community. Widows, particularly widows who may have come to Jerusalem from the Jewish Diaspora and did not have family connections there, were vulnerable in a patriarchal society. The early Christian community probably followed the Jewish practice of having something like 'soup kitchens' for needy people. In caring for widows they were following the injunctions of their Jewish religious traditions (see, for instance, Ex 22:21; Deut 10:18; Is 1:17; Jer 7:6; Ez 22:7; Ps 94:6).

Who were the Hellenists and the Hebrews in the Christian community (Acts 6:1)? The Hellenists were most probably Christian converts from among the Diaspora Jews resident in Jerusalem, while the Hebrews were converts from Jews who were natives of Palestine. The Hellenists spoke Greek and the Hebrews spoke Hebrew or Aramaic.[12] Many think that, besides speaking different languages, there were also differences in culture and theological emphases. The Hellenists were more acculturated to Greco-Roman culture and probably had a more liberal attitude to the role of the Law and the Temple in Jewish life and practice. So the dispute over the distribution of food in Acts 6:1 may be symptomatic of a deeper division in the early Christian community. Among the Christians in Jerusalem there may well have been different positions with regard to the importance of the Jewish Temple and participation in Temple worship. The crisis in Acts 6:1 foreshadows the crisis which came later over the question of the circumcision of Gentiles admitted to the Christian community.

The 'Twelve' (term used only here in Acts) address the immediate problem by calling together 'the whole community' (Acts 6:2). One of the functions of the Twelve is to preserve the *koinōnia* of the community. They (under pressure of work?) feel they must be (more?) free from 'ministry at tables' (*diakonein trapezais*) to devote themselves to prayer and the 'ministry of the word' (*diakonia tou logou*) (Acts 6:2, 4). Prayerful 'service of the word' (see Lk 1:2) should probably be understood as discerning prayer to discover where the active word of God is leading the Church's mission (see Acts 6:7; 12:24). This cannot be neglected at a time when the community is in danger of being consumed by internal issues. The serving at tables is usually understood as something like working in a soup kitchen – in view of the issue in question. But it could mean serving at financial tables with responsibility for distribution of funds to the needy (see NRSV footnote – 'keep accounts').

While the Twelve give directions, they leave it to the community to make the selections (Acts 6:3). They ask that those chosen be 'of good standing, full of the Spirit and of wisdom'. These qualities may seem superfluous for the function immediately envisaged (serving at tables). In Luke's subsequent story, however, Stephen and Philip appear as preachers and workers of 'signs and wonders,' doing the same things on mission as the apostles did in Acts 2–5. Seven are chosen by the community and presented to the apostles for approval, appointment and commissioning (Acts 6:5-6). They all have Greek names, which is an indication that leaders are being appointed for the Hellenistic branch of the community.[13]

Stephen is singled out as 'a man full of faith and the Holy Spirit' (see Acts 6:8-10). He will be a pivotal figure, linking mission in Jerusalem with mission beyond Jerusalem. The apostles prayed and laid hands on the Seven (Acts 6:6). This is meant to remind us that this new development is taking place under the guidance of the Spirit.[14] The laying on of hands also symbolises solidarity between persons, transfer of power, and self-identification of one person with another in respect of status, office and value. Thus the Seven become associates of the apostles in the mission of the Church. Luke establishes the continuity of mission at this important transition point. Traditionally, the Seven are called 'deacons,' but this word is not used in Acts 6:1-7.

Acts 6:7 is a minor summary, reminding us again of community growth, which forms an inclusion with the reference to growth in Acts 6:1. Tension and growth often go hand-in-hand in mission. Even Jewish priests (perhaps those belonging to lower priestly ranks) are among those joining the Christian community.

10. Stephen's Mission, Arrest, Trial and Death (Acts 6:8–8:3)

Acts now takes up the story of how Stephen engaged in mission among the Hellenistic Jews in Jerusalem, which leads to his arrest, trial and execution. As mentioned above, the Stephen story marks a major turning point in Acts.

a. Stephen's Mission, Arrest and Trial (Acts 6:8-15)

Stephen is described in terms reminiscent of Jesus and the apostles: he is filled with the Spirit; full of grace and power; he does 'wonders and signs'; his activity generates opposition. Opposition to him comes from Hellenistic Jews who frequent the synagogue(s) for the Jews from the Diaspora in Jerusalem among whom Stephen was probably carrying on his mission (Acts 6:9). In reading the sequence of events dealing with Stephen's arrest and trial (Acts 6:11-14), we realise that Luke is drawing a close parallel between the experience of Jesus and the experience of Stephen: the people are stirred up against Stephen (Acts 6:12; Lk 23:13-25); he is accused of blasphemy (Acts 6:11; Mk 14:64); false witnesses accuse him (Acts 6:13; Mk 14:56-57); the elders and the scribes came upon him (Acts 6:12; Lk 20:1); they led him away to their council (Acts 6:12; Lk 22:66); one of the false accusations concerns the threat to destroy the Temple which Jesus is alleged to have made (Acts 6:14; Mk 14:58).[15] The parallelism is continued in Acts 6:15 – they fixed their eyes on him (compare Lk 4:20) and saw that his face was like the face of an angel (compare Lk 9:29). We will see that Luke will continue drawing parallels between Jesus and Stephen when he narrates his execution in Acts 7:54–8:3.

b. Stephen's Speech (Acts 7:1-53)

Stephen's speech (in response to a question by the high priest) is by far the longest speech in Acts, which in itself is an indication of its importance for Luke. It is, for the most part, a long recital of the history of salvation from Abraham to the foundation of the Temple. Many think the speech is mainly a Lukan composition, inserted in his work at an important transition point and aimed at the reader to explain key insights, not only for the Stephen episode, but indeed for Luke-Acts as a whole.[16]

We could say there are four major points Luke wants to highlight in Stephen's speech. Firstly, the history of God's dealings with the people is a history of fidelity to his promises, which reach their real fulfilment in the Christ event. Everything that God was doing in the history of his people was pointing to fulfilment in the Christ event, which includes the mission of his disciples. Jesus is the promised prophet like Moses; in him, the 'Righteous One,' the Law is fulfilled; and he has replaced the Temple as the place on earth where God encounters humans. Secondly, looked at from another perspective, the history of God's people is a history of infidelity on their part. It is a long story of resistance to God's advances, even to the point of killing God's prophets. This resistance has reached its climax in the rejection and killing of Jesus, the Messiah sent by God to fulfil the promises. Thirdly, one element of this infidelity which the speech highlights is the people's tendency to idolatry, to a type of worship which is based on the assumption that God can be confined to a Temple made by human hands and can thus be controlled and manipulated by the worshippers. But the sovereign God cannot be confined to the land of Israel or to a Temple made by human hands.

Notice how the speech points out that most of the great events of salvation history took place *outside* the promised land. (Abraham was called when he was in *Mesopotamia*; God favoured Joseph, and through him the patriarchs, in *Egypt*;

Moses found favour with God in *Egypt* and he was in the *wilderness of Sinai* when he experienced Yahweh in the burning bush; God led the people out of Egypt, guided them in the *wilderness* and gave Moses 'living oracles' for the people while they were at *Sinai*). This particular emphasis is important at a stage in Luke's story when the Good News is about to take the first step in breaking away from its Jewish moorings and the Christian missionaries are about to set out to proclaim God's presence and salvation outside Jerusalem and even in foreign lands.

Fourthly, central to Stephen's speech is the comparison between Jesus and Moses, whom Jews regarded as the foremost prophet and the one through whom the Law was given. Stephen speaks of Moses as a type for Christ. To accept Moses and the Law inevitably must lead to the acceptance of Jesus, the Moses-like prophet, whom God has raised up in fulfilment of prophecy. The career and mission of Moses and the career and mission of Jesus (including the mission of the risen and exalted Jesus which continues through the mission of the Church) follow the same path.

The speech can be divided in four parts: (i) The *Patriarchal Period* and the Rejection of Joseph (Acts 7:2-16); (ii) The *Mosaic Period* and Moses' Rejection by Israel (Acts 7:17-43); (iii) From *Joshua to Solomon* and the Misguided Act of building the Temple (Acts 7:44-50); (iv) Stephen's *Indictment of the Jews* who have brought to a climax the infidelities of the past in rejecting Jesus (Acts 7:51-53). In each part we see the contrast between what the faithful God is doing and how the unfaithful people are responding. And each part (particularly the Mosaic stage) is pointing forward to Jesus in whose coming God's fidelity and the people's infidelities reach a climax.

(i) Patriarchal Period (Acts 7:2-16): Stephen concentrates on two figures in the patriarchal period, Abraham (Acts 7:2-8) and Joseph (Acts 7:9-16). He begins with *Abraham* whose story was regarded as the beginning of salvation history. God

called Abraham and made him a promise. Stephen seems to be emphasising that God called Abraham in a foreign land and Abraham encountered God when he was a wanderer, constantly moving on from his settled abode, and not having a permanent foothold in the promised land (Acts 7:5). Note how God is the main actor in the story of Abraham and the fulfilment of the promise made to Abraham belongs to God (Acts 7:7). The faith of Abraham, so important in the Genesis story, is not mentioned. The later stages of the people's history will show us how God was working out this promise, but the real fulfilment of the promise is given to Abraham's posterity (*sperma*) (Acts 7:5), who, in Stephen's mind, is Jesus. The promise to Abraham includes the opportunity to participate in the true worship of God (notice how the quotation in Acts 7:7 makes this point by incorporating a phrase from Ex 3:12). As we shall see later in the speech, this aspect of the promise is not fulfilled in the building of the Temple or in Temple worship; for Stephen the fulfilment is found in the worship in and through Jesus.[17]

Stephen moves with great rapidity to the patriarch *Joseph* where his real interest lies. In contrast to the obedient Abraham, the patriarchs manifested their opposition to God through their rejection of Joseph, motivated by jealousy (Acts 7:9). But the faithful God was with Joseph (Acts 7:9), delivering him from his afflictions and giving him favour with Pharaoh in the land of Egypt (foreign soil) and thus keeping the promise to Abraham alive. Through Joseph, the rejected one, Jacob and his family experienced salvation in Egypt. Jacob and the other patriarchs died in Egypt, having no inheritance in the promised land except for the tomb bought from the heathen Canaanites.[18] The parallel between what happened in the life of Joseph and what happened in the life of Jesus and his followers is obvious in Stephen's speech. The favour and wisdom which Joseph enjoyed calls to mind Lk 2:52. Rejection by the patriarchs, but acceptance and empowerment by God (Acts 7:9), reminds us of the kerygmatic contrast which was characteristic of the speeches in Acts 2–5. The patriarchs acted out of jealousy (Acts 7:9), as did those who rejected Jesus at work in his apostles (Acts 5:17).

(ii) Mosaic Period (Acts 7:17-43): The life and mission of *Moses* is central to Stephen's speech. The Mosaic Period is an important step in the working out of God's plan and promise. But almost everything in the life and mission of Moses is meant to point forward to the life and mission of Jesus (including his mission through his followers) which fulfil God's plan and promise.[19] Acts 7:17-19 rapidly connects the period of the patriarchs with the period of Moses. Stephen's treatment of the story of Moses falls into three periods of forty years (see Acts 7:23, 30), in each of which God closely directed Moses' life. The period of Moses' birth, nurture and education culminated in his first visit to his fellow Israelites and his rejection by them (Acts 7:20-29). The period of Moses' time in the wilderness was a time when he experienced the call of God and was empowered and sent to be the leader and liberator of his people (Acts 7:30-34). The period of the Exodus and the Wilderness, which was Moses' second visitation to his people as leader and saviour, was again a time of rejection, despite the signs and wonders he worked and the 'living oracles' (Law) which were given through him (Acts 7:35-43).

The first period of Moses' life is based on a free summary of the Exodus text. Stephen is making the point that Moses was brought up in a Gentile palace, not among the people of God and still less in the holy land. He resembles Jesus in his favour before God and growth in wisdom (see Lk 2:52) and in being powerful in his words and deeds (see Lk 24:19). When he was forty years old, Moses visited his fellow Israelites (Acts 7:23). He appears as the defender of the oppressed (Acts 7:24), a peacemaker and reconciler (Acts 7:26). This also fits in with the picture of Jesus we get in Luke's writings. However, what Moses was doing was misunderstood by his kinsfolk. The rejection of Moses is not just verbal, but physical: he is 'pushed aside' in the act of reconciling his kinsfolk (Acts 7:27, 39). He flees and becomes a stranger in a foreign land (Acts 7:29), where he will experience the presence and the call of God.

In the second forty-year period in Moses' life (Acts 7:30-34) the focus is again on the climax of the period, the incident of the burning bush which is Moses' call and empowerment for mission as God's agent in liberating his oppressed people. Moses experiences God in a foreign land, but the ground on which he stands is holy (Acts 7:33). In Luke's understanding, Moses' experience of God at the burning bush, in which he is empowered and sent back again as saviour of God's people, corresponds to Jesus' experience of God in the resurrection/ascension, when he is empowered and sent back (through the mission of the disciples) to visit God's people a second time with the offer of salvation.

The final period of Moses' life and mission (Acts 7:35-43) covers the exodus and wilderness experiences. Acts 7:35 again reminds us of the kerygmatic contrast we have seen in the speeches of Acts: Moses is rejected by the people as ruler and judge, but is sent by God as both 'ruler and liberator' (Jesus is called 'leader and saviour' in Acts 5:31). He led the people out with 'wonders and signs' (Acts 7:36; see also Acts 2:22; 5:12; 6:8). Moses was the one through whom 'living oracles' were gifted to the congregation in the wilderness (Acts 7:38). A climax is reached in Acts 7:37 when we are told that Moses spoke of the coming of a prophet like himself (see Deut 18:15). Of course, in Luke's understanding Jesus is the one who fulfils this prophecy (see Acts 3:22-26). Moses is rejected a second time (Acts 7:39 – the same verb 'push aside' as in 7:27). Stephen goes on to say that the rejection took the form of idolatry in the wilderness. The incident of the golden calf is recalled, an idol which is the work of their hands (Acts 7:41). At this point Stephen gives a quotation from the Book of Amos to make the point that the people worshipped idols rather than Yahweh in the wilderness (Acts 7:42-43).[20] The Mosaic period ends on the note of idolatry, the misguided concentration on the work of human hands. That becomes the main theme of Stephen's treatment of the last period in his historical survey, with particular reference to a misguided understanding of the Temple and the worship carried on in it.

(iii) From Joshua to Solomon (Acts 7:44-50): Stephen's only interest here is to contrast the Tent of Testimony of the wilderness period with the Temple built by Solomon in Jerusalem. For Stephen, the moveable Tent was seen as something transitory and temporary, destined to be replaced, like the Law, when the promises were fulfilled in Christ who is the authentic Meeting Place between God and humans. The building of the permanent Temple in Jerusalem is seen as a backward and misguided step by Stephen. Solomon's Temple was not part of the fulfilment of the promise to Abraham. Like the idolatrous calf in the wilderness, it was something made by human hands (Acts 7:48; see Acts 17:24). It led people to treat Yahweh as an idol, a god who is confined to one place to be controlled and manipulated by the will of the worshippers. Stephen quotes Is 66:1-2 (LXX) to support his argument that the sovereign God cannot be confined or controlled in this way. Saying that God is not confined to Jerusalem is important at this stage in Luke's story as the missionaries are about to leave Jerusalem and proclaim the Good News farther afield. In expressing such strong reservations about the Temple worship, the Hellenist Stephen would have gone a lot farther than the apostles in their preaching. We saw that they frequented the Temple for worship and preaching. Stephen and the Hellenistic preachers may have been the first to see the implications of some of the things Jesus said about the Temple. Stephen stands in the line of those prophets who warned the people about turning the Temple into an object of false security (see, for instance, Jer 7:1-15; 26:1-6).

(iv) Indictment of the Jews (Acts 7:51-53): Using biblical images to describe the people's stubborn resistance (see, for instance,

Ex 32:9; 33:3; Jer 9:25; 6:10; Ez 44:7), Stephen launches into an open attack on his accusers and judges. Israel's history of infidelity and resistance to God has reached its climax in the refusal of the leaders to accept Jesus. They killed the 'Righteous One' (Acts 3:14; 22:14; Lk 23:47), as their ancestors murdered the prophets. Like their fathers before them (see, for instance, Is 63:10) they resist the Holy Spirit in rejecting the Spirit-filled leaders (especially Moses), the prophets, and now the prophet like Moses. Despite the fact that the leaders were privileged in receiving a Law 'promulgated by angels' (this underlines its sacred character), they did not keep it. They failed to see that the Law, like the Temple, pointed to Jesus the Messiah.

c. Stephen's Martyrdom (Acts 7:54–8:3)

Stephen's harsh indictment of the members of the Sanhedrin fills them with anger, while he is filled with the Holy Spirit (Acts 7:55). As at the beginning of Stephen's trial, so now Luke draws a close parallel between Jesus and Stephen at the time of his death. He wants to show the Christian martyr following in the footsteps of the Master and also the Jewish leaders rejecting the second offer of salvation as they did when they crucified Jesus. In Stephen Jesus is being rejected and dying again. The heavens are opened and Stephen has a vision of the Son of Man standing at the right hand of God (Acts 7:55-56; Lk 3:21; 22:69). Like Jesus (Lk 4:29) and Paul (Acts 14:29), Stephen was cast out of the city to be killed (Acts 7:58). His death was probably more a lynching than an execution carried out after sentence was passed. Luke very skilfully introduces the young Saul into the narrative (Acts 7:58; 8:1). At the very point when the mission's outward movement from Jerusalem is about to begin, the one who will play the most prominent role in this outreach is mentioned. Jesus committed his spirit to the Father at the time of his death (Lk 23:46); Stephen commits his spirit to the risen Lord at the time of his death (Acts 7:59). Jesus prayed for forgiveness for his persecutors (Lk 23:34); Stephen did the same (Acts 7:60). The death of the first Christian martyr is described as a 'falling asleep' (Acts 7:60). We are told that some devout men buried Stephen and mourned over him (Acts 8:2; see Lk 23:50-53). Notice how Luke links the death of Stephen to the persecution which follows by delaying the mention of his burial (Acts 8:2) till he had said something about the persecution in Acts 8:1. It seems the 'severe persecution', resulting in a scattering to Judea and Samaria (Acts 8:1), was directed at Hellenists like Stephen who enraged Jews because of their radical attitude to the Law and the Temple. The not-so-radical apostles were not touched. Having the apostles remain in Jerusalem probably serves Luke's interest in preserving the link between the mother church in Jerusalem and other evangelised areas. Luke immediately highlights Saul's role in the persecution (Acts 8:3). It almost seems that Saul is the sole persecutor! We are being prepared for the story of Saul's conversion in Acts 9.

Reflection on Acts 2:42–8:3

As stated in the introduction, my missionary interests influence what I see in the text. As I read the text I hope to find meaning and energy for engagement in mission today. What light might the account of the mission in Jerusalem shed on the missionary challenges facing us?

I am particularly struck by the way Luke has skilfully interwoven material on the community's internal life with material about its external mission. Community and mission must never be separated, as one without the other leads to lopsided attitudes and practices.[21] Note how the phrase 'with one accord' (*homothymadon*) is used in speaking of the community's internal life and external mission (see Acts 2:46; 4:24; 5:12; see also 1:14; 8:6; 15:6). I think of ways we can break the connection between community and mission. When I was on overseas mission I often saw time spent in the community house as a break from mission. In missionary congregations we often made a distinction between those on overseas mission and those in the home base who were asked to play a supportive role for the real missionaries. A distinction between maintenance and mission also led to drawing a clear line between the pastoral care of the faithful and missionary outreach to those outside the Church. The close connection between community and mission in Acts challenges these false dichotomies. Every Christian community, be it a diocese, parish, religious congregation or small group, is called to be both a sign and agent of the communion God wishes for our world. Communion is not only the goal of mission but also the way of mission. The aim of mission is the formation of communion among diverse peoples bound together in faith and love. We do this, not just by preaching and working for others, but also by the way we relate among ourselves in our missionary Church. Building communion among ourselves is an essential part of the missionary task.[22] If we are not signs of true communion in our mutual relationships, our preaching will sound very hollow. Of course, in building communion among ourselves, we must be aware of the danger of becoming cosy, inward-looking groups, focused only on ourselves. True Christian communion will always impel us to missionary outreach and witness in service of the wider world. Communion must always be the source and fruit of mission.

The sentence which opens the large section in Acts on mission in Jerusalem lists the distinguishing marks of Christian communion: 'They devoted themselves to the apostles' teaching and fellowship, to the breaking of bread and the prayers' (Acts 2:42). Every Christian community on mission has to ask how it measures up to these criteria. Hearing of the apostles' teaching, we are prompted to reflect on the role of leaders in the community. The teaching authority in the Church is responsible for fostering communion and guarding against the disintegration of communion. The apostles did this by constantly putting the focus on Jesus Christ and his Spirit. In the Ananias and Sapphira incident (Acts 5:1-11) we hear of Peter detecting deceit, hypocrisy, collusion and self-glorification in the community and taking steps to counter attitudes and practices which harm communion. Acts 6:1-7 shows us a Church leadership preserving communion and inviting participation from the whole community. The apostles were not slow to adapt community structures in response to changing circumstances. And they trusted the community to make right choices in presenting candidates for ministry. If the missionary Church is to evangelise successfully today, it must develop more participative structures and draw on gifts and talents in the whole community. The apostles were willing to involve others in financial administration, an area which is sometimes kept under the strict control of Church leaders today. The service of leadership is a gift to the Church and we are blessed today with the leadership of Pope Francis in fostering communion and promoting mission.

The second distinguishing mark of the Church is *koinōnia* (fellowship), expressed especially in the sharing of goods and care for the poor and marginalised. This is a reminder to us that the poor and excluded ones must always be put at the heart of Church life and mission. Working for justice is a constitutive dimension of preaching the Gospel of Jesus. Pope Francis constantly promotes a Church of the poor – a Church for the poor, excluded and exploited, including the exploited earth. The Church will always need the radical witness of people like Barnabas and Francis of Assisi, who gave their all to the poor, as a reminder to the whole Church that option for the poor is central to its mission.

Thirdly, the Church is called to be a praying community. The discerning prayer of the community (Acts 4:23-31) in the face of mounting opposition is a model for missionary prayer today when it may seem that things are not working out as they should. It is a prayer of trust in the faithful God who remains in control and whose salvific plan will prevail. This prayer draws us into identification with Jesus and helps us keep the focus on his life and message. It also opens us to the power of the Spirit of mission who enables us to be bold and courageous in sharing the Good News of Jesus.

Finally, Acts 2:42 turns our attention to the centrality of the Eucharist in the life and mission of the community. In celebrating the Eucharist we experience the hospitality of God, the bonds of our communion with God and each other are strengthened and we commit ourselves to be an open, hospitable community. We offer ourselves to be channels of God's hospitality and communion in an inhospitable and fragmented world, nourished for our missionary journey by the Bread of Life. As the Second Vatican Council said, the Eucharist is 'the source and summit of the Christian life'.[23]

In Acts 2:42–8:3 we are given a powerful picture of Spirit-filled witness in the face of mounting opposition. As co-witnesses with the Spirit (Acts 5:32), the disciples are prophetic figures walking in the footsteps of Jesus the Prophet. Mission becomes a sharing in the paschal experience of Jesus who suffered and died in fidelity to his mission, but who always trusted in a loving Father and in the power of the kingdom of God over the power of evil in its many forms. Again, Luke emphasises the identification of Jesus with his missionaries through his use of parallelism, seen most clearly in the story of Stephen the martyr. In the commissioning ceremony for new missionaries we have the practice of giving them the mission cross. 'The missionary cross or crucifix is no mere ornament depicting Christianity in general. Rather, it is a vigorous commentary on what gives the Gospel its universal appeal. Those who receive it possess not only a symbol of their mission but a handbook on how to carry it out.'[24]

Christian mission calls for great boldness (*parrēsia*) which is granted by the Spirit in response to prayer (Acts 4:29-31). The basic meaning of this Greek word is 'frank and open speech,' even in threatening situations. It is one of the favourite words of Pope Francis in speaking of Christian life and mission today. 'The Holy Spirit also grants the courage to proclaim the newness of the Gospel with boldness (*parrēsia*) in every time and place, even when it meets with opposition.'[25] There are still places in our world where

Christians are suffering for their faith and some have paid the ultimate price in living and proclaiming the Gospel. Wherever Christians live they are called to bear witness to Gospel values by what they say and do, and that is not always easy. It takes courage to practise one's faith openly in a post-Christian world with its secular agenda. It takes courage to stand in solidarity with the poor and those forgotten in the mad rush for ever-greater economic prosperity. It takes courage to speak about care for the exploited earth when most say that policies for environmental protection will hinder economic growth. It takes courage to welcome migrants and refugees who are generally seen as people who are stealing our jobs and threatening our way of life. It takes courage to speak out about the sacredness of all life and the rights of the unborn in situations where abortions are readily available. Reading about the courageous mission of the early Church in Acts can inspire us and remind us where the source of missionary courage is found. Knowing that the risen Jesus is with us, even in moments of suffering and opposition, will ensure that we remain people of hope and joy (see Acts 5:41).

NOTES

[1] 'The four features characteristic of Jerusalem communal life selected by Acts show both continuity with Judaism and distinctiveness that marked off Jews who believed in Jesus from other Jews. These aspects were in tension, pulling in opposite directions: The first held the Christians close to their fellow Jews whom they met in the synagogal meetings; the second gave to the Christian *koinōnia* identity and the potentiality of self-sufficiency. External factors of rejection and reaction, however, would have to take place before Christians would constitute a distinguishably separate religious group...' (Brown, *An Introduction to the New Testament*, 289).

[2] See Michael Mullins, *The Acts of the Apostles* (Dublin: Columba Press, 2013), 78.

[3] Some think that in Acts 3:20-21 we have a remnant of a very early Christology which sees the second coming as the time when Jesus becomes Messiah.

ACTS OF THE APOSTLES

4   For 'And in your descendants all the families of the earth shall be blessed' (Acts 3:25 NRSV) read 'And in your *seed* all the families of the earth shall be blessed'. The singular 'seed' (*sperma*) could be taken in a collective sense, referring to the people of Israel. But Luke may well understand it to refer to the risen Jesus, the source of universal salvation.

5   For brief background information on the Sadducees, see Mullins, *The Acts of the Apostles*, 81. It is interesting to note that the only reference to the Sadducees in Luke's Gospel is Lk 20:27-33, also in a context of controversy about resurrection.

6   'There is a certain parallelism that Luke used in this episode with the passion narrative of his Gospel. In both instances the religious authorities gather to adjudicate in the morning (Luke 22:66; Acts 4:6); Peter plays a special role (Luke 22:56; Acts 4:13); there is lack of evidence of guilt (Luke 23:4, 14-15; Acts 4:21) and a similar reaction of the people (Luke 19:47; Acts 4:21)' (Fitzmyer, *The Acts of the Apostles*, 297).

7   'Luke depicts Peter proclaiming the exclusive role of Jesus Christ in that divine plan for human salvation. He does not envisage the modern problem of salvation for human beings who have never heard of Christ or who are devotees of other religions, like Hinduism, Buddhism' (Fitzmyer, *ibid.*, 302).

8   On private ownership in the early Christian community, see Tannehill, *The Narrative Unity of Luke-Acts*, vol. 2, 73; Fitzmyer, *The Acts of the Apostles*, 313; John Gillman, *Possessions and the Life of Faith. A Reading of Luke-Acts* (Collegeville: Glazier, 1991), 95-100. Taking into account all the material in Luke's writings about attitudes and practices with regard to wealth and possessions, one can't conclude that Luke is questioning the right to private property. However, one can't meet the Lukan Jesus without being reminded that attachment to possessions can pose a danger to discipleship and without being challenged to take a long hard look at one's use of property and wealth in a world where many do not have the basic necessities of life. What Pope Francis says about the social role of all forms of private property fits well into the Lukan mind-set: 'The right to private property can only be considered a secondary natural right, derived from the principle of the universal destination of created goods. This has concrete consequences that ought to be reflected in the workings of society. Yet it often happens that secondary rights displace primary and overriding rights, in practice making them irrelevant' (*Fratelli Tutti*, no. 120).

9   'Just as Satan played an important role at the beginning of the Period of Jesus (Luke 4:1-13), so he plays a parallel role now at the

beginning of the Period of the Church under Stress. Whereas the disciples, after their prayer, were all "filled" with the Holy Spirit (4:30), Ananias is "filled" with Satan; he has become Satan's plaything' (Fitzmyer, *The Acts of the Apostles*, 323).

10 Johnson, *The Acts of the Apostles*, 87.

11 For a good treatment of the historical value of Acts 5:1-11, see Fitzmyer, *The Acts of the Apostles*, 316-320. He points out that the main emphasis is not on the deaths of Ananias and Sapphira, but on how God works through the apostles, and Peter in particular, in handling a scandalous activity.

12 On the 'Hebrews' and 'Hellenists' in the early Christian community, see Johnson, *The Acts of the Apostles*, 105; Brown, *An Introduction to the New Testament*, 293-295; Fitzmyer, *The Acts of the Apostles*, 347-348.

13 Some see significance in the number 'seven'. It is the number of completion, perhaps seeing this group of seven, who speak Greek (the world language), as a sign of the universal mission soon to take place. The number 'twelve' has already been used as a reminder that the Christian community is the restored Israel.

14 'Although the development of church structure reflects sociological necessity, in the Christian self-understanding the Holy Spirit given by the risen Christ guides the church in a way that allows basic structural development to be seen as embodying Jesus Christ's will for his church' (Brown, *An Introduction to the New Testament*, 295).

15 Luke has no hesitation in shifting some of the elements of Jesus' trial, which he found in his Marcan source, to the trial of Stephen, because in his mind the trial of Jesus was being re-enacted again in the experience of the disciple Stephen.

16 'Luke has intruded this discourse into the trial of Stephen. It breaks the connection of 6:1-15 with 7:55-60. It contains relatively little which can be construed as answering the charges he faces and, in fact, when it does touch on them, it seems rather to confirm rather than deny them (vv.35-36)' (Crowe, *The Acts*, 47; see also Johnson, *The Acts of the Apostles*, 119).

17 Tannehill (*The Narrative Unity of Luke-Acts*, vol. 2, 92, note 34) points to the close connection between Lk 1:73-75 and Acts 7:6-7. In both these texts, the fulfilment of the promise to Abraham is understood in terms of freedom from oppression resulting in unhindered worship.

18 Acts 7:16 confuses or conflates what the Pentateuch says about the buying of burial plots by the patriarchs, and about the burial of Jacob at Hebron and the burial of Joseph at Shechem (see Gn 23:17-20; 33:18-19; 49:30-31; 50:13; Jos 24:32). Shechem is perhaps

highlighted in Stephen's recital of history at this time because it was in the locality of Samaria and Mt Gerizim, the antithesis of Jerusalem. In a short time (Acts 8), Luke will be recounting the story of the spread of the Good News to Samaria.

[19] Johnson (*The Acts of the Apostles*, 136-137) thinks that attention to the Moses-Jesus comparison is of the utmost importance for understanding Luke's two-volume work. Having pointed out the similarities between Moses and Jesus, he goes on to say that Stephen's speech provides 'Luke's most explicit interpretation of his entire narrative, and shows us the logic of its two-fold structure. Appearing at the very end of the Jerusalem narrative (indeed itself ending the narrative) it provides the reader with the key to understanding everything that has happened in the story of Jesus and the apostles up to this point. The Jerusalem narrative has been all about the second offer of salvation, posing the question whether the people would accept the prophet this time or not.'

[20] Luke uses the Greek version (LXX) of Amos 5:24-27 which is quite different from the Hebrew version. While the Greek version sees the worship in the wilderness in a negative light, the Hebrew version sees it in a favourable light and contrasts it with the syncretism and formalism in the worship of Amos' day. Luke changes the LXX slightly to insert a reference to Babylon as a reminder that the later Babylonian exile was a punishment for the people's infidelities.

[21] 'Communion and mission are profoundly connected with each other, they interpenetrate and mutually imply each other, to the point that *communion represents both the source and the fruit of mission: communion gives rise to mission and mission is accomplished in communion'* (Pope John Paul II, *Christifideles Laici. On the Vocation and Mission of the Lay Faithful in the Church and in the World,* Rome, 1988, n. 32).

[22] Building communion between the different Christian confessions is also essential for Christian mission today, as Pope Francis points out in *Fratelli Tutti,* no. 280.

[23] *Lumen Gentium (Dogmatic Constitution on the Church),* no. 11 in Austin Flannery, ed. *Vatican Council II: The Conciliar and Post Conciliar Documents* (New York: Costello Publishing, 1996).

[24] William Frazier, quoted in Bosch, *Transforming Mission,* 122.

[25] *Evangelii Gaudium,* no. 259; see also Pope Francis, *Gaudete et Exsultate. On the Call to Holiness in Today's World* (London: Catholic Truth Society, 2018), no. 129-139.

CHAPTER 4

MISSION IN JUDEA AND SAMARIA
(ACTS 8:4−11:18)

In this section of Acts, Luke is moving on to the next phase of universal mission, as outlined in Acts 1:8. The Good News is taken beyond Jerusalem and begins to take root in Samaria and Judea. Luke is simplifying what surely was a more complicated process of historical growth. The summary statement in Acts 9:31 speaks of the growth of the Church 'throughout Judea, Galilee and Samaria'. But Luke tells us nothing about a mission in Galilee. In Acts 9:2 we are told of Saul's intention to arrest 'any who belonged to the Way' in Damascus. Again we have not been told of any missionary expansion to Damascus. Furthermore, while the missionary activity in Acts 8:4–11:18 is taking place in and around Samaria and Judea, Luke's mind is racing ahead to the next phase of Christian mission. He is preparing the ground for the spread of the Good News to the Gentiles ('to the ends of the earth'), which is related in the second part of Acts. He does this by telling two conversion stories – the conversion of Saul on the road to Damascus (Acts 9:1-19), who will play the key role in the spread of the Gospel to the Gentiles, and the conversion of Cornelius in Caesarea (Acts 10:1–11:18), the event which convinces Peter that the Good News has to be shared with Gentiles.

Philip's Mission in Samaria and Judea (Acts 8:4-40)

In dealing with the missionary activity of the Hellenist Philip, Luke selects two episodes, one giving an account of the powerful spread of the Good News in 'the city of Samaria', north of Jerusalem (Acts 8:4-25) and the other dealing with the conversion of the Ethiopian eunuch on the road to Gaza, going south from Jerusalem (Acts 8:26-40). He ends both these episodes with a summary statement about missionary activity in a much wider area (see Acts 8:25 and 8:40). We are left with the impression of mission radiating out from Jerusalem in different directions. From now on, in the story of Acts, events begin to take place farther and farther away from Jerusalem. We return to Jerusalem only when events in Samaria, Caesarea, Antioch, and in the Gentile Christian communities, necessitate such a return. In the story of the Ethiopian eunuch, in particular, Luke emphasises that this new missionary expansion from Jerusalem is due to the impulse and direction of the Holy Spirit. Both the episodes in Acts 8 also represent an outreach to people who are marginalised and do not enjoy the privileges of full participation in the people of God. Such an outreach is very much in line with the practice of Jesus in his mission as reported in Luke's Gospel.

Philip's Mission in Samaria (Acts 8:4-25)

There was a history of mutual hostility and distrust between Jews and Samaritans. After the conquest of the northern kingdom of Israel by the Assyrians in 721 BC, the land was planted with foreigners from many parts of the Assyrian Empire. The Samaritans were descendants of intermarriage between these foreigners and the local population. Jews regarded them as mixed-blood heretics whose faith in the true God had been greatly corrupted. The Samaritans had their own temple on Mount Gerizim. For them, only the Pentateuch was Sacred Scripture and only Moses was to be honoured as God's prophet. Hostile clashes between the Jews and Samaritans were not infrequent. Jesus himself in Luke's Gospel did not enter Samaritan territory or engage in mission among the Samaritans. But he made positive remarks about Samaritans, even holding them up as models for his followers (Lk 10:33-37; 17:11-19). When he experienced Samaritan hostility, he refused to retaliate as some of his disciples wanted (Lk 9:52-54). Now Jesus, in the person of Philip his missionary, reaches out to the Samaritans with the message of salvation. The mission among the Samaritans in Acts 8:4-25 can be seen as a process of reconciliation between the two peoples, a bringing together of Jews and Samaritans in the fellowship (*koinōnia*) of the restored people of God. It is a movement towards the greater step of bringing Jews and Gentiles together in the Christian community, which will become the question of vital importance as the story of Acts continues.

Acts 8:4 tells us that the Samaritan mission began because the Hellenist Christians were expelled from Jerusalem, not because of any great missionary planning or human calculations. However, in Luke's mind, God was behind this development. Philip's mission in Samaria, which includes teaching about the kingdom of God and Jesus the Messiah (Acts 8:12), along with healing and casting out unclean spirits (Acts 8:6-7), reminds us of the Gospel mission of Jesus and the mission of the apostles in Jerusalem in the early chapters of Acts. The crowds listened 'with one accord' (*homthymadon*) (Acts 8:6). A word, which Luke has used to describe the harmony and togetherness of the Jerusalem community (see Acts 1:14; 2:26; 4:24; 5:12), is now being used for Samaritans who are being incorporated into the community.

Joy (Acts 8:8) is characteristic of the response to the Good News in Luke's writings. In hearing Philip and seeing the signs he worked, people forsake their eager adherence to Simon the magician who was regarded as having the power of God (Acts 8:9-13). Even Simon himself was converted. All of this underscores the success of Philip's mission and the power of the kingdom of God at work in it. In the ancient world, magic was often understood as an attempt to control transcendent powers through precise rituals and recipes with automatic and predictable results. 'For Luke, magic is consistently associated with demonic powers, and therefore part of the resistance put by "the other kingdom" to the kingdom of God (Acts 8:20; 13:10; 19:13-20).'[1] But Acts 8:13 also points out that Simon was very much taken by Philip's ability as a miracle worker, an interest that wasn't altogether healthy, as the story will go on to point out.

Peter and John are now sent by the apostles in Jerusalem to see what was happening in Samaria (Acts 8:14-24). Luke's main interest at this point is to show that the new missionary initiative of Philip receives the approval and confirmation of the apostles and the Jerusalem community.[2] Continuity in the story of universal salvation is once again on Luke's mind. As the story develops, we will see the same concern for continuity with and approval by the Jerusalem church (see Acts 9:26-31; 11:1-18 and 11:22). After arrival in Samaria, the two apostles pray that the Samaritans might receive the Holy Spirit (Acts 8:15) and when they laid hands on them they received the Spirit – sometimes called the 'Samaritan Pentecost' (Acts 8:17). Luke adds an explanatory note (Acts 8:16) that the Samaritans had only been baptised in the name of Jesus and had not yet received the Holy Spirit. Immediately, a question arises for us: 'Is the Holy Spirit not given in Christian baptism, as Acts 2:38 indicates?' The same question arises with regard to Acts 10:44-48 (where the Spirit is given to people *before* the reception of baptism) and, to a lesser extent, Acts 19:5-6 (where believers were first baptised in the name of Jesus and *afterwards* Paul laid hands on them and the Holy Spirit came upon them).

Some explain the 'difficulty' by saying that in these three cases the focus is on the external manifestation of the Spirit (in such experiences as 'speaking in tongues' and 'prophesying'), rather than the internal reception of the Spirit in baptism (as the principle of Christian unity, love and joy). Later theology understood the reception of the Spirit in Acts 8:17 in terms of the reception of the Spirit in the sacrament of confirmation through the imposition of the hands of the bishop. However, it would be reading too much into the text to understand the visit of Peter and John in terms of a modern bishop's confirmation visit. The best explanation is that Luke, in the three texts mentioned (Acts 8:15-17; 10:44-48; 19:5-6), is not addressing the question of the relationship between baptism and the reception of the Spirit, but is emphasising that the Spirit is given through the Church (especially through the Twelve or their emissaries), to show how new developments in mission are assimilated into the mainstream Christian movement, and to point out how these developments took place under the supervision and direction of the Twelve.[3]

But we should not conclude that the Spirit is controlled by ritual or office. The Spirit is God's gift and not subject to any person or to the performance of any rite. That's the main point in the verses which follow (Acts 8:18-24). Simon still has a magician's mentality. He thinks that the Spirit can be controlled and given as one pleases, provided one has the skill, technique or recipe for doing this. Using words associated with the worship of false gods (see Deut 29:18), Peter reacts strongly, telling Simon that God's gift can't be bought and calling on him to repent. Simon capitulates and asks Peter to pray for him (Acts 8:24). Some see Simon's response to Peter as completely inadequate as there is no explicit mention of confession of sin and repentance. However, there is nothing in the text which would lead us to believe that Simon was insincere and continued in his perverse ways. He gave his name to the sin of simony and later tradition depicts him as an arch villain who was a strong rival and opponent of Peter. In some early Christian literature he is regarded as the founder of Gnosticism, one of the early Christian heresies.

The conclusion of the story of the Samaritan mission in Acts 8:25 serves two functions. Firstly, it generalises the single episode of Acts 8:4-24 in speaking of a wider mission in Samaria. Secondly, it has the apostles Peter and John taking part in this mission to reinforce its ratification by the Jerusalem church. The Greek text has the indefinite 'they' rather than 'Peter and John' which could mean that the apostles engaged in mission along with Philip.

Conversion of the Ethiopian Eunuch (Acts 8:26-40)

We have just read an account of mission north of Jerusalem. Now attention shifts in the direction of missionary activity south of Jerusalem, within Judea on the road going down to Gaza. The conversion of the Ethiopian eunuch is one of the most dramatic stories in Luke's writings. As the man is an Ethiopian, this could be understood as the first Gentile conversion in Acts. However, many would say that Luke does not present it as such because that would upstage the climactic event of Cornelius' conversion in Acts 10.[4] Luke's main interest in presenting the story of the Ethiopian eunuch is to give us a striking example of missionary activity in the area of Judea. He highlights the man's interest in and attraction to the Jewish faith, thus putting him closer to the Jewish (rather than the Gentile) camp. He is to be numbered among the 'God-fearers' in synagogues who, we shall see, were quite responsive to Paul's missionary preaching. As the Ethiopian is returning from worshipping in Jerusalem, he is reading the Jewish scriptures (Acts 8:27-28). He is a man of great importance, holding a high position in the court of the Ethiopian queen (Acts 8:27). He is a eunuch, however, one numbered among those on the margins of the Jewish community who are excluded from full participation in God's people (see Deut 23:1; but Is 56:3-5 promised that eunuchs who are faithful to the demands of the covenant could hope for some share in God's final salvation). The compassionate God of Jesus Christ reaches out to this excluded and marginalised person in the mission of Philip.

The divine prompting and guidance are highlighted very much in this story, more than in the previous story. Philip sets out for the wilderness (a most unlikely place for mission!) in response to the prompting of an angel (Acts 8:26-27a); the Spirit prompts him to draw near at the very moment the eunuch happens to be reading a passage suitable for Christian preaching (Acts 8:29); they come to water (in a desert!) at just the right time in the story (Acts 8:36); the Spirit takes Philip away after the eunuch's baptism (Acts 8:39). Luke leaves us in no doubt that God is the principal agent in this missionary story.

Philip, prompted by the Spirit to draw near, heard the man reading Is 53:7-8, taken from the fourth Servant Song in the Book of Isaiah (Acts 8:29-33). These Servant Songs exercised a profound influence on early Christian thinking about Jesus (see, for instance, Rm 10:16; 1 Pt 2:21-25; Jn 12:38). Luke is quoting the LXX version of Is 53:7-8. The Greek sentences in Acts 8:33 can be translated and understood as follows: 'In his humiliation his judgement was taken away' (that is, his condemnation by others was removed by God). 'Who will describe his family'? (This is an expression of wonder at the vast progeny of believers that will result from Jesus' exaltation as Messiah). 'For his life is taken away from the earth' (that is, his life was taken up from the earth in his resurrection).[5] This way of translating Acts 8:33 provides a reference to the death and resurrection of Jesus, along the lines of the kerygmatic contrast in the earlier speeches of Acts. In response to a question from Philip, the eunuch invites guidance in interpreting the passage (Acts 8:31). His question is about the person referred to in the prophet's text (Acts 8:34). Using the text as the point of departure, Philip proclaims the Good News of Jesus to him. The further question of the eunuch (Acts 8:36), which amounts to a request for baptism, may be a conventional formula for the admission of a candidate for baptism in the early church (see also Acts 10:47).[6] The eunuch is baptised by Philip (Acts 8:38) and then he and Philip quickly part ways in an atmosphere of joy (Acts 8:39).[7] The incident ends with a generalising comment about further missionary activity by Philip in the western part of Judea (Acts 8:40).

Many see parallelism between the story of the Ethiopian eunuch and the story of the two disciples on the road to Emmaus (Lk 24:13-35). Both episodes involve a journey away from Jerusalem, the use of the Scriptures in throwing light on the person and mission of Jesus, a 'sacramental action' as the climax of the story, and the sudden disappearance of the main protagonist. Both passages have much to say to us about meeting Christ today in the Scriptures and in the sacraments.

Saul's Conversion, Initial Preaching, and Contact with the Apostles (Acts 9:1-31)

In Acts 8 we have heard how the Good News spread to Samaria and Judea. In the chapters which immediately follow, most of the action takes place in Lydda (Acts 9:32-35), Joppa (Acts 9:36-43) and Caesarea (Acts 10). But in Acts 9:1–11:18 Luke's attention is also shifting to the next phase in the onward journey of the Good News, that is, the outreach to the Gentiles. He gives a lot of attention to events which prepare the ground for the mission beyond Samaria and Judea to 'the ends of the earth' (Acts 1:8). We have two conversion stories which taken together represent the pivotal centre of Luke's story in Acts. The story of Saul's conversion (Acts 9:1-19a) brings him out of the shadows and closer to the position on centre stage which he will occupy for the second half of Acts. For Luke, Paul is the great missionary hero who plays the major role in the journey of the Good News to 'the ends of the earth'. The conversion of Cornelius' household (Acts 10:1–11:18), in which Peter is the major human actor, is, for Luke, *the* event that signals and legitimises the mission to the Gentiles.

> The close parallelism between the transactions in Acts 9 and 10 – convert's vision, reluctant inductor's vision, then their encounter, followed by the convert's baptism and reception of the Spirit – suggests that Luke has assimilated the two stories to some extent so that the foremost Gentile missionary and the first Gentile conversion could stand side by side at the pivotal centre of his composition.[8]

Saul's Conversion (Acts 9:1-19a)

Luke relates the story of Saul's encounter with the risen Lord not once but three times in Acts (see Acts 9:1-19a; 22:3-21; 26:9-18). That in itself is an indication of the importance of this event for Luke. Each time, the account of this event is situated at an important turning point in the story of Acts. In Acts 9 it occurs as the mission to the Gentiles is about to take off; in Acts 22 it is related at the time of Paul's arrest in the Temple which begins a series of events pointing him in the direction of Rome; in Acts 26 we have the third narration just before Paul sets out for Rome. Acts 9 gives a direct narration by Luke, but in Acts 22 and Acts 26 Luke has Paul himself tell the story in speeches when he is defending himself, first before the Jewish crowd in the Temple and then before King Herod Agrippa in the presence of the Roman governor Porcius Festus. So, the genre of each account is different. While the three accounts agree on the basic fact that Saul encountered the risen Lord on the road to Damascus and this meeting changed his life radically, there is quite a bit of variation in detail between the different versions. For instance, the accounts do not agree on what Saul's companions saw and heard (compare Acts 9:7 with Acts 22:9); Ananias tells Saul what the Lord has in store for him in Acts 22:13-16 (which he does not do in Acts 9:17); the Lord himself commissions Saul on the road in Acts 26:16-18 and there is no mention of Ananias or Saul's baptism in this final account.[9]

Acts 9:1-2 picks up Acts 8:3 with its focus on Saul's violent persecution of the Church. Saul in his zeal against Christians seeks authorisation from the high priest to go to Damascus to bring back men and women who belonged to the Way. Damascus was about 240 kilometres NE of Jerusalem. It was part of the Decapolis, a league of autonomous city-states within the jurisdiction of the Roman province of Syria, and had a sizeable Jewish population. It is not certain that historically the high priest had the presupposed powers of extradition. Here Christians are called those 'who belong to the Way,' seemingly an early designation for the Christian movement (for the absolute use of 'Way' see Acts 19:9, 23; 22:4; 24:14, 22). This reminds us that Jesus in Luke's Gospel invited people to follow him on the way to Jerusalem and adopt his way of life.

The present episode takes place in the context of a journey which is significant in Luke-Acts (compare Lk 24:13-35; Acts 8:26-40). Acts 9:3-6 describe the theophany as Saul journeyed towards Damascus. Light (see, for instance, Ps 4:6; Is 55:13; 1 Jn 1:5-6) and lightening (see, for instance, Ex 19:6; 2 Sm 22:15; Ps 17:14) are common symbols for the divine presence. In Acts 22:6 it is a 'great light' and in Acts 26:13 it is said to be 'brighter than the sun'. The voice from heaven recalls such texts as Ex 19:16-20 (voice from Sinai) and especially Ex 3:3 (voice from the burning bush). The repetition of the name ('Saul, Saul') reminds us of God's urgent call, command, mission or promise to a chosen one: Gn 22:11 ('Abraham, Abraham'); Gn 46:2 ('Jacob, Jacob'); Ex 3:4 ('Moses, Moses'); 1 Sm 3:4, 6, 10 ('Samuel, Samuel'). The dialogue, which clarifies the import of the experience, is very similar in each of the three versions (compare Acts 22:7; 26:14).

The risen Lord remains active in the story of Acts and identifies with his disciples; to persecute them is to persecute him. In Lk 10:16 we have the same identification of Jesus with those sent in his name. Saul addresses the one he experiences as 'Lord' (*Kyrios*). He recognises that he is involved in a theophany, even though he does not know who is calling on him. In response to Saul's request for a name, the risen Lord identifies himself as Jesus. In this account (and in Acts 22:10) the only thing Saul is told to do by the Lord is to go into the city and await further instructions (compare Acts 26:16-18 where Saul at this stage receives his commission immediately from the Lord).

The effect of the vision on Saul's companions (Acts 9:7 – hearing the voice, but seeing no one) is the reverse to what we find in Acts 22:9 (the companions saw the light but did not hear the voice). In Acts 26:13-14 the light shines around

Saul and his companions and all fall to the ground, but only Saul sees the light and hears the voice ('*I* saw a light from heaven,' '*I* heard a voice saying to me'). What Luke is probably emphasising in all three accounts is the unique and personal character of Saul's experience; it wasn't the same for the others. Saul was called by name. He is told to enter Damascus where he will be told what to do (Acts 9:6).

In Acts 9:8-9 we have the picture of the powerful persecutor completely immobilised – blind, disorientated and having to be led by the hand. Ironically, he who came to overpower the disciples of Jesus and lead them bound out of Damascus is now overpowered himself and has to be led into Damascus! Not eating or drinking for three days may be understood as a period of preparation (see, for instance, Ex 34:28) or repentance (see, for instance, Jer 14:12). We are reminded of the disciples' preparation in Acts 1 before the Spirit descended on them. The physical emptiness of fasting gets one in touch with the emptiness in the heart which needs to be filled with the Spirit.

In Acts 9:10-16 we have another vision, that of Ananias in Damascus. We have seen that visions are an important way for Luke to underline the intervention and activity of God. This is doubly emphasised by stories of 'double visions' and 'vision within vision'. We will have the same prominence of visions in Acts 10:1–11:18 when Luke is narrating the story of the conversion of the Gentile Cornelius. Note the very detailed instructions given to Ananias about where to find the praying Saul (Acts 9:11). Everything is being stage-managed by the risen Lord. As in Luke's Gospel, important turning points in the story in Acts are in the context of prayer (see also Acts 1:24; 6:6; 10:2-4, 9, 30; 11:5; 13:3; 14:23). In his prayer, Saul has a vision of Ananias coming in and laying hands on him to heal him. Ananias' reluctance (Acts 9:13-14) is another indication that the step to be taken is due to God's initiative, not human reason or calculation. The reluctance motif will occur again in Peter's vision in Acts 10. Acts 9:15-16 are important in the story as they say something about Saul's future role.

Saul is referred to as a 'chosen instrument' or a 'vessel of election' to carry the Lord's name (Acts 9:15). In 2 Cor 4:7 Paul speaks of apostles as 'earthenware vessels', which underlines the fragility of the one called to be an apostle. Three classes are mentioned before whom Saul will bear witness to the Lord's name: 'Gentiles,' 'kings,' and 'the people of Israel'. The accent in Acts 9:15 is not only on Paul's missionary journeys, but also on the public witness he will bear when he is arraigned before Gentile and Jewish tribunals. Like the apostles in Jerusalem (Acts 5:41), Saul will suffer for the sake of the name of Jesus (Acts 9:16). Suffering was the lot of Jesus in fulfilling his mission (Lk 9:22; 17:25; 22:37; 24:7, 26) and he foretold the sufferings of missionary disciples in tribunals of kings and governors which will be for them an opportunity to testify (Lk 21:12-19). Saul the fierce persecutor will become the one fiercely persecuted. Note the Lukan 'divine necessity' (*dei*) in Acts 9:16, another reminder that all of this is part of the working out of God's plan of universal salvation.

In Acts 9:17-19a we have the encounter between Saul and Ananias, two people brought together by the experience of the risen Lord in visions. Conversion for Saul meant being incorporated into the community he has been persecuting. Saul's incorporation into the community is important for Luke's emphasis on continuity in mission. This incorporation is indicated by the laying on of hands (physical touch), being filled with the Spirit, receiving baptism, and being addressed as 'brother'. The laying on of hands also brings about the healing from blindness, probably meant to include a removal of spiritual blindness. The taking of food may be an indication that his time of preparation (or penance) is over. Note that Ananias says nothing to Saul about his commission as a missionary (as he does in Acts 22:14-15). Nevertheless, Saul does not waste time getting involved in missionary witness in Damascus.

Does Luke see the event on the road to Damascus as a conversion or vocation story? We can say that for Luke it was an experience of both conversion and call. But the 'conversion' of Saul is not to be understood as conversion from a dissolute or ungodly way of life. Saul was a deeply religious person whose religious zeal led him to persecute the disciples of Jesus. Nor would Saul have understood his following of Jesus as a change of allegiance from one religion to another. As he will point out later, he accepted Jesus the Messiah 'for the sake of the hope of Israel' (Acts 28:20). But his faith commitment to God underwent a radical transformation and reorientation as a result of a deeply personal meeting with the risen Christ.

Luke in Acts 9 wants us to ponder the dimensions of this remarkable conversion in which a fierce persecutor of the Church became a committed disciple and witness to Jesus. Such a totally unexpected transformation and 'turn-about' in Saul's life was not the result of any process of personal soul-searching, but could only be attributed to the overwhelming power of God at work in mission. In his letters Paul speaks of how the grace of God transformed him from a violent persecutor of the Church into one who was completely captivated by Jesus Christ (1 Cor 9:1; 15:8-10; Gal 1:13-17; Phil 3:4-16; see also 1 Tm 1:13-16). At the heart of Saul's Damascus 'conversion' experience was a call to mission. The way Luke describes it reminds us of the call of Moses (see Ex 3:4) and Samuel (1 Sm 3:1-10). In his letter to the Galatians (1:15-16) Paul himself describes it in terms similar to the call of Jeremiah (Jer 1:5) and the Servant of Yahweh (Is 49:1-6).[10]

Saul's Initial Mission in Damascus (Acts 9:19b-25)
The action in Acts 9:19b-25 and Acts 9:26-30 has a similar sequence: preaching, rejection, threats and hasty departure.[11] We note in Acts 9:19b that Saul is now 'with the disciples'. Immediately (Acts 9:20) he engages in mission. Going to the synagogues first will be the practice of Paul's later missionary activity. He proclaimed that Jesus was the 'Son of God' (Acts 9:20) and proved (from the Scriptures?) that Jesus was the 'Messiah' (Acts 9:22). In this context the two titles may mean

more or less the same thing (the Israelite king, and consequently the Messiah, was regarded as a 'son of God'), though some see the title 'Son of God' here as an indication of Jesus' unique relationship to Yahweh.[12] Acts 9:21 underlines again the radical change and transformation that has taken place in Saul. Saul, growing in strength, confounds and amazes the 'Jews'. This is the first time in Acts that 'the Jews' are spoken of as a group separate from the followers of Jesus. In Paul's later mission the 'Jews' are his constant opponents. The Jews plot to kill Saul who makes a dramatic escape in a basket lowered through an opening in the city wall (Acts 9:23-25). We see that the prediction of Acts 9:16 is already coming to pass. Paul refers to this escape from Damascus in 2 Cor 11:32-33, but there it is the governor of the Nabatean King Aretas who is the one who wants to apprehend Paul. The reference in the Greek text of Acts 9:23 to the period of time spent in Damascus is quite vague and is translated differently in the various English versions: 'after a long time,' 'after some time,' 'after many days'. This is of interest to those trying to establish Saul's exact movements in the years immediately following his conversion.[13]

Saul's Visit to Jerusalem (Acts 9:26-31)
The reluctance motif again surfaces in Acts 9:26. This time it is the Jerusalem community who out of fear is reluctant to accept the one who had persecuted the Church. Barnabas appears again in his role as encourager and mediator, the role for which he is best remembered (Acts 9:27; see also 4:36; 11:22-23, 25-26). He tells the reluctant disciples about Saul's Damascus experience and how he had already preached boldly in the name of Jesus. The phrase 'to go in and out' (Acts 9:28) connotes intimate companionship and partnership (see Acts 1:21). Here we touch on what is perhaps Luke's main concern in Acts 9:26-30. He wants to establish the link between Saul and the apostles in Jerusalem, between their mission and his mission. Crowe says this is the last time in Acts that the apostles appear as the leaders of the Church:

'In their final appearance in that role they set their seal of approval on the work of the man who will eventually replace them on centre stage.'[14]

Saul speaks 'boldly' in the name of the Lord (Acts 9:27-28). Boldness marked the apostles' preaching (Acts 2:29; 4:13, 29, 31) and it will mark Paul's later mission (Acts 13:46; 14:3; 18:26; 19:8; 26:26; 28:31). In Jerusalem Saul directs his attention to the Hellenists with whom he was associated at the time of Stephen's death. They now try to kill their former ally, so the believers have to help Saul make a quick escape once again. He goes back to his home town of Tarsus, via Caesarea (Acts 9:30). In Paul's later missionary activity in Acts, the sequence of preaching, danger and escape will often recur.

At this point Luke gives us one of his short summaries (Acts 9:31). It highlights the progress and growth of the Church. This is the first time in Acts that the word 'Church' is used for the scattered communities as a whole, rather than a local community. The Church lived in peace and was built up (by God), living in the fear of the Lord and the comfort of the Holy Spirit. We get the impression that this peace is due to the fact that the Church's greatest persecutor has been converted!

Peter's Judean Mission and the Conversion of Cornelius' Household (Acts 9:32–11:18)

Having introduced Paul, the one who will be the main *human agent* in the spread of the Good News of Jesus Christ to the Gentiles, Luke now turns his attention to *the event* which he regards as the major turning point setting in motion the mission to the Gentiles, that is, the conversion of Cornelius and his household (Acts 10:1–11:18). The missionary who is at the centre of this key event is not Paul, the former persecutor who may still have been regarded with some suspicion even in Luke's day, but the leader of the apostles, Peter. As we shall see, however, in Luke's mind the initiative for this step lies not with any human person in the early Church, but with God. The God who took the initiative in transforming Saul the persecutor into Paul the missionary, now leads Peter through the event which signals and initiates the next major phase of the Church's mission, that of bringing the Good News to 'the ends of the earth' (Acts 1:8). Having Peter on mission in Lydda and Joppa is bringing him in the direction of Caesarea where Cornelius lived.

Peter's Mission in the Coastal Area of Judea (Acts 9:32-43)

In Acts 9:32-43 we find Peter on a 'mission tour' in Judea, more precisely in Lydda (25 kilometres NW of Jerusalem) and Joppa (19 kilometres further on). He is visiting Christian communities which had been evangelised by others and confirming their missionary work. The two miracles he performs lead to the growth of these communities. In both the healing of Aeneas and the raising of Tabitha, Luke is drawing parallels with the ministry of Jesus. Note that Luke is adhering to his practice of pairing a story of a man with the story of a woman (see Chapter 2, note 6 above). He is also reintroducing Peter the missionary as a prelude to the all-important event in Caesarea (some 48 kilometres N of Joppa).

The cure of Aeneas (Acts 9:32-35) reminds us of Jesus' cure of the paralytic in Lk 5:17-26 (compare, for instance, Jesus' word to the paralytic and his immediate response in Lk 5:24-25 with Peter's word to Aeneas and his response in Acts 9:34). Note how Peter points out that it is Jesus himself who is healing through the apostle's mission (Acts 9:34). The man is told to 'get up' and he immediately 'got up'. The verb used (*anistēmi*) is also used to refer to the raising of Jesus (see, for instance, Lk 24:46; Acts 10:41) – a hint that Aeneas' healing is a resurrection experience for him. The cure acts as a stimulus to further conversions to the Lord in Lydda and the Plain of Sharon (Acts 9:35 – this verse sounds hyperbolic).

Acts 9:36-43 tells the story of the raising to life of Tabitha (Dorcas), a woman disciple at Joppa. It is emphasised that

Tabitha was particularly charitable (Acts 9:36, 39) – another example of concern for the needy in the early Christian community. After Tabitha died and was laid out in the room upstairs, Peter is summoned to Joppa from Lydda (Acts 9:37-38). Peter comes and through his prayers (Acts 9:40) raises her to life. The way this miracle story is told reminds one of 1 Kgs 17:17-24 (the story of how Elijah raised the son of the widow of Zarephath – upper chamber; prayer of Elijah; the prophet presents the boy to his widowed mother) and 2 Kgs 4:32-37 (the story of how Elisha raised the Shunammite woman's child to life – the roof chamber; being alone with the dead person; prayer of the prophet; opening of the eyes).[15] Luke presented Jesus as an Elijah-like prophet, so now Peter, the one through whom the power of Jesus is operative, is being presented in the same way. Lest we miss the parallelism, Luke tells this story of the raising of Tabitha in terms very similar to the raising of the daughter of Jairus in Lk 8:40-42, 49-56 (the parallelism is even closer if we keep in mind Mk 5:49-56 which Luke was probably using as his source at this point): Jesus and Peter are requested to come; Jesus and Peter take the person by the hand; the person gets up/sits up. Peter puts the people outside (Acts 9:40), as did Jesus (Mk 5:40). Again we are told that the miracle is a stimulus to conversions to the Lord (Acts 9:42). In Acts 9:40-41 we again have the resurrection verb *anistēmi* used twice. The story ends on the note of Peter staying in the house of Simon, a tanner (Acts 9:43). This links the story with the story of Cornelius' conversion (see Acts 10:5, 17, 23, 32). The tanner's trade made one ritually impure. Could it be an indication that Peter continues Jesus' association with outcasts?[16]

The Cornelius Episode (Acts 10:1–11:18)

In his narrative to date, Luke has already indicated that the salvation offered by God is for all without exception (Lk 2:32; 3:6; 4:25-27; 24:47; Acts 1:8; 2:21). Now he has reached the point in his story where this becomes the major question.

Luke knows that the outreach to Gentiles was the most important and decisive step in the mission of the early Church, and we will see how he is at pains to point out that the step was taken because it was the will of God and God's reaching out to the Gentiles through the Christian mission is in continuity with God's salvific activity up to that point.

We could look on the Cornelius episode as a *drama* which unfolds in *five scenes*: (1) The Vision of Cornelius (Acts 10:1-8); (2) Peter's Vision (Acts 10:9-16); (3) Peter's Reception of Cornelius' Messengers (Acts 10:17-23a); (4) Proceedings in Cornelius' house (Acts 10:23b-48); (5) Report by Peter to the Jerusalem Church (Acts 11:1-18). In this drama God is the hidden, but principal actor. God takes the initiative and directs operations through visions, angels and his Spirit. At the end of the drama, Peter makes it quite clear that he was acting under the direction of God and to act in a way other than he did would be going against and hindering the manifest will of God (see Acts 11:17).

We see Peter throughout this drama struggling to keep pace with God and slowly growing in an understanding of God's action and intention in mission. He moves from hesitation and reluctance (Acts 10:14) through perplexity and confusion (Acts 10:17-19) to clarity and conviction about God's designs (see Acts 10:28, 34-35, 47; 11:16-17). He reaches this clarity through God's enlightenment and by listening to the experience of Cornelius. Cornelius, the other human person who has a main part in the drama, appears from start to finish as one who is open to the ways of God, eager to listen to what God's messengers have to say. We also have a supporting cast in the drama. Cornelius is surrounded by his household who like him are open to what God wants to do among them. Peter is accompanied by some Jewish believers from Joppa (Acts 10:23, 45-46; 11:12) who play the important role of witnesses to what God is doing among the Gentiles. It seems they were also the ones who baptised Cornelius and his household, thus receiving the first Gentiles into the Christian community (Acts 10:48). A small Christian community is there to receive the group of Gentiles as new members of the Church. The community dimension in mission is always important for Luke.

The story begins in *Scene I* (Acts 10:1-8), not with the experience of Peter the missionary in Joppa, but with the experience of Cornelius the Gentile in Caesarea.[17] From the way Cornelius is described he seems to be a 'God-fearer,' that is, a Gentile adherent to the synagogue, interested in the Jewish faith and performing typical works of Jewish piety, without accepting circumcision or observing some other Jewish practices (see Acts 10:2, 22). He very much resembles the benevolent centurion in Lk 7:2-10, who is highly praised by the Jews as one who loves their people and built their synagogue. Cornelius has a vision at the ninth hour (3 p.m.), the hour of evening prayer for Jews; in Acts 10:30 he says he was praying at the time. Remember how Luke constantly puts important events in the context of prayer.

The appearance of an angel immediately underscores the initiative of God. Cornelius, called by name, has the usual reaction of fear to an experience of the divine (see Lk 1:12, 29-30; 24:5, 37; Acts 24:25). Cornelius' prayers and almsgiving, traditional acts of Jewish piety (see, for instance, Tob 12:8-9; Mt 6:1-18) are said to be like a memorial offering which causes God to remember a person (Acts 10:4, 31). Some rabbis speculated that prayer, charity and the study of the Torah are spiritual sacrifices. The only instruction Cornelius receives is to send for Simon Peter and he is given the exact address of Peter's whereabouts in Joppa (Acts 10:6; compare 9:11). This reminds us again of the centurion who sent messengers to bring Jesus to help his seriously ill servant (Lk 7:3). Cornelius obeys immediately (Acts 10:7-8), sending three members of his household, even though he knows precious little about what God has in store for him. The picture we get of Cornelius is that of a person who is open and willing to do without question what God directs. He does not show the hesitation or reluctance which characterises Peter's initial response.

In *Scene II* (Acts 10:9-16) we switch to Joppa where Peter has a vision on the roof, as the messengers from Caesarea are making their way towards Joppa. Luke is again using the device of the double vision, which we saw in Acts 9, to emphasise that everything is happening as a result of the divine initiative and direction. Again, we have the context of prayer (Acts 10:9), which for Luke is meant to be the opening of the human person to what God is doing. The mention of Peter's hunger prepares us for the content of the vision which took place when Peter fell into a trance (Acts 10:10). 'The heaven opened' (Acts 10:11) is a phrase denoting a theophany or revelation of God (see, for instance, Lk 3:21; Acts 7:56). Notice the reserved language characteristic of many biblical visions: 'something *like* a large sheet... being lowered to the ground by its four corners.' *Skeuos* can mean 'instrument,' 'container,' 'vessel,' 'tent,' 'thing,' which makes it difficult to visualise what Luke is saying here. It is more important to concentrate on the contents of the *skeuos* – the list in Acts 10:12 which is meant to be inclusive of all animals, clean and unclean (see Gn 1:24; 6:20; Lev 11:46-47; Rm 1:23). The heavenly command to eat (Acts 10:13) implies that the hungry Peter is not to distinguish between clean and unclean creatures.

Peter strongly objects (Acts 10:14) in words reminiscent of Ezekiel who also objects to eating unclean food (see Ez 4:14). Purity and dietary regulations were 'a badge of identity among the peoples and a sign of their special covenantal relationship with God'.[18] So transgression of such regulations was seen as a denial of one's identity and religion. The main point of the vision is stated in Acts 10:15, which should probably be taken in the sense that everything created by God (including 'unclean Gentiles') is clean. The statement of the heavenly voice about clean and unclean foods has a deeper meaning which Peter begins to fathom only as the story develops. The threefold occurrence of the vision (Acts 10:16) underlines the importance of the divine intervention and command, and perhaps also Peter's difficulty in understanding what is happening.

Scene III (Acts 10:17-23a) tells us of Peter's reception of the messengers from Cornelius. They arrive at the gate of Simon the tanner's house and ask for Simon Peter at an opportune time, when Peter is still trying to figure out what his vision was all about (Acts 10:17-19). Hearing what they have to say will clarify things somewhat for Peter. But Peter also has the help of the Spirit in coming to greater understanding. The Spirit prompts him to meet the messengers and go with them without hesitation, 'for I have sent them' (Acts 10:19-20). We are not let forget that God is the main actor in this all-important drama. The Spirit in bringing people (Jew and Gentile) together is clarifying the meaning of Peter's vision. The Greek phrase *mēden diakrinomenos* can be translated 'without hesitation' (NRSV), but it can also be translated 'without making discrimination' or 'without debate'. All of these meanings fit the context: Peter is not to hesitate in following God's lead; he is not to make distinction between Jew and Gentile; he is not to keep agonising and debating with himself or others as to what he should do. It is possible that Luke intended all these meanings here.

Peter, in obedience to the Spirit, meets the messengers and invites them to state their purpose in coming (Acts 10:21). Perhaps Peter's request for more information could be seen negatively as an indication that he is still slow to move. But it's better to see it positively as an indication that Peter is starting to move from an argumentative to a listening mode. The meeting between Peter and Cornelius will take place in an atmosphere of mutual listening which enables a listening to God (see Acts 10:29, 33). The messengers simply repeat the message Cornelius received from the angel in his vision with a slight expansion, that is, 'to hear what you have to say' (Acts 10:22). They also say that Cornelius is 'well spoken of by the whole Jewish nation' (compare Lk 7:4-5). Peter invited them into the house and gave them lodgings (Acts 10:23a). This is seen as the first sign that the meaning of the vision is beginning to dawn on Peter. He, a Jew, has no hesitation in receiving Gentiles and presumably dining with them.

Gentiles are not to be seen as unclean and a source of ritual contamination.[19]

Scene IV (Acts 10:23b-48) is the important scene in the house of Cornelius at Caesarea. It can be further divided into three parts: (a) the reception of Peter by Cornelius (10:23b-33); (b) the speech of Peter (10:34-43); (c) the descent of the Spirit on the Gentiles and their baptism (10:44-48). Some believers from Joppa accompany Peter to Caesarea (Acts 10:23b). In Acts 10:45 we learn that they are Jewish, so they could be seen as representatives of the Jewish Christian community about to receive the band of Gentile Christian converts. They also play the role of witnesses and in Acts 11:12 we see that Peter associates them with himself in entering the Gentile's house. There we are also told that there were six companions of Peter. The expectant Cornelius had assembled a group of relatives and close friends to receive Peter (Acts 10:24). Peter deflects homage from himself when Cornelius seeks to worship him, as if he were angelic or divine (Acts 10:25-26; compare Acts 14:15). The command 'get up/stand up' (*anastēthi*) in Acts 10:26 reminds us of the same command to Aeneas (Acts 9:34) and Tabitha (Acts 9:40). This 'resurrection' word could be an indication that Cornelius like them is about to experience the power of the resurrection through Jesus.

Crossing the threshold of the Gentile house was a momentous step, symbolising a great breakthrough in Christian mission.[20] We note that Peter takes this step conversing with Cornelius (Acts 10:27). Peter's first words to the assembled group (Acts 10:28-29) show that he has advanced in understanding what God is doing in the unfolding events. He is now making a connection between his vision and his visit to a Gentile household. God had sanctioned this unusual step for a Jew. Rather than immediately preaching to Cornelius and his household, Peter wants to first listen to what Cornelius has to say (Acts 10:29). Cornelius recounts his vision (Acts 10:30-34). All of this repetition serves to clarify (for Peter and the readers) what God wants and to remind us once again that God is the principal actor in this drama. Cornelius actually indicates that he and his household are listening to God through Peter (Acts 10:33).

In Acts 10:34-43 we have Peter's last missionary discourse in Acts. It has some of the elements of the previous discourses: an introduction linking the speech to the context; the Jesus proclamation (kerygma). It has no appeal for conversion, as Cornelius is already 'converted,' that is, turned towards God. There is only a brief reference to the fulfilment of the Scriptures (Acts 10:43). The present speech picks up and greatly amplifies the theme of universalism which was hinted at in Peter's Temple speech (see Acts 3:21, 25). It begins and ends on a universal note (Acts 10:35-36, 42-43). This speech also has features not mentioned in the earlier discourses of Peter: the earthly ministry of Jesus (Acts 10:38-39); Jesus as the future judge (Acts 10:42). Acts 10:34-36 (with its focus on universality) is the introduction to the speech which connects it to the context.[21] Peter shares the key insight which is now dawning on him: God is impartial and righteous people of every nation are acceptable to him. Jesus' preaching to Israel was/is a message of peace which is destined for all nations; he is Lord of *all* (Acts 10:36). Peace is an important Lukan theme (see Lk 1:79; 2:14; 7:50; 8:48; 10:5-6; 19:38, 42; 24:36; Acts 7:26; 9:31). Perhaps it is highlighted here because peace/reconciliation between Jew and Gentile through the message of Jesus is in view.

The remainder of the speech (Acts 10:37-43) is a proclamation of Jesus (kerygma) to Cornelius and his household. In Acts 10:37-41 Peter looks back at what has happened and gives us a summary of the Gospel story as found in the first volume of Luke's work: beginning with the baptism of John; ministry in Galilee ('Judea' in Acts 10:37 seems to refer to the district of the Roman province of Syria, which includes Galilee); death and resurrection in Jerusalem. Note how it is underlined that *God* was the main actor in the story of what happened to Jesus, an emphasis which fits in with the stress on the initiative of God in the Cornelius story.

On the occasion of his baptism, *God* anointed Jesus with the Spirit and with power (Acts 10:38a; see Lk 3:21-22; 4:18; see also Is 61:1-2). *God* was with Jesus during his earthly ministry and worked through him (Acts 10:38b). *God* raised Jesus from the dead after people had put him to death by hanging him on a tree (Acts 10:39b-40). Note again the contrast between what people did to Jesus and what God did for him, which was a constant refrain in Peter's earlier discourses. *God* also chose witnesses, who can testify both to Jesus' earthly ministry (Acts 10:39) and his resurrection (Acts 10:41; see also Lk 24:30, 34; Acts 1:3-4, 8; 1:21-22). In Acts 10:42-43 Peter turns his attention more to the present and the future. Forgiveness of sins through Jesus' name can now be experienced by everyone who believes (Acts 10:43). Jesus has been appointed by God as the (future) judge of the living and the dead and the missionaries are bearing witness to that (Acts 10:42; see Acts 17:31). Peter's speech ends on a universal note ('living and dead,' 'everyone'), as it began. In Acts 10:43 we have a very general reference to the fulfilment of the Scriptures (prophets), a prominent element in the earlier Petrine preaching. As a 'God-fearer' Cornelius would have had some acquaintance with the prophets of Israel.

In Acts 10:44-48 we see that the Spirit is still ahead of Peter whose role is basically to cooperate with and confirm what the Spirit is doing. The Holy Spirit falls on the group of Gentiles in Cornelius' house even before Peter has finished talking! This is usually referred to as the 'Gentile Pentecost'. The Jewish (circumcised) believers who accompanied Peter witness this (they hear the Gentiles speaking in tongues and praising God, which is taken as a sign of the outpouring of the Spirit); their reaction is one of amazement that the Spirit descends *even* on Gentiles (Acts 10:45-46). Peter realises that what is happening is the same as what happened to the Jewish apostles and disciples on the day of Pentecost (Acts 10:47). He feels that the only course of action is to confirm God's acceptance of the Gentiles through the rite of baptism. See comments on Acts 8:16 above on the relation between the coming of the Spirit and the reception of baptism. We have the picture of Jewish Christians baptising Gentiles and receiving them into a community of faith in which cultural boundaries are transcended. Peter, in response to the Gentiles' invitation, stays for some time in what Jews would consider a legally unclean place (Acts 10:48) – another sign of the all-inclusive hospitality of God.

Scene V (Acts 11:1-18), the final scene in the drama, tells how Peter reported the Cornelius episode to the Jerusalem church which puts its seal of approval on what happened. Acts 11:1-4 sets the scene. News that 'the Gentiles had also accepted the word of God' reached the apostles and disciples in Jerusalem. The indications are that the news was received favourably. But Peter is criticised by 'the circumcised believers' who object that he has gone to the Gentiles and eaten with them (Acts 11:2-3). The issue is mingling with unclean Gentiles and eating food with them, which is a source of ritual impurity for Peter and indeed for the whole Jewish Christian community.[22] Those who object have the same mentality that Peter had in Acts 10:14 – a strong reluctance to transgress any Jewish regulation with regard to ritual purity and a determination to argue about the issue. Peter can do no more than tell 'in order' (*kathexēs*, 'step by step' – Luke uses the same word in Lk 1:3 about his own orderly account) the story of what happened to him, to make the point that what he did was done, not on his own initiative, but in obedience to the will of God and the movement of the Spirit.

In Acts 11:5-17 we have the story told from Peter's point of view. Notice he starts, not with Cornelius' vision, but with his own experience, including his own reluctance and tendency to debate and object (thus identifying with his critics), and goes on to explain how he gained greater insight as the events unfolded and as he listened to the experience of Cornelius and his household. He brings his critics through his own experience of growing in clarity and understanding until they too can praise God for giving the Gentiles 'the repentance that leads to life' (Acts 11:18). This retelling in Acts 11:5-17 is basically the same as the story in Acts 10 with a few small changes. Peter says there were six Jewish Christians with him and in the retelling he associates them with his own actions very closely (see Acts 11:12 – 'we entered'). The Holy Spirit falls on the Gentiles as Peter begins to speak (Act 11:15), not as he was finishing his speech. Could it be that Peter wants to offset any conclusion that he convinced the Gentiles by his eloquence?

Finally, Peter appeals to a saying of the Lord about being baptised with the Holy Spirit to throw light on and justify what has happened (Acts 11:16; see Acts 1:5; Lk 3:16). Peter again emphasises that the Gentiles have received the Spirit just as the Jewish Christians received the Spirit at Pentecost (Acts 11:17). He ends with a question: 'Who was I that I could hinder God?' The critics and debaters are reduced to silence, to an attitude of listening (to what God is doing) which leads to praise (Acts 11:18). They glorify God as people in Luke's Gospel do in response to Jesus' mighty deeds (see Lk 5:25-26; 7:16; 13:13; 17:15). Their comment is similar to the reaction of the Jewish witnesses in Acts 10:45: 'God has given *even to the Gentiles* the repentance that leads to life.' Note that repentance is a gift of God, not simply our work (see Acts 5:31 which speaks of repentance granted to Israel). But, as we shall see, the issue is not closed; it will raise its head again in Acts 15 when the Gentile mission is well under way through the ministry of Paul and Barnabas.

The Cornelius episode is a major turning point in Luke's story of Christian mission. It surfaced basic questions and issues which took quite some time to articulate and resolve. Should Jewish Christians reach out to Gentiles in the first place? What are the implications of accepting Gentiles into a Jewish Christian community? Can Jews and Gentiles in the Christian community share meals together? Are Gentiles to be asked to adhere to Jewish laws and practices? Can Gentile believers have equal status with those who first believed? At the root of all these questions is the basic question of identity: Who are we as followers of Jesus Christ? Perhaps we could say that the reception of Gentiles into the Christian community was accepted in principle as a result of the Cornelius episode. But, as we shall see, when Gentiles started to come into the community in large numbers as a result of the missionary work of people like Paul, the questions came up again with new force and were the major issues at the Council of Jerusalem (Acts 15). Christians had to go through the at times painful experience of redefining themselves as people belonging to a universal religion, rather than an ethnic religion.

Reflection on Acts 8:4–11:18

The account of Philip's mission in Samaria (Acts 8:4-40) triggers some thoughts and questions for me in reflecting on mission today. How do we handle setbacks in mission which might lead us to think that our mission is folding up? The mission in Samaria began when a severe persecution in Jerusalem threatened to bring the Church's mission to an end. But this major setback became the stepping stone to a new missionary outreach which was not due to human planning and calculation. It was guided and empowered by the Spirit of mission, as Luke brings out explicitly in his story of Philip and the Ethiopian eunuch. The incident with Simon the magician reminds us that we do not control the Spirit; rather, we must open ourselves in freedom to be led by the Spirit.

Over the years I have been quite involved in drawing up and promoting plans of action for mission. We have used various programmes from the world of management to bring greater efficiency to our missionary work. And we should use any help we can get to be more organised and efficient in implementing our decisions. But I wonder have we got the right balance between the discerning and managerial approaches in mission. Do we give sufficient attention to processes which help us to be open to the Spirit at work among us? In arriving at decisions in our missionary life and work, how much time is spent listening rather than talking and debating?

In Acts 9 we hear of Saul, who was quite zealous and efficient in stamping out what he saw as a dangerous sect in Judaism, being rendered powerless and told to wait for the guidance of the Lord. In Acts 10 we hear how Peter, who liked to argue and put forward objections, has to learn to listen and respond to the Spirit of mission who always seems to be one step ahead of him. So, while we should use managerial skills in implementing our major missionary decisions, we need to learn the way of spiritual discernment in reaching these decisions in the first place. Pope Francis, in calling us to be Spirit-filled evangelisers, warns against the danger of over-planning in our mission: 'There is no greater freedom than that of allowing oneself to be guided by the Holy Spirit, renouncing the attempt to plan and control everything to the last detail, and instead letting him enlighten, guide and direct us, leading us wherever he wills. The Holy Spirit knows well what is needed in every time and place. This is what it means to be mysteriously fruitful!'[23] I will have more to say about a discerning approach in mission when we consider how the Church arrived at major decisions at the Council of Jerusalem (Acts 15).

Through his experience on the road to Damascus, Saul was transformed into the greatest missionary and theologian the Church has seen. The Damascus experience could be called a peak experience which determined Paul's discipleship and mission. He revisited that experience time and time again, particularly at critical moments, in order to find meaning and energy for his life and mission in changing circumstances. He recalls the experience in Acts 22:3-21 (after he had been arrested in the Temple area) and Acts 26:9-18 (before he is sent as a prisoner to Rome). In his letters also we hear him speak of his Damascus experience at critical moments (see 1 Cor 9:1; 15:8-10; Gal 1:12-17; Phil 3:4-16; 1 Tm 1:12-16).

In our life and mission, we need to be in touch with our own peak experience(s), when we had a clear sense of the meaning and direction of our lives, when we felt energised and enthused to commit ourselves to someone or some higher cause. A past peak experience can be like a diviner's rod for us as we seek meaning and energy in the midst of confusion and change. Let us explore a little further the dimensions of Saul's peak experience. It was fundamentally a meeting with the risen Lord which initiated a deep relationship and identification with the Lord, to the extent that Paul could say, 'It is no longer I who live, but Christ lives in me' (Gal 2:20). That was what impelled and sustained Paul in mission.

I once heard a missiologist say that the basic question for any missionary is, 'Who is Jesus Christ for me?' In our mission do we witness to a person who is alive, one whom we have personally experienced in our own lives, rather than a historical person we read about in books? Pope Francis never tires of telling us that a personal encounter with Jesus is the basis for our Christian life and mission. He begins his Apostolic Exhortation on the Proclamation of the Gospel in Today's World with the words, 'The Joy of the Gospel fills the hearts and lives of all who encounter Jesus.'[24] Saul's call to mission flowed naturally from his meeting with the Lord. Immediately after his baptism we find him on mission in Damascus and Jerusalem. This is another reminder that our missionary call is rooted in baptism, not priestly ordination or religious profession. Every baptised Christian is called to mission. Saul's meeting with the risen Lord was also a conversion experience, a radical transformation and reorientation of his life brought about by the free gift of the Lord, not by his own efforts.

To be on mission today involves an ongoing conversion to the Lord who comes to meet us in the events of our lives and in the people to whom we are sent on mission, especially the poor and excluded ones of our world. The Jesus who met Saul on the road to Damascus is the one who identifies with the persecuted and downtrodden. He still identifies with those who are suffering, oppressed, excluded (see also Mt 25:31-46).

The poor are not just on the receiving end of our mission; they are also our evangelisers through whom we meet the Lord calling us to a transformation and reorientation of our lives.

Reaching out to the Gentiles was the most momentous step for the early Church, but also a most challenging and frightening step. Though Luke presents Jesus commissioning his disciples to be his witnesses to the ends of the earth (Acts 1:8), the evidence suggests that historically it took quite some time for disciples to realise fully that the Good News of Jesus must be proclaimed to all peoples. Reflecting on the Gospel message in the light of changing circumstances raised profound and at times unsettling questions for the Jewish Church. But grappling with these questions brought deeper insight about the meaning of the Gospel and the meaning of mission.

Every time Christianity encounters a new culture, philosophy, ideology or scientific theory, new questions arise about the appropriate Christian response. By grappling with these questions we too can be led to a deeper understanding of and commitment to the Gospel. And what gives us the courage to face these questions is our belief that the Spirit of God is guiding and empowering us in our mission, just as he led Peter to face the challenge of crossing the threshold of a Gentile house. The Cornelius episode reminds us that God is present and active in every situation even before the missionary arrives. The attitude of the missionary on entering a new situation should not be defensive. We should be on our guard against rejecting something because it is outside our familiar religious experience and understanding. Initially Peter is defensive because he is bound by his traditional convictions and practices. The reasons that made Peter hesitate sound very plausible: 'I want to do the right thing; I want to keep the law; I don't want to go against what we traditionally do; I wouldn't like to upset people who may not agree with what I'm doing; I want more time to figure out what's going on.' Often seemingly good reasons block us from recognising where God is leading us in mission.

Speaking of obedience to the Gospel as the ultimate standard, and to the Magisterium which guards it, Pope Francis warns us against a rigid resistance to change: 'It is not a matter of applying rules or repeating what was done in the past, since the same solutions are not valid in all circumstances and what was useful in one context may not prove so in another. The discernment of spirits liberates us from rigidity which has no place before the perennial "today" of the risen Lord.'[25] Like Peter, we too have to learn to listen first to the experience of those to whom we are sent on mission. We try to sense the presence and activity of God in every new situation and challenge in order to cooperate and keep pace with the movements of God's Spirit. I am not saying that missionaries should just listen and remain silent. As we have already seen, courageous witness to Jesus Christ is essential in mission. In the Cornelius episode, Peter, having listened, shares the story of Jesus and what Jesus is offering to those who believe in him. The Cornelius episode is about respectful listening and mutual sharing in which the voice of the Spirit is heard. After our consideration of Acts 15 we will return to this topic and reflect on the challenges of inculturation and intercultural living in Christian mission.

Finally, in this whole section of Acts we get strong reminders about the ecclesial dimension of mission. Philip is not a missionary doing his own thing. His missionary outreach is confirmed by leaders of the Jerusalem community who even join Philip in his work of evangelisation. Before Saul engages in mission in Damascus he is received into the Christian community by Ananias and Luke emphasises his close contacts with the Damascus and Jerusalem communities. The community dimension is also prominent in the Cornelius episode. Jewish disciples receive Gentile believers into the one community of Jesus' followers. Peter reports to the community in Jerusalem what happened in Caesarea and they confirm the extraordinary step he took. What we learn from all of this is that mission is always ecclesial – carried out on behalf of the Church and in dialogue with Church leadership, thus being a sign of the community which is Church. Baptism is the rite of admission into the community. Philip baptised the Ethiopian eunuch, Ananias baptised Saul, and Peter along with the Jewish disciples baptised Cornelius and his household. In reflecting on the place of sacraments in our communal life, perhaps the incident with Simon the magician in Samaria can warn us against a formalistic celebration of rites. Sacraments are not ways of dispensing and controlling God's free gifts through the performance of rituals. They are privileged moments in the community for meeting the risen Lord who strengthens and sustains us in our discipleship and mission.

NOTES

[1] Johnson, *The Acts of the Apostles*, 147.

[2] This is the first indication of a changing role for the apostles in the story of Acts. They are not just the initiators of mission, but also the verifiers of new missionary outreaches undertaken by others. Here we see Peter and John working as evangelists in an area opened for mission by Philip (see also Acts 9:32-42 where Peter visits those already evangelised in Lydda and Joppa). However, in this regard we should not overlook the key role of Peter in the conversion of Cornelius, the event that sanctioned the Gentile mission. (On the changing role of the apostles in Acts see Tannehill, *The Narrative Unity of Luke-Acts*, vol. 2, 102).

[3] On the significance of the coming of the Spirit in Acts 8:15-17; 10:44-45; 19:5-6, see Fitzmyer, *The Acts of the Apostles*, 400-401.

[4] See Johnson, *The Acts of the Apostles*, 159; Fitzmyer, *The Acts of the Apostles*, 410.

[5] See Tannehill, *The Narrative Unity of Luke-Acts*, vol. 2, 111.

[6] Acts 8:37 (see footnote in NRSV) is not found in the best manuscripts. It is probably an addition to the original text to underline the need for faith in receiving baptism.

[7] Philip's transportation by the Spirit is perhaps meant to recall a characteristic of Elijah's prophetic ministry (1 Kgs 18:12). In 1 Kgs 18:46 we hear of Elijah running in front of the chariot of a powerful person (compare Acts 8:30). Drawing similarities between Philip and Elijah reinforces the parallelism between Philip and Jesus who, for Luke, is the Elijah-like prophet (see Lk 4:25-26 and the many references and allusions to Elijah in Lk 9).

8 Richard J. Dillon, 'Acts of the Apostles' in *The New Jerome Biblical Commentary,* ed. R. E. Brown et al. (London: Chapman, 1989), 744.

9 For a comparison between the three accounts, see Fitzmyer, *The Acts of the Apostles,* 141-144.

10 Fitzmyer (*Ibid.,* 420) has this to say about Saul's Damascus experience: 'This is the story of the call of Saul. It is not an account of his psychological "conversion," as it is often characterised, but the story of how divine grace transforms even the life of a persecutor... It is not the story of the conversion of a great sinner, but rather of how heaven can upset the persecution of God's people.' Johnson (*The Acts of the Apostles,* 167) says: 'As with the story of Pentecost, Luke has the daunting challenge of putting in narrative terms what is essentially an internal transformation... Reduced to basics, what happened involved the (by definition incommunicable) personal experience of the risen Lord, and the ritual acceptance into the community. To give narrative life to that bald statement, Luke employs models and symbols available to him in the tradition.'

11 See Dillon, 'Acts of the Apostles' in *The New Jerome Biblical Commentary,* 744; Tannehill, *The Narrative Unity of Luke-Acts,* vol. 2, 122; Fitzmyer, *The Acts of the Apostles,* 438.

12 See, for instance, Fitzmyer, *ibid.,* 435; Kurz, *Acts of the Apostles,* 157.

13 In trying to determine what happened in the period after Paul's conversion, historical critics compare Acts 9:19b-30 and Paul's own comments in Gal 1:11-24 and 2 Cor 11:32-33. Johnson (*Acts of the Apostles,* 173-174), having mentioned points of substantial agreement in this regard between Acts and the Pauline letters, draws attention to the following disagreements: '(a) Paul makes a point about the passage of time between his independent ministry in Arabia and Damascus, and his first trip to Jerusalem, whereas Luke allows us to imagine a passage of time, but gives the impression of only a short one. (b) Paul says he was opposed by King Aretas in Damascus, whereas Luke attributes his troubles to a plot by the Jews of that city. (c) Paul insists that on his first visit he saw none of the apostles except Cephas and James, whereas Luke has simply that he saw the "apostles". (d) Paul does not leave room for a period of ministry within the Church in Jerusalem, whereas Luke explicitly emphases it. (e) Paul has Barnabas accompany him on the trip only "after fourteen years," and simply as another companion like Titus, whereas Luke has him as the essential mediator between Paul and the apostles.' Some try to harmonise the various pieces of information, but without great success. We need to keep in mind the different concerns of Luke and Paul in

telling the story. Luke wants to emphasise Paul's connection with Jerusalem in order to signal that his missionary outreach in the Gentile world is in continuity with what had happened among the restored people of God in Jerusalem. Paul in Galatians was anxious to assert his independence of the Jerusalem leadership in an effort to insist that he did not receive his message from a human source; it came from an experience of the risen Lord (Gal 1:16). Again we are reminded that Luke's main concern is not to give exact historical information, but to highlight the meaning of what happened.

14   *The Acts*, 68.

15   See Tannehill, *The Narrative Unity of Luke-Acts*, vol. 2, 126-127, for a detailed list of the similarities between the text in question (Acts 9:36-43) and the following texts: 1 Kgs 17:8-24; 2 Kgs 4:18-37; Lk 7:11-17 (raising of the widow's son at Nain); Lk 8:41-42, 49-56 (raising of the daughter of Jairus).

16   Peter is 'moving geographically and ethnically closer to the edge, to the place by the sea in Joppa, where he resided with the ritually impure tanner Simon, ready to hear the call from the Gentile city of Caesarea' (Johnston, *The Acts of the Apostles*, 186).

17   Caesarea was built by Herod the Great in 37-34 BC. It had a large Gentile population and was the centre of Roman administration in Judea from AD 6. There is archaeological evidence for an Italian cohort stationed in Syria around AD 69, but there is no evidence supporting the presence of the unit in Caesarea for the period AD 41-44.

18   Mullins, *The Acts of the Apostles*, 119.

19   Tannehill (*The Narrative Unity of Luke-Acts*, vol. 2, 136) underlines the importance of hospitality and shared meals in the Cornelius episode (see Acts 10:23, 27, 48; 11:3). They not only show that community is now possible between Jew and Gentile, but also indicate that mission to Gentiles can now begin because of the removal of the obstacle of unlawful association with Gentiles. All of this should be seen against the backdrop of Jesus' table fellowship in Luke's Gospel as a sign of the all-inclusive hospitality of God.

20   The Greek text of Acts 10:25 is better translated 'when Peter entered,' rather than 'on Peter's arrival' (NRSV). Luke tells us twice (Acts 10:25, 27) that Peter entered the Gentile's house. It seems he wants to linger on that significant, boundary-crossing moment.

21   The Greek in Acts 10:36-37 is awkward and can be translated in a number of ways. Contrast the NRSV translation with the following translation of Johnson (*The Acts of the Apostles*, 189), which takes

Acts 10:36 with what goes before rather than what follows: 'He sent the message to the children of Israel. He proclaimed the good news of peace through Jesus Messiah. He is Lord of all! You know the word that spread through all of Judea, beginning from Galilee after the baptism that John preached ...' Fitzmyer (*The Acts of the Apostles*, 459-460) takes the words *humeis oidate* ('you know'), which begins Acts 10:37 in the Greek text, to refer to the Christian reader of Acts and not to Cornelius.

[22] 'Table-fellowship with non-Jews was seen as betrayal of the special identity of the Jews and a sharing in the ways, even in the idolatry of the Gentiles' (Mullins, *The Acts of the Apostles*, 122).

[23] *Evangelii Gaudium*, no. 280.

[24] *Ibid.*, no. 1; Francis expands on that in nos 264-267 of the same document.

[25] *Gaudete et Exsultate*, no. 173.

CHAPTER 5

LAUNCH OF THE GENTILE MISSION
(ACTS 11:19–15:35)

Overview

Mission to the Gentiles has now been sanctioned by God through the Cornelius episode. We recall once more the words of Jesus when he commissioned his disciples: 'You will be my witnesses in Jerusalem, in all Judea and Samaria, and to the ends of the earth' (Acts 1:8). We have heard the story of the first two phases of this missionary programme, the outreach to Jews and Samaritans. The remainder of the Acts of the Apostles is about mission 'to the ends of the earth'. In Acts 11:1–28:31 the focus falls almost exclusively on the missionary outreach to the Gentiles carried out by Paul and those associated with him. This does not mean that missionary outreach to Jews now comes to an end. Though Paul was adamant about his special call to preach to the Gentiles, on his arrival in a new city or area he usually reached out first to Jews in their synagogues. We will hear him twice making solemn declarations about turning from unresponsive Jews to Gentiles who are more eager to listen (Acts 13:44-49; 18:5-7), yet when he arrives in Rome at the end of all his journeying he first meets with the Jewish leaders in that city. Given how he continued to approach Jews after his previous declarations, his final statement in Rome about turning to Gentiles (Acts 28:25-29) should not be taken as the definitive end of outreach to Jews. Mission 'to the ends of the earth' is to all nations, including Jews. Acts 11:1–28:31 could be divided into seven major sections:

1. Acts 11:19–14:28: Mission from Antioch to Cyprus and Asia Minor
2. Acts 15:1-35: Council of Jerusalem
3. Acts 15:36–19:41: Major Missions of Paul
4. Acts 20:1–21:16: Paul's Farewell Journey to Jerusalem
5. Acts 21:17–23:35: Paul's Imprisonment and Witness in Jerusalem
6. Acts 24:1–26:32: Paul's Defence and Witness in Caesarea
7. Acts 27:1–28:31: Paul's Last Journey and Ministry in Rome

These are not clear and watertight sections, as one section flows easily into the next and Luke has the habit of anticipating future developments. Luke was thinking in terms of the developing narrative rather than dividing his material into neat blocks. The important thing is to read each passage in the context of the wider story. My division of the remaining material of Acts into chapters for this book is somewhat subjective and is influenced to some extent by a desire to avoid having a mixture of relatively short and long chapters, but I am careful not to lose sight of the overall unfolding story. The present chapter, entitled 'Launch of the Gentile Mission,' covers the foundation of the Church in Antioch, its mission to Asia Minor through its representatives Paul and Barnabas, and the Council of Jerusalem which addressed questions arising from the success of the Gentile mission from Antioch. The story of Peter's miraculous escape from prison (Acts 12:1-23) is also covered in this chapter with a consideration of the role it plays in the ongoing narrative.

Foundation of the Church in Antioch (Acts 11:19-30)
Acts 11:19 picks up the story of the scattered Hellenists (see Acts 8:1), which had been 'interrupted' by the stories of the conversions of Saul and Cornelius. These 'went from place to place, proclaiming the word' (Acts 8:4). Having told us of the Hellenist Philip's evangelising work in Samaria and Judea,

Luke now speaks of those who went farther afield – to Phoenicia, Cyprus and Antioch – and who at first spoke the word to Jews only (Acts 11:19). Luke at this stage is particularly interested in those who went to Antioch in Syria, the third most important city in the Roman Empire (after Rome and Alexandria). It was a predominantly Gentile city with a mixed population of native Syrians and settlers (for example, Macedonians, Cretans, Cypriotes, Argives and Jews). This cosmopolitan city will become an important mission centre in Luke's story and so he gives particular attention to its foundation. 'It will be the sponsoring Church for the western mission (13:1-3), the place where the debate over Gentile membership will come to a head (14:26–15:2), and the place where, after an extended tenure (11:26; 15:35), Paul and Barnabas finally separate (15:36-40). Finally, Paul will make a separate visit to the Church (18:22) before beginning his final European tour.'[1]

Some Hellenist Christians of Cypriot and Cyrenean origin took the bold step of preaching the word to Greeks (that is, non-Jews) in Antioch (Acts 11:20).[2] It is quite possible that this preaching to Greeks in Antioch had been going on even before Peter's meeting with Cornelius and his household. But Luke has placed the major emphasis in this regard on the Cornelius episode, because he wants to highlight the initiative of God in the outreach to the Gentiles, as well as Peter's prominent role, and the sanction of the apostles in this most decisive development. By placing the story of the foundation of the Church in Antioch and its initiative in reaching out to Gentiles *after* the Cornelius event, Luke has firmly rooted this step in 'apostolic tradition' and thus ensured continuity. The Lord was in this initiative and Luke notes its success by once again referring to increase in number (Acts 11:21, 24b, 26; see Acts 2:41, 47; 4:4; 5:14; 6:7).

Hearing about this development, the church in Jerusalem sent Barnabas to Antioch as its delegate (Acts 11:22-24). Luke's main interest here is to emphasise that the initiative in Antioch had the approval of the apostles and the Jerusalem church, and to forge links between these two Christian communities. Barnabas' joy is a typical Lukan reaction to the experience of God's gracious presence and activity (Acts 11:23; see, for instance, Lk 13:17; 19:6). True to his name and nature (see Acts 4:36; 9:27), Barnabas encourages the Christians in Antioch in their life and mission. In Acts 11:24 Barnabas is described in terms reminiscent of Stephen – 'a good man, full of the Holy Spirit and of faith' (see Acts 6:5, 8). Barnabas also takes a decision which turned out to be most important. He went to Tarsus and brought Saul to Antioch to get involved in mission there (Acts 11:25-26). This is the second time Barnabas introduced Saul to mission (see Acts 9:26-29). For a year Barnabas and Saul exercised a teaching role in the community, probably instructing new Gentile converts (Acts 11:26). Putting Barnabas and Saul at the heart of the community in Antioch prepares for their call to mission farther afield (see Acts 13:1-3). In Acts 11:26 Luke gives us an interesting piece of information. At Antioch the disciples were first called 'Christians' (*Christianoi*). This may well have been a somewhat derogatory nickname used by others for the followers of Jesus who proclaimed him as the *Christos*, the anointed Messiah (something like the name 'Moonies' for the followers of the Korean religious leader Sun Myung Moon).[3]

The story of the arrival of prophets from Jerusalem, one of whom spoke of a severe famine about to happen, and the consequent visit of Barnabas and Saul to Jerusalem to bring relief to the needy churches in Judea (Acts 11:27-30), are meant by Luke to highlight once more the close ties between the Jerusalem and Antioch communities. The 'prophets' in the early Church were charismatic preachers who were either attached to a particular local church or wandered from place to place (See Acts 13:1; 21:10; 1 Cor 12:28-29; 14:29, 32, 37; Eph 2:20; 3:5; 4:11). Agabus appears again in Acts 21:10 where he also makes a prediction. The 'world' (*oikoumenē*) (Acts 11:28) should be taken to mean 'empire' in this case. We know there were widespread famines during the reign of Claudius (AD 41-54). We are told that the church in Antioch decided to send relief to the believers in Judea and selected Barnabas and Saul to bring this relief to the 'elders' (*presbyteroi*) (Acts 11:29-30). This is the first time in Acts we hear of 'elders'. They should not be seen as the successors of the apostles; rather they are local church leaders (see also Acts 14:23; 15:2, 4, 6, 22, 23; 16:4; 20:17; 21:18).[4]

In 1 Cor 16:1-4, 2 Cor 8-9 and Rm 15:25-32 Paul speaks of the collection 'for the saints in Jerusalem,' which was organised in the latter part of his missionary career as a symbol of unity as well as practical assistance. It seems beyond doubt that at some time in his career Paul brought a gift of money to the church in Jerusalem. But when it comes to the timing, motivation and significance of the collection, it is not easy to harmonise fully what Luke says in Acts 11:29-30 with what we read in Paul's letters.[5] What is uppermost in Luke's mind at this point in his story is the forging of strong links between Jerusalem and Antioch through the movement of personnel and material resources between the two communities. This interest is also evident in Acts 12:25 when Luke says that Barnabas and Saul brought John Mark with them on their return from Jerusalem to Antioch.[6]

What is said of the community in Antioch in Acts 11:19-30 reminds us of some of the characteristics of the Jerusalem community as described in the summaries in the early chapters of Acts: a community increasing in number (Acts 11:21; see 2:47); experiencing the grace of God (Acts 11:23; see 4:33); sharing possessions with the needy (Acts 11:29; see 4:45); listening to the teaching about Jesus (Acts 11:26; see 2:42). This is probably Luke's way of saying that the new community at Antioch is an authentic realisation of the messianic people. It also reinforces his continuity theme.

Peter's Escape from Prison and Herod's Death (Acts 12:1-25)

We have been told about Saul's conversion and commission to bring the Good News to the Gentiles. God has sanctioned the Gentile mission in the Cornelius episode and the

Jerusalem community has recognised that. The Christian community has been established in Antioch as an eminently suitable base for the Gentile mission. Strong links have been forged between Jerusalem and Antioch. Barnabas has brought Saul from Tarsus to Antioch to get him involved in mission. We now fully expect Luke to get on with telling the story of the Gentile mission from Antioch. But Luke abruptly switches the focus back to Jerusalem to tell us of the martyrdom of the apostle James and to relate the story of Peter's miraculous escape from prison during the persecution of church leaders by King Herod Agrippa I (AD 41-44) and the subsequent story of Herod's death. Why does Luke introduce these stories at this point in his narrative? One could put forward at least three reasons for this.

Firstly, before he begins the story of Paul's mission to the Gentiles, Luke wants to give us a powerful reminder that God is with his missionaries and nothing can hinder their mission.[7] He makes this point vividly and dramatically in the story of Peter's miraculous escape from prison (Acts 12:6-17) and the story of Herod's sudden and ignominious death (Acts 12:20-23). Note how the angel of God is present and active in each case. Secondly, Luke wants to connect and interlock the stories of his two great missionary heroes – Peter, the most prominent missionary in the first part of Acts, and Paul, the one whose mission in bringing the Good News to the ends of the earth receives almost exclusive attention in the second part of Acts. Having Saul in Jerusalem at the time of Peter's escape suggests that Peter and Paul's paths crossed at this time. Thirdly, Acts 12 is probably meant to mark Peter's exit from the narrative of Acts in an appropriate way. 'He left for another place' (Acts 12:17), but we are not told where he went. After this, Peter makes just one brief appearance in Acts 15:7-11 to share with the Council of Jerusalem what he had learned from the Cornelius episode. From now on, attention is given to the leadership role of James (the brother of the Lord) in the Jerusalem church (see Acts 12:17; 15:13, 19; 21:18). So Luke wants Peter to make his exit from the stage with a flourish. We can almost hear the applause.

The story of Peter's miraculous escape from prison (Acts 12:6-11) is the centrepiece of Acts 12. It is bracketed by references to the praying community (Acts 12:5 and 12:12-17). These in turn are flanked by passages with the focus on Herod (Acts 12:1-4 and 12:18-23). All of this is bracketed by the coming of Barnabas and Saul to Jerusalem (Acts 11:30) and their return to Antioch (Acts 12:25). The only verse not accounted for in this arrangement is Acts 12:24, which is one of Luke's short summaries to indicate the growth and advance of the word despite the effort to blot it out. Acts 12 presents the second of three rescues from prison in Acts (see also Acts 5:18-20; 16:23-29). It also presents another fulfilment of Jesus' prediction in Lk 21:12 that his followers would be handed over to prisons and brought before kings.

Herod Agrippa I was the grandson of Herod the Great. He found favour with the Romans and for four years (AD 41-44) succeeded in ruling most of his grandfather's territory. His persecution of the Church was probably directed at its leaders. His motivation in acting was to please the Jews (Acts 12:3). The Jewish historian Josephus tells us that this Herod did try to ingratiate himself with the religious leaders, especially the Pharisees. He had the apostle James killed by the sword – probably beheaded which in Jewish thinking was a shameful form of death, particularly suitable for apostates (see Deut 13:15). Herod then moved against Peter, whom he had arrested on the occasion of the feast of Unleavened Bread/Passover, to be kept in prison till he could be dealt with after the feast. The detailed description of the elaborate security measures (Acts 12:4, 6) is meant to heighten the wonder of the subsequent escape. The fervent prayer of the Church for Peter (Acts 12:5, 12) is an important element in this story, as the power of God is operative in the context of prayer. Remember how Jesus received strength through prayer at the time of his arrest and passion (see Lk 22:39-46).

What Luke wants to tell us in Acts 12:6-11 is that God was the principal agent in the release of Peter from prison. Luke often introduces an angel when he wants to speak about the intervention of God (see Lk 1:11, 26; 2:9, 13; 22:43; 24:23; Acts 8:26; 10:3, 7, 22; 11:13; 12:7-15, 23; 27:23). In Acts 12 we have an angel rescuing Peter and striking Herod, his persecutor. Light (Acts 12:7) is also a symbol for the divine presence (see Acts 9:3; 22:6, 9-11; 26:13). Peter seems to be in a trance and doesn't realise what is happening (Acts 12:9). The angel has to give him very detailed instructions, almost to the extent of having to dress him (Acts 12:7-8)! Peter and the angel pass guards unimpeded and the iron gate leading into the city opens before them (Acts 12:10). Once outside the prison the angel departs and we find Peter 'coming to himself' and talking to himself (Acts 12:11). Luke wants us to listen to what Peter is saying to get the basic point of his story, that is, the Lord's hand has been in Peter's release. The historical kernel of the story is a release/escape of Peter from prison which the community rightly understood in faith as God's saving action on behalf of Peter.[8]

Peter makes his way to the community assembled in prayer at the house of Mary, the mother of John Mark (Acts 12:12). There is a certain comic aspect to Peter's difficulty in getting into the house (Acts 12:13-16). 'Luke's own pleasure in the art of storytelling is obvious ... an angel gets Peter out of Herod's cell, but Peter himself cannot get through the locked gate to the Christian household because he is mistaken for an angel!'[9] Rhoda, in her joy, leaves Peter standing at the door. Those inside think she is mad or that Peter's (guardian) angel is outside. When Peter finally gets in, he tells them that the Lord brought him out of prison; this message is to be delivered to James and the believers (Acts 12:16-17). Then he departed to an unknown destination.[10]

We should not miss the parallelism between the experiences of Peter in Acts 12:1-17 and the experiences of Jesus in his arrest, death and resurrection.[11] Both were arrested during the time of the Passover celebration (Lk 2:1 and Acts 12:2); a

'King Herod' had a role in each event (Lk 23:6-12 and Acts 12:1); angels announce that Jesus has been released from death (Lk 24:23) and an angel is God's messenger in releasing Peter from the threat of death (Acts 12:7-10); when the women brought the news of Jesus' resurrection to the apostles, it was regarded as nonsense (Lk 24:11) and when Rhoda reported that Peter was out of prison she was told she was mad (Acts 12:14-15); the disciples' disbelief for joy in Lk 24:41 could be compared to Rhoda's reaction in Acts 12:14; when Jesus appears to the disciples, they think they are seeing a ghost (Lk 24:37), while the disciples in Acts 12:15 understand Peter's reappearance as the appearance of his angel; after Jesus converses with the disciples he withdraws (Lk 24:51) and Peter does the same in Acts 12:17. So it seems that Luke is telling us that Peter the missionary is reliving the paschal experience of Jesus. The life of the true missionary will always have the imprint of that experience.

Acts 12:18-23, which deals with the aftermath of Peter's escape, is mainly concerned with the death of Herod, the Church's persecutor. This is to reinforce the basic point that God overcomes the evil forces which threaten to hinder or blot out the power at work in mission. The Jewish historian Josephus' account of Herod's death differs in some respects from that of Luke, but they both agree in interpreting Herod's sudden death as a punishment for not rejecting the flattery of people who regarded Herod as a god.[12] 'Being eaten by worms' may be a feature taken over from 2 Mac 9:5-12 which describes the death of Antiochus IV Epiphanes, another persecutor of God's people.

Acts 12:24 is one of Luke's minor 'growth summaries,' highlighting the dynamism of the word of God. It is placed here to make the point that the word advances despite persecution. As mentioned above, Acts 12:25, which forms an inclusion with Acts 11:30, gets Barnabas and Saul back to Antioch so that the focus can return to their missionary work after the 'digression' of Acts 12.

Mission from Antioch to Cyprus and Asia Minor (Acts 13:1–14:28)

In Acts 13-14 we have the first example of planned 'overseas mission'. This section of Acts is traditionally referred to as Paul's first missionary journey (AD 46-49).[13] But the community dimension of this missionary outreach should not be overlooked. Barnabas and Saul are not acting on their own initiative. Rather, they are commissioned by a Church to go on mission as its representatives (Acts 13:1-3) and on completion of the task assigned to them they report back to the community (Acts 14:27-28). Unlike Paul's later missionary activity, the mission in Acts 13-14 is not confirmed by what we read in the undisputed Pauline letters, though 2 Tm 3:11 refers to Paul's sufferings in Antioch, Iconium and Lystra. In Acts 13-14 Luke gives us a good insight into Paul's missionary career. Patterns occur which will be repeated in Paul's later missionary activity. Luke is at pains to show that Paul's mission, under the direction of the Spirit (Acts 13:4), continues the mission of Jesus and the mission of Peter. He does this through an extensive use of parallelism, as we will see in considering the various episodes.[14] Saul starts the journey as the junior partner of Barnabas and ends it as the leader of the missionary team. At the end of Acts 14 Paul has been given centre stage in Luke's story and will hold that position right up to the end of Acts. The influx of large numbers of Gentiles as a result of the mission in Acts 13-14 brings to the surface once more the crucial issue of the identity of the Christian community and the place of the Gentiles in that community, an issue which will be addressed in Acts 15.

Commissioning of Barnabas and Saul (Acts 13:1-3)

The story of this missionary journey begins in the heart of the praying community in Antioch. We are given a list of the community's 'prophets and teachers' (leaders) – Barnabas and Saul bracket the list (Acts 13:1). 'Prophets' and 'teachers' performed similar functions in the community – for instance, exhortation, interpretation of the Scriptures, charismatic utterances (see Rm 12:6-7; 1 Cor 14:26, 28-29). The word of the Spirit in Acts 13:2 was probably uttered through one of these prophets. Again we are reminded of the presence, initiative and guidance of the Spirit at another important turning point in mission. The community experiences this guidance in a context of prayer and fasting which expresses openness to the Spirit and a need for the Spirit's guidance. The laying on of hands signifies the community's association and solidarity with Barnabas and Saul. The whole community is involved in the commissioning of Barnabas and Saul (compare Acts 1:15-26; 6:1-6; 15:22). In Acts 14:26, the community's action is seen in terms of commending the missionaries to the grace of the Lord. So, just as the Spirit of mission descended on the chosen Jesus while he was praying Lk 3:21-22, the same Spirit descends on Barnabas and Saul in the context of community worship, choosing and empowering them for mission.

Mission in Cyprus (Acts 13:4-12)
In Acts 13:3 we were told that the missionaries were sent out by the Church, whereas in the following verse we read that the Holy Spirit sends them out. The Holy Spirit acts in and through the Church. The Spirit also launched the mission of Jesus (Lk 3:22; 4:1, 14, 18) and the mission of Peter (Acts 2). From Seleucia (the seaport for Antioch) the missionaries set out for Cyprus with John Mark as an assistant (Acts 13:5). They start evangelising on the east side of the island (Salamis) and work their way across to the west side (Paphos). Right from the beginning we are told of one of Paul's main strategies in mission, that is, to head first for the synagogues of the Jews (Acts 13:35; see also Acts 13:14, 46; 14:1; 16:13, 16; 17:1, 10, 17; 18:4, 19; 19:8; 28:17). He worked on the principle that the Good News had to be proclaimed to Jews first, because Jesus was the fulfilment of the promises to Israel (see Acts 13:46). While Paul often got a cold reception from the leading Jews in the Diaspora synagogues, it seems

his message found a responsive note among Gentile converts to Judaism and 'God-fearers' (that is, Gentiles at the margins of the synagogue who were attracted to Judaism without converting fully).

Barnabas was a native of Cyprus (Acts 4:36) and the Good News had already been proclaimed to Jews in Cyprus by Hellenists who had been expelled from Jerusalem (Acts 11:19). In fact, disciples from Cyprus were among the first to preach to Greeks in Antioch (Acts 11:20). Nothing is said about the Christian community in Cyprus and we are given precious little information about the preaching of Barnabas and Saul in Salamis and throughout the island. Luke is anxious to move on to Paphos to concentrate on the encounter between Saul, an authentic prophet (see Acts 13:1), and the Jewish magician and false prophet, Bar-Jesus (Elymas). This man was seemingly in the retinue of Sergius Paulus, the Roman proconsul who wanted to hear the missionaries, and he tried to prevent the proconsul from accepting the Good News (Acts 13:6-8).

The confrontation between Saul and Elymas (Acts 13:9-12) reminds us of the confrontation between Peter and Simon the magician in Acts 8:18-24. As we saw in dealing with Acts 8, magic is associated with demonic powers and is part of the resistance of the kingdom of Satan to the kingdom of God at work in the mission of Jesus and his followers. This is even more accentuated in Acts 13. Paul is 'filled with the Holy Spirit' (Acts 13:9), while Elymas is a 'son of the devil', an 'enemy of righteousness,' 'full of all deceit and villainy,' one who is 'making crooked the straight paths of the Lord' (Acts 13:10). Again, in this conflict the power of the kingdom of God is a clear winner. The victory is symbolised in the powerful word of Paul leading to the temporary blindness and helplessness of Elymas (Acts 13:11). This clash between the power of the kingdom of God and the power of the devil reminds us of Jesus' clash with Satan in the wilderness at the beginning of his mission, when Satan tried to hinder his mission (Lk 4:1-13). All this parallelism underlines the fact that the mission of Paul is in continuity with the mission of Jesus and the mission of Peter.

Elymas' blindness is probably symbolic of spiritual darkness and unbelief. The proconsul, seeing what had happened, believed because he was astonished by the teaching about the Lord (Acts 13:12). There may be a secondary apologetic motif running through Acts 13:4-12. Luke presents the Roman administrator of high rank as an intelligent man who was open to the Christian message (Acts 13:7) and responded positively to it. Rome has nothing to fear from Christians and being a Christian is not incompatible with being a citizen of the empire.

From Acts 13:9 onwards, Luke will call his chief missionary Paul rather than Saul (except in the conversion accounts in Acts 22 and 26). The change to his Roman name marks the time when Paul begins to move more freely among non-Jews. Change of name is often associated with change of status or identity. From now on also, Paul assumes leadership in the missionary team (Acts 13:13); his name will be put before that of Barnabas (Acts 14:14 is an exception).

Mission in Antioch of Pisidia (Acts 13:13-52)

Luke gets us from Cyprus through Perga in Pamphylia to Antioch in Pisidia in less than two verses (Acts 13:13-14). This Antioch was about 160 kilometres inland through hazardous mountain terrain. At Perga John Mark returned home to Jerusalem, but we are not given the reason. Whatever it was, Paul was not impressed (see Acts 15:38). Again Paul and Barnabas headed for the local synagogue in Antioch. It was the Sabbath day and after the readings in the synagogue service they were invited to give the homily (Acts 13:14b-15). This leads into Paul's discourse in Antioch of Pisidia (Acts 13:16-43), which is his one and only recorded missionary sermon to Jewish listeners.[15]

Luke sees Paul's experience in Antioch of Pisidia as a parallel to Jesus' experience in Nazareth at the beginning of his ministry (Lk 4:16-30). Both Jesus and Paul, at an early point in their mission, and after an encounter with the power of Satan, give a significant address in a synagogue on the Sabbath day. In both cases, after an initial favourable response, things turn sour and they experience opposition (Lk 4:22; Acts 13:42-45). Both, arguing from Scripture, speak of a mission beyond Israel (Lk 4:23-27; Acts 13:46-47). Both were forced out of the town (Lk 4:28-30; Acts 13:50-51). Both episodes are programmatic in that they enunciate the programme of the ministry they inaugurate. There can be little doubt that Luke once again wants to impress upon us that there is an essential continuity between the mission of Jesus and the mission of Paul. Jesus is still on mission in the ministry of Paul.

The discourse of Paul (Acts 13:16-41), addressed to Israelites and (Gentile) God-fearers (see Acts 13:16b), has most of the elements of Peter's missionary speeches in Jerusalem: the Jesus kerygma, the proofs from the Scriptures, and the appeal for conversion. It is also similar to Stephen's discourse in Acts 7:1-53 in that both root what they want to say about Jesus in a survey of God's dealings with Israel in the past. However, Stephen concentrated on the promise made to Abraham, the experience of Joseph and particularly the story of Moses, with little or no attention to the period of the monarchy. Paul, on the other hand, is interested in focusing on David and the promises made to him, with minimal attention to the periods of the patriarchs and Moses. While the tone of Stephen's speech is negative and threatening, the tone of Paul's speech is positive and inviting. Paul goes out of his way to identify with his listeners as fellow Israelites.

By this speech Luke illustrates the principle that the Good News of salvation, intended for all nations, is first offered to Israel to whom the promises have been made. We can divide the speech into three parts, each part beginning with an address to the audience (who are called fellow 'Israelites' in Act 13:16, 'my brothers, you descendants of Abraham's family' in Acts 13:26, and 'my brothers' in Acts 13:38): (i) *Acts 13:16-25* gives a summary of Israel's history culminating in the promises to David which find fulfilment in Jesus; (ii) *Acts 13:26-37* is the Jesus kerygma, whose resurrection is the fulfilment of the promises to David; (iii) *Acts 13:38-41* concludes the speech with a summons to faith and the offer of forgiveness.

Historical Survey (Acts 13:16b-25): Paul starts with the people's experience of election. Note that God is once again seen as the main actor and the focus is on what God did for his people. Paul gets through the time covering the patriarchs, the exodus and the period of the judges in double quick time (Acts 13:17-20). Through all this time, the chosen Israel experienced God's salvation, care and favour. It is better to read 'he cared for' in place of 'he put up with' in Acts 13:18 (see NRSV footnote).[16] When Paul gets to the period of Samuel and the monarchy, he quickly focuses on David and the promise to him, because that is where his interest lies. In Acts 13:22 David is extolled with a quotation which is really a combination of three Septuagint texts (Ps 88:21; 1 Sm 13:14; Is 44:28). In speaking of Jesus as David's posterity (Acts 13:23), Paul has in mind the promise made to David that the Lord will raise up an offspring after him and establish his kingdom forever (see 2 Sm 7:12-16; Ps 89:29, 36-37; Ps 132:11-12, 17). Luke also recalls this promise in the story of the annunciation to Mary (Lk 1:32-33). For Jesus as *Saviour*, see also Lk 2:11 and Acts 5:31. In Acts 13:24-25 we have reference to John the Baptist, the prophet who preached repentance and bridged the Time of Promise and the Time of Fulfilment (see especially Lk 16:16; also Lk 1:17; 3:2-20; 5:33; 7:18-33; 9:7-9, 19; 11:1; 20:4-6; Acts 1:5, 22; 10:37; 11:16). Acts 13:25 repeats John's own testimony that Jesus was superior to him (Lk 3:16), which was also a major theme in the Lukan infancy narratives.

Jesus Kerygma (Acts 13:26-37): In the historical survey Paul has already introduced Jesus as the one who fulfils the history of Israel, in particular the promise made to David.

Now he goes on to focus on the death and especially the resurrection of Jesus, because it is in the resurrection of Jesus that the promise to David is fulfilled for the descendants of Abraham's family and (Gentile) God fearers (see Acts 13:26). In Acts 13:27-30 we have the kerygmatic contrast between what people did to Jesus and what God did for him, which we have seen as a feature of all the missionary discourses in Acts. We get the ignorance motif again in this speech which is conciliatory in tone. The people did not recognise who Jesus was or understand the words of the prophets who pointed to him (Acts 13:27; see Acts 3:17). Yet, ironically, they actually fulfilled these prophecies by condemning Jesus. We also have the innocence motif (Acts 13:28) which is a feature of Luke's passion story (Lk 23:4, 14, 22). How God in the resurrection reversed the rejection of Jesus is stated clearly and simply in Acts 13:30.

Paul immediately speaks of the witnesses to the resurrection (Acts 13:31) in words that recall Acts 1:21-22 and 10:41. Paul does not number himself among these first witnesses, but he quickly goes on to speak about his task of announcing the Good News that what God promised to Israel has been fulfilled for his present hearers through the resurrection of Jesus (Acts 13:32-33a). Now Paul backs up what he is saying by quoting three texts from the Scriptures which he says are fulfilled in the resurrection event. *Ps 2:7* (Acts 13:33b) is taken from a royal psalm, probably addressed to the Davidic king on the day of his coronation when he was declared God's adopted son. When applied to the resurrection, the thinking may be that God declared Jesus his Son, giving him life and a share in his dominion over the whole world (see Lk 3:22; Acts 4:25-26; Heb 1:5; 5:5 which also apply Ps 2 to Jesus). *Is 55:3* in its LXX form (Acts 13:34b) is taken to mean that the 'holy promises' made to David are given to 'you' (plural), that is, through the resurrection of Jesus the fulfilment of the promises made to David becomes a reality for the present generation. *Ps 16:10* (Acts 13:35) fulfils the same purpose it had in Peter's Pentecost speech (Acts 2:27), that is, to make the point that this psalm must have been speaking about someone other than David, because David died and experienced corruption (Acts 13:34a, 36; Acts 2:29-30). The psalm refers to Jesus whom God raised from the dead so that his body did not experience corruption (Acts 13:37).

Summons to Faith and the Offer of Forgiveness (Acts 13:38-41):
The offer of the forgiveness of sins to those who believe (Acts 13:38) is central to the proclamation of the Good News in Luke's writings (see Lk 24:47; Acts 2:38; 5:31; 10:43). Acts 13:38-39 is close to what Paul says in his letters about justification through faith in Jesus rather than by observance of the Law (see Rm 2:13; 3:24-26; 4:2, 5; 5:1, 9; 8:30, 33; 1 Cor 8:11; Gal 2:16; 3:11, 24). Note the universal dimension in Acts 13:39 ('everyone') (compare Acts 10:43). The speech ends in Acts 13:40-41 with a prophetic warning about the danger of unbelief, backed up by a quotation from Hab 1:5 which speaks of the consequences of failing to recognise what God is doing in one's midst. In the original context of Habakkuk the failure in question was the failure to recognise the Chaldean invasion as a punishment of God.

The initial response to Paul's preaching was very favourable (Acts 13:42-43). The crowd wanted to hear more and Paul and Barnabas are invited back to speak again on the following Sabbath. It seems that some already believe or at least are open to the 'grace of God' being offered through the missionaries (Acts 13:43). The role of divine grace in the process of conversion and justification is an important emphasis in the Pauline letters. But, as in the case of Jesus' initial proclamation in the synagogue of Nazareth (Lk 4:22), the mood changes and on the following Sabbath we have people divided in their response to the missionary preaching. The division in response to the Good News is a Lukan theme (see the programmatic statement in Lk 2:34).

On the one hand, the Jews, out of jealousy (see Acts 5:17; 7:9; 17:5), contradict the missionaries and revile them. The context suggests that the positive response of the Gentiles to

Paul's message is a stumbling block to the Jews in Antioch of Pisidia. The response of Paul and Barnabas to this is to speak boldly about a turning to the Gentiles (Acts 13:46-47). According to the divine plan and order, the Good News must first be proclaimed to the Jews (Acts 13:46; see Rm 1:16; 2:9-10). Since the Jews are disqualifying themselves from eternal life by their lack of openness to the Good News, however, the missionaries now feel free to turn to the Gentiles in Antioch and concentrate on them. This step is not motivated solely by the Jewish rejection, as the Gentile mission was envisaged from the beginning (see Lk 2:30-32; Acts 1:8). The claim that in God's plan the Good News is also meant for the Gentiles is backed up by a quotation from Is 49:6 (LXX) (Acts 13:47). This is taken from the second Servant Song in which the Servant is told that, along with restoring the tribes of Jacob and preaching to the scattered ones of Israel, he is to be a 'light for the Gentiles'.

Paul especially is now the Servant, that 'light to the Gentiles' through whom the universal mission is being realised. To put it in another way, in and through Paul, Jesus the Servant becomes the light of the Gentiles. This is the first of three solemn turnings from Jews to Gentiles; the second happens in Corinth (Acts 18:6) and the third in Rome (Acts 28:28). As mentioned already, none of these turnings should be taken as a definitive closing of the door to Jews in the mission of the Church. Envy, contradiction and revilement lead to persecution and expulsion from the region (Acts 13:50). Paul is reliving the experience of Jesus who was driven out of Nazareth (Lk 4:29) and of the apostles who faced murderous rage (Acts 5:33). The Jews who opposed the missionaries were able to get influential men and women on their side. The shaking of dust off the feet of the two missionaries (Acts 13:51) is an act of disassociation (see Lk 9:5; 10:11) and a sign that the unbelieving Jews are like pagan Gentiles who are not part of the restored Israel.

On the other hand, Luke highlights the Gentiles' response of joy and praise to the word of God's salvation (Acts 13:48).

By becoming believers the Gentiles show that they are destined in God's plan for eternal life. Acts 13:49 is a typical Lukan summary statement about the success of the mission (see Acts 2:41, 47; 6:7; 9:31; 11:24; 12:24). The mission in Antioch of Pisidia ends on a high note despite rejection and persecution. The disciples (probably the new converts) were filled with joy and the Holy Spirit (Acts 13:52).

Mission in Iconium, Lystra and Derbe (Acts 14:1-20)

Luke does not go into much detail about the mission in *Iconium* (145 kilometres east of Antioch), but simply says, 'the same thing occurred in Iconium' (Acts 14:1). Again we have the experiences of success and rejection after the missionaries had preached in a Jewish synagogue. Both Jews and Greeks (Gentiles) believed. But unbelieving Jews stir up opposition to the missionaries (Acts 14:2). Paul and Barnabas continue to speak boldly about the free gift ('grace') of God's salvation through Jesus who confirmed their mission by working 'signs and wonders' through them (Acts 14:3; compare Acts 4:29-30 where disciples pray for boldness in preaching and ask that God perform signs and wonders in the name of Jesus). In Acts 14:4 we have reference again to the division which is the result of preaching the Good News. Some Jews and Gentiles sided with the Jews who were stirring up trouble, while others sided with the apostles.[17] Division again leads to persecution from Jews and Gentiles (the Jewish rulers get special mention!) with an attempt to stone the missionaries who are forced farther afield to Lystra (28 kilometres from Iconium) and Derbe (88 kilometres from Lystra), cities of Lycaonia (Acts 14:5-6). They continued proclaiming the Good News (Acts 14:7). A recurring pattern in Acts is that persecution does but hinder mission but is the occasion for the expansion of evangelisation.

The mission in *Lystra* tells of the first encounter of the Good News with an entirely Gentile environment. Luke wants to impress on us that the impact of the Gospel message on Gentile religion and culture was quite remarkable. The passage opens with a miracle story (Acts 14:8-10), which parallels Peter's cure of the cripple in Acts 3:1-10 (which in turn has similarities with Jesus' cure of the paralytic in Lk 5:17-26). Common features include: one who was crippled from birth (Acts 3:2; 14:8); the intent gaze of the healer (Acts 3:4; 14:9); the one who was healed jumping up and walking (Acts 3:8; 14:10). Both healings took place in the vicinity of a temple (Acts 3:2; 14:13) and lead to speeches which begin by correcting a misunderstanding about the source of the healing power (Acts 3:12; 14:15). One could also add that Paul's command to the cripple to get up is similar to what Peter said to the bedridden Aeneas (Acts 9:34) and the deceased Tabitha (Acts 9:40). Luke is once again emphasising his 'continuity in mission' theme. The faith of the one healed is highlighted (Acts 13:9); faith and salvation/healing go together (see Lk 7:50; 8:12, 48, 50; 17:19; 18:42; Acts 3:16).

The reaction to the miracle greatly exceeds what we expect and amounts to a spontaneous outpouring of Hellenistic religiosity. The crowds declare that Paul and Barnabas are gods in human form and the priest at the local temple wants to offer sacrifice to them (Acts 14:11-13).[18] As the people are speaking in their local language, Paul and Barnabas seemingly are a little slow to realise what is happening. Every cross-cultural missionary knows how language differences can lead to confusion! The mistake the people of Lystra made was to regard Paul and Barnabas as gods, rather than messengers of the true God, and the missionaries set about putting things right. They tear their clothes as an expression of emotional shock (see Gn 37:34; 2 Sm 13:31; Mk 14:63; Mt 26:65) and, like Peter before them (Acts 3:12; 10:26), they deflect from themselves honour which is due to God alone (Acts 14:14-15).

The short speech in Acts 14:15-17 has a number of themes which will be orchestrated at much greater length in Paul's later discourse in Athens (Acts 17:22-31): the appeal to turn from 'worthless things' (idolatry) to the worship of the 'living God'; God as the creator of all things; God's past tolerance of the mistaken ways of the Gentiles; God's revelation of himself in the things he has made. This approach to Gentile religion is similar to Jewish apologetics with its appeal for conversion from foolishness to the living God (see Jer 2:5; Wis 13:1; Rm 1:20; 1 Th 1:9-10). The missionaries just about succeed in preventing the people from offering sacrifice to them (Acts 14:18).

But how the fortunes of the missionaries change within a few verses! Having just been treated as a god, Paul is now stoned and left for dead outside the city walls (Acts 14:19-20). In 2 Cor 11:25 Paul recalls that he was stoned once. Jews from Antioch and Iconium arrive and stir up trouble for Paul and Barnabas. As the Jews aggressively watched and stalked Jesus, so now they are hunting his missionaries. The opposition to the missionaries is escalating just as it did during the earlier mission in Jerusalem. In Antioch of Pisidia Paul and Barnabas are cast out, in Iconium there is an attempt to stone them, and in Lystra Paul is actually stoned. The disciples gathered around Paul who was left for dead (Acts 14:20). Are we to imagine Paul jumping up miraculously and striding back into the city, thus illustrating once again the fact that nothing can stop the spread of the Good News? The next day Paul and Barnabas are on the road again to *Derbe*. We are told nothing about the mission in Derbe beyond that it was successful (Acts 14:21).

Return to Antioch in Syria (Acts 14:21-28)
On their homeward journey to Antioch in Syria, Paul and Barnabas retraced their steps through the very places where they had been violently expelled, which was a remarkable display of courage. Luke highlights two activities of the missionaries on the return trip, which show their care for the churches they founded. Firstly, they encourage the new communities under pressure 'to continue in the faith', reminding them that we must enter the kingdom of God through many tribulations (Acts 14:22). Note the Lukan

'must' (*dei*) in Acts 14:22, an indication that sufferings are taken up into the working out of the salvific plan of God. The Lord told Ananias that he will show Paul 'how much he must (*dei*) suffer for the sake of my name' (Acts 9:16). All of this is to be seen in the context of what is said in Luke's Gospel about the necessity of Jesus' sufferings (Lk 9:22; 17:25; 24:7, 26). Secondly, Paul and Barnabas appointed elders (*presbyteroi*) in each local church and entrusted them to the Lord with prayer and fasting (Acts 14:23), as they themselves had been commended to the grace of God in an atmosphere of prayer and fasting (Acts 13:1-3). Luke may be using later terminology for these early Church leaders. *Presbyteroi* do not appear in the undisputed Pauline letters nor the Deutero-Pauline letters, but they are mentioned in the Pastoral letters (see Ti 1:5; 1 Tm 5:17, 19).

Paul and Barnabas pass through Pisidia and Pamphylia and we are told they preached the word in Perga (Acts 14:24). Having completed their 'work' (see Acts 13:2), the missionaries set sail for Antioch in Syria and report back to the church which had sent them out in the first place. In their report they don't concentrate on the many sufferings they endured. What they want to share is the marvellous news about 'all that *God* had done with them, and how he had opened a door of faith for the Gentiles' (Acts 14:27). Note once again that God was seen as the main actor throughout the missionary journey; he was 'with them', working through their words and deeds (see Acts 10:38 where Peter tells Cornelius that God was with Jesus as he went about doing good).

What the missionaries want to highlight especially is the fact that believing Gentiles are coming into the Church in large numbers. A door being opened for the one on mission is a Pauline concept (see 1 Cor 16:9; 2 Cor 2:12; Col 4:3). The reference to faith picks up one of the important themes of the missionary journey just completed (Acts 13:8, 12, 39, 41, 48; 14:1, 9, 22, 23 – many of these texts refer to the faith of Gentiles and not just Jews). It also prepares for the emphasis

Peter will put on faith as a means of cleansing for Gentiles and the way to salvation for both Gentiles and Jews (Acts 15:9, 11). The sojourn of the missionaries in Antioch reinforces their link with that church and creates a pause in the narrative before the discernment in Acts 15 about the Gentile mission.

The Council of Jerusalem (Acts 15:1-35)

There can be no doubt that Acts 15:1-35 is one of the key passages in the Acts of the Apostles. The fact that the author has brought together all his main characters in this story should alert us to its importance. What happens in Acts 15:1-35 is the culmination of many events in Luke's story to date: the call of Saul to be the great missionary to the Gentiles (Acts 9:1-19); the Cornelius episode in which Peter, in response to God's initiative, takes the first vital step in the outreach to the Gentiles (Acts 10:1-11:18); the missionary activity of the Antioch community through their representatives, Paul and Barnabas (Acts 13:1–14:28). Gentiles are now being accepted into the Church in large numbers without any obligation to live according to the Law of Moses. That is giving rise to issues and questions which must now be faced and resolved definitively, for example, 'Is circumcision one of the necessary requirements for salvation in Jesus Christ? How can Jewish Christians freely associate with Gentile Christians whom they regard as ritually unclean?' It seems questions like these remained live issues long after the Cornelius episode.

Historical Note on Acts 15:1-35

Scholars encounter difficulties in trying to reconstruct the historical situation underlying the Council of Jerusalem, taking into account what we read in Acts and the Pauline letters. Firstly, at the beginning of the meeting in Acts (15:1, 5), the issue is circumcision for the Gentiles. Yet, the decree from the meeting (Acts 15:23-29) makes no explicit mention of circumcision! Secondly, Paul never mentions this Jerusalem decree in his letters, which we would expect in Rm 14 and 1 Cor 8-10, at least, where he deals with tensions over dietary regulations and the question of food offered to idols. Thirdly, it is quite impossible to harmonise Acts 9:26–15:29 and Gal 1–2 with regard to Paul's visits to Jerusalem. Fourthly, it is difficult to harmonise Gal 2:1-14 and Acts 15:1-35 with regard to the meetings and debates concerning the Gentile mission. Luke speaks of one major meeting in Jerusalem which resolved all the issues and which took place after a dispute in Antioch about circumcision for Gentiles. Paul speaks of two different occasions – his earlier meeting with the leaders in Jerusalem about the circumcision question (Gal 2:1-10) and his later dispute with Peter and Barnabas in Antioch about table fellowship between Jewish and Gentile Christians (Gal 2:11-14). If Paul knew of the Jerusalem decree (reported in Acts 15) when he wrote Galatians in AD 54, it is surprising he did not refer to it in connection with the issue of table fellowship between Jews and Gentiles in the Antioch community.

Many think that in Acts 15:1-35 Luke has fused two separate meetings in Jerusalem about the Gentile mission which were historically distinct in topic and time. *Meeting 1* took place between Paul and Barnabas and the Jerusalem leaders at which it was agreed that circumcision should not be imposed on Gentile converts. That meeting (circa AD 49) is the background for Acts 15:6-12 and Gal 2:1-10. *Meeting 2* took place also in Jerusalem sometime after the clash between Paul and Peter in Antioch which is reported in Gal 2:11-14. This meeting discussed the issue of table fellowship in mixed communities of Jews and Gentiles, and a letter embodying its decree was sent from Jerusalem to Antioch and the churches in Syria and Cilicia. That meeting is the background for Acts 15:13-29. Paul and Barnabas were not present at that meeting, though Luke thought they were. Paul had probably departed on mission to the Aegean region when news of this meeting's decree reached Antioch. So, Paul was not aware of the decree till much later, which would account for the fact that he does not mention it in dealing with dietary regulations and the question of food offered to idols in Rm 14 and 1 Cor 8-10. Some say he heard about the decree for the first time as late as AD 58 when he went to Jerusalem after all his missionary work (see Acts 21:25).

It seems, then, that Luke gives us a rather simplified and idealised picture of developments concerning complicated issues which were potentially very divisive, but which challenged the Church to clarify basic questions about its identity and mission. We are primarily interested in the meaning Luke sees in these developments and their significance for Christian mission, rather than in questions of purely historical interest.[19]

Luke's Message in Acts 15:1-35

Prelude to the Meeting (Acts 15:1-5): These verses set the scene for the Jerusalem meeting and clarify the basic issue to be discussed. The problem arises with the arrival of individuals from Judea in Antioch, a church engaged in the Gentile mission (Acts 15:1). These visitors say that Gentile males in becoming Christian must be circumcised or else they can't be saved. This demand is repeated a short time later in Jerusalem by members of the Pharisee party within the Christian community (probably Pharisees who were converted to Christianity) (Acts 15:5). The fact that there were Pharisees among converts to Christianity is another indication of the success of Christian mission. We have the Lukan 'must' (*dei*) which is a signal that God's plan is in view. The objectors are claiming that in God's plan people had to become Jews first if they wanted to be Christians and thus experience salvation.

The issue gave rise to quite a bit of 'dissension' and 'debate' in Antioch and Paul and Barnabas, the champions of the Gentile mission, were in the thick of it. They find themselves in a delegation appointed to go to Jerusalem to discuss the matter with 'the apostles and elders' there (Acts 15:2). Luke has the delegation pass through Phoenicia and

Samaria, the outward path of the original evangelisation. They report the success of the Gentile mission to Christian communities on the way. We will see that narration of experience is a very important element in shaping the decision in Acts 15:1-35. The believers' joyous response (Acts 15:3) is a signal of God's saving presence. This widespread support has the effect of creating the impression that those demanding circumcision for the Gentiles are a fringe group. The same effect is created by telling us about the warm welcome of the delegation by 'the church and the apostles and the elders' (Acts 15:4). Again we have the narration of 'all that God had done with them'. The focus is on what God is doing and what God wants, and that will receive increasing emphasis during the meeting.

Sharing Experiences (Acts 15:6-12): It's not entirely clear from the Lukan account who attended this meeting. Acts 15:6 suggests that only the leaders met together, but Acts 15:12, 22 lead us to believe that a much wider group was present. It seems the meeting started in the same atmosphere of debate and argumentation (Acts 15:7a) which characterised the discussion in Antioch (Acts 15:2). Things start to change when Peter (who makes a sudden reappearance in Luke's story) stands up to speak (Acts 15:7b-11). It is important for Luke that Peter, the hero of the first part of Acts and the leader of the apostles, is at hand to confirm the Gentile mission. Basically, Peter shares his experience in the Cornelius episode and highlights that God was acting in that event. God is the subject of the action in Acts 15:7b-9. The opening words of Peter's speech in Acts 15:7b could be translated as follows: 'You know that from early days among you God chose the Gentiles to hear the message of the Good News through my mouth and to believe.' This translation puts the emphasis on God's choice of the Gentiles, rather than on God's choice of Peter to initiate the Gentile mission. The experience of God's election, which is at the heart of Israel's self-understanding (see Num 16:5; Deut 4:37; 7:7;

21:3; Jos 24:15), is now extended to Gentiles through Jesus Christ. Acts 15:8-9 echo the ideas and language of the Cornelius episode (Acts 10:1–11:18): the impartiality of God who can see into the heart and consequently is not swayed by externals (Acts 10:34-35); God who cleanses (Acts 10:15); no distinction between Jews and Gentiles (Acts 10:14-15, 20; 11:12); God giving the Spirit to Gentiles, just as he gave to Jewish Christians (Acts 10:44, 47; 11:15, 17); openness in faith to what God is doing (Acts 10:33).

Peter's point is that the Gentiles have been cleansed inwardly by the gift of the Spirit and faith. They are not to be regarded as people who are somehow unclean and who can defile Jews who come in contact with them. Peter ends his speech with a direct challenge to those who insist that circumcision is essential for salvation (Acts 15:10-11). They are putting God to the test – the verb 'to put to the test' is used in the Old Testament with the meaning of challenging or resisting the manifest will of God (cf. Ex 17:2; Deut 6;16; Ps 95:9). 'Yoke' was used in Judaism as a symbol of the Law placed on Israel (see Mt 11:29-30), and Peter points out that the people of Israel were unable to keep the Law. He goes on to say in Acts 15:11 that the source of salvation for everyone (Jew and Gentile) is not the Law, or any particular practice like circumcision, but 'the grace of the Lord Jesus' (probably to be translated 'the grace which is the Lord Jesus'). Acts 15:10-11 has been called a 'snapshot' of Paul's teaching in Galatians and Romans about justification through the free gift of God in Jesus Christ and not by works of the Law (see also Acts 13:38-39).

What Peter has done in his speech is to share his discerned experience, emphasising the initiative of God in the Gentile mission and the basic equality between Jew and Gentile when it comes to the way of salvation. *God* is the one who has decided. That will becomes the basis of the meeting's decision; they can do nothing else but confirm what God has already decided (see Acts 15:28). Acts 15:12 links Peter's speech and the speech of James (Acts 15:13-21). It also notes the changing mood of the meeting. Those who had been debating and arguing now begin to listen in silence. The assembly is coming to realise that their task is to listen to the voice of the Lord and get a sense of his guidance. They listen as Barnabas and Paul relate their experience in the Gentile mission, how God in 'signs and wonders' had been working through them (see Acts 14:27; 15:4).

Speech of James (Acts 15:13-21): James responds to the experiences of mission 'on the ground' which have been shared. He plays a leadership role and his view certainly carries a lot of weight in the meeting. What he says here may represent a change of mind on his part. Gal 2:12 suggests that he had some connection or sympathy with those who emphasised the observance of Jewish practices for Gentiles. What he does in his speech is to agree with Peter, relate the experiences which have been shared to God's will as revealed in the Scriptures, and then indicate the way the issue is to be resolved. He begins by encouraging the listening atmosphere (Acts 15:13). Acts 15:14 repeats in different words what Peter said about the election of the Gentiles (Acts 15:7). God, taking the initiative, 'visited' (*epeskepsato*) the Gentiles – this verb in Luke's Gospel is shorthand for God's intervention in history (see Lk 1:68, 78; 7:16; 19:44). God visited for a purpose, that is, to take from among the Gentiles 'a people (*laos*) for his name'.

In Luke's writings *laos* has been used almost exclusively for Israel as the 'people of God' (see Lk 1:17, 68, 77; 2:32; 7:16, 29; 20:1; 22:66; 24:19; Acts 2:47; 3:23; 4:10; 5:12; 7:17, 34; 13:17). By using that term now in referring the Gentiles, Luke is extending its meaning and even redefining it, because now membership in God's people does not depend on race or ritual practice, but on faith. 'For his name' virtually means 'for himself'. It implies God's ownership of his chosen people (see, for instance, Deut 28:9-14: Jer 14:9). In Acts 15:15-18 James goes on to refer to Amos 9:11-12 (editing the text slightly with phrases from Jer 12:15 and Is

45:21). The Amos quotation is from the Greek text of the Old Testament (a prophecy of restoration of the house of David so that 'all other peoples may seek the Lord' and join the people of God), which is quite different from the Hebrew text of this passage (a promise of Israel's return from exile and the subjugation and possession of the nations in a restored kingdom). In effect, Amos 9:11-12 (LXX) speaks of the Gentiles becoming part of a reconstituted people of God. God's name has been called over all the Gentiles (Acts 15:17; note the link with Acts 15:14). The Amos prophecy is fulfilled because Jesus, the Davidic heir, has been raised up and installed at God's right hand. What James is saying is that 'the words of the prophets' agree with and confirm what has been learnt in the experience of mission about God's intention and initiative.[20]

In Acts 15:19-21 James goes on to speak about practical steps to be taken. Are we to understand that James makes an authoritative decision and settles the matter on his own? The verb *krinō* in Acts 15:19 can have a number of meanings: to decide, decree (with authority), assess, estimate, judge or discern. Perhaps 'I discern' best suits the context as in Acts 15:22 we see that the apostles, elders and the whole Church had a part in decisions taken at the meeting. Ultimately the decision belongs to the Spirit and the role of all at the meeting is to discern what the Spirit has decided (see Acts 15:28).

James says that the Gentiles turning to the Lord are not to be harassed (Acts 15:19). There is no explicit mention of the circumcision issue. Rather in Acts 15:20 the focus goes on measures to make possible common life (*koinōnia*) between Jewish Christians and Gentile Christians. The requirements for table fellowship are reduced to four: abstention from *things polluted by idols* (that is, abstention from eating meat that had been offered at the shrine of idols before being sold in the market – see 1 Cor 8-10); abstention from *fornication* (*porneia* can mean sexual immorality in general; in this case it probably means marriage within close degrees of kinship which is prohibited by Jewish law, or possibly mixed marriages with unbelievers – see 2 Cor 6:14); abstention from *what is strangled* (that is, meat of animals not slaughtered in the prescribed way; the animal must have been butchered in such a way that all the blood was drained from it – see Lev 17:14); abstention from *blood* (that is, food made from the blood of animals; Jews did not eat blood products because blood was considered the 'seat of life' which belonged to God). These four prescriptions of the Law were also binding on aliens residing among Jews (see Lev 17:8–18:18). Later rabbis believed they were enjoined on Noah's sons, the ancestors of the entire human race. The point of Acts 15:21 seems to be that Gentile converts, who had some connection with the synagogue, will know what the Jewish law required of aliens wanting to mix with Jews. The measures in Acts 15:19-21 do not mean that Gentile Christians are bound by some precepts of Jewish law. The argument is rather an appeal to Gentile Christians for a sympathetic understanding of Jewish Christian sensitivities, so that common life is possible in mixed communities. The Council of Jerusalem recognises the freedom of Gentiles from Jewish law but also protects the religious culture of the Jews. The apostolic decree is also found in Acts 15:29 and 21:25 with some changes in wording and order.

Letter to Gentile Christians (Acts 15:22-35): The resolution of the meeting is enshrined in a letter to Gentile Christians in Antioch, Syria and Cilicia. Acts 15:22-23a is Luke's introduction to the letter, which paraphrases part of the letter. Judas Barsabbas (otherwise unknown) and Silas (probably to be identified with Silvanus, the future missionary companion of Paul – see Acts 15:40; 1 Th 1:1; 2 Cor 1:19), who were leaders in the Jerusalem church, are sent with Paul and Barnabas as delegates to Antioch. The team itself reflects the unity between the two local churches. For Luke, Silas in particular will be one more reminder of the link between Paul's mission and the Jerusalem church. In the text of the letter (Acts 15:23b-29) the Jerusalem church disassociates itself from the demands of those who have unsettled the minds of the Gentiles (Acts 15:24). There is a unanimous decision to send delegates who will deliver the letter and explain its contents and the delegates are introduced (Acts 15:25-27). Note the respect for the beloved Barnabas and Paul, who engaged in the Gentile mission and risked their lives for the sake of the Lord. The measures proposed to make community life possible are repeated in Acts 15:29. While Acts 15:19-20 could be taken to mean that James was the one who made the key decision, Acts 15:28 indicates that the outcome of the meeting was a joint decision of the Holy Spirit and the community. Once again it is a matter of the community catching up with what the Spirit is doing in the Gentile mission.

In Acts 15:30-35 we are back in Antioch where the issue first arose. When the letter is delivered and read in the community, the reaction is joy (Acts 15:30-31), always a sign of God's presence in Luke's writings. The letter is received as an 'exhortation' (*paraklēsis*), rather than a burden or imposition. Judas and Silas are more than postmen; they exercise a ministry of encouragement in the Antioch community (Acts 15:32). After some time they are seen off in an atmosphere of peace as they return to Jerusalem. 'Peace' in this case is not only a farewell greeting, but the effect of the resolution of an issue which had caused much dissension in Antioch (Acts 15:2). In Acts 15:35 we see Paul and Barnabas once more rooted in the life of the Antioch community (see Acts 11:26; 13:1; 14:26-28). However, it will not be long before the Spirit of mission leads them once more out of that community.

Reflection on Acts 11:19–15:35

For quite some time, missionary congregations have experienced a sharp drop in the number of members from countries of western culture, their traditional home bases. Practically no new candidates from these countries are coming forward and the number of active members who originate from these places is decreasing significantly through retirement and death. On the other hand, we are seeing an increasing number of members and candidates from the local churches where these congregations have been on mission for many years. Of the world's 1.1 billion Catholics today, more than two thirds now live in the Global South. Some would say that the centres of Christian missionary outreach are now to be found in Asia, Africa, South America and Oceania, and missionaries from these places are needed to re-evangelise the traditional Christian countries.

I recall all of this as I read how the new church in Antioch, which was evangelised and established by Hellenist Christians from Jerusalem (Acts 11:19-30), quickly became a great centre of missionary outreach, sending out its representatives to proclaim the Good News in many places (Acts 13:1–14:28). We saw how Luke is careful to forge strong links between the 'mother church' in Jerusalem and the 'daughter church' in Antioch through the exchange of personnel and resources between the two communities. The picture emerges of an exchange between 'sister churches' giving and receiving in the missionary enterprise. This is perhaps a better model for mission today, rather than seeing a shift in missionary centres or a reversal of roles between 'mother churches' and 'daughter churches'.

Every local church is and remains a missionary centre, no matter how its circumstances have changed. Every continent and country is a place of mission where the Good News needs to be proclaimed in a broken world often driven by values contrary to those of Jesus Christ. No local church is self-sufficient, having within itself the means and experience to fulfil its mission in a world where local missionary challenges more often than not have global dimensions. No local church can regard help from other local churches as a temporary arrangement till it gets its own house in order. There is need for ongoing, mutually enriching exchange between local churches in the cause of mission. The missionary Church is a communion of local churches on mission together.

Since the Second Vatican Council (1962-65), the Church is facing the challenge of becoming a truly World Church, open to embrace peoples of all cultures and express Christian faith and practice in the categories of all cultures and not just one culture.[21] The Jewish Christian church was faced with the challenge of accepting and integrating the expression of the Gospel in the way of life of one other culture (Greco-Roman culture); the Church today is called to promote the inculturation of the Gospel in all cultures.

Too often in the past, a western cultural expression of Christian faith and practice was imposed on all local churches. The newer model of mission stresses the need for each local church to explore how Christian faith and practice can be expressed in a way that resonates with the authentic values and aspirations of their culture. In encountering every culture, including western culture, the Gospel both affirms the authentic values of the culture and challenges cultural values which are opposed to the values of the kingdom of God. Every cultural expression of the Gospel has its strengths and weaknesses. One cannot make one's own culture the norm of Christian faith and practice, and impose it on others. Different cultures can express different aspects of the Christian message and way of life, all contributing to the richness of our Christian tradition.

The exchange between local churches today takes place in the context of the great movement of peoples due to the ease of international travel, global commerce and mass migration, often arising from the pressures of economic necessity, the experience of discrimination or persecution, and violent conflict in their homelands. Many local churches today are no longer mono-cultural. While visiting urban parishes in Britain to promote mission, I was often surprised to find a wide variety of cultures in the weekend congregations. In such situations the challenge is to build truly multicultural communities which bear witness to the Gospel in multicultural settings. A multicultural Christian community where all feel at home and where people of different cultures relate in a mutually enriching way can be a powerful sign of the Christian message in a world often torn apart on the basis of race and culture.

Acts 15 has much to teach us about what is involved in Christian inter-cultural living. The Jewish Christians were told not to impose their own cultural practices (for example, circumcision) on Gentiles who wanted to join the Christian community. On the other hand, these Gentiles are told to respect Jewish Christian sensitivities. If common life in mixed communities is to be possible, there has to be tolerance and respect for each other's cultural practices. There has to be 'give and take' and compromise in matters which are not of the essence of Christian faith. In our multicultural communities today we have to approach those of other cultures as people from whom we can learn a lot, rather than people we have to 'educate' to be like ourselves.[22]

Reading Acts 15:1-35 also leads us to reflect again on the process of making decisions in mission. Many of these decisions are far-reaching and are invested with a lot of emotion. In some situations they may involve letting go of cherished ministries in order to focus on a more limited set of mission priorities with the resources available to us. They may mean departure from areas where our group has been on mission for very many years, or the clustering and even closure of parishes. In making decisions like these, more often than not, we analyse the situation carefully, debate the reasons for and against, and consult the experts. Then, having made our decision, we pray that God will bless the decision *we* have made and help us carry it out. But, if we believe the Spirit is guiding us in all situations, should we not first prayerfully discern where the Spirit is leading us in the decision we face? Having made a major decision, how often can we say, 'it has seemed good to the Spirit and to us' (Acts 15:28)? We need to develop a discerning approach in mission. Pope Francis constantly encourages the practice of prayerful discernment and adopts a discerning approach in the many difficult decisions he faces.[23]

Acts 15:1-35 gives us the components of the process of discernment. Firstly, the 'whole Church' (Acts 15:22) is involved in the decision-making process. In discernment the maximum participation of all concerned is to be encouraged. Secondly, the focus must remain on what God is doing and what God wants, rather on what we would like. The Pharisee party had the focus on themselves and their own traditional practices which meant they were not free and open to seeing things differently. In discernment we need God to show us our 'un-freedoms' which block us from following the lead of the Spirit. Thirdly, the mood in the meeting changed from one of debate and argumentation to respectful listening. In debating, we are focused on what we want to say; in listening we are more attuned to what God might be saying.[24] Fourthly, during the meeting a lot of attention was given to the sharing of experiences. In listening to the story of others and telling our own story in a context of faith, we build up the sense of a common story in which God is present. Fifthly, James relates the experience shared by Peter to the word of God in the Scriptures. In the discernment process there is dialogue between experience and the revealed word of God. One throws light on the other. Finally, in discernment people should be on the lookout for confirmatory signs that the decision taken is in accordance with God's designs. The decision of the Jerusalem Council gave rise to joy and peace. Among other signs are renewed heart, stronger sense of purpose and enthusiasm, greater unity, and confirmation by legitimate authority rightly exercised.

The processes of inculturation, inter-cultural living and prayerful discernment are not easy. They often challenge us to move out of our comfort zones, let go of self-interests, and journey in faith without knowing for sure how things will turn out. They are part of the paschal experience which is at the heart of Christian life and mission, the call to identify with Christ in dying to self in order to experience new life. In Acts 13-14 Luke makes that point mainly through the sustained parallelism between the mission of Jesus and the mission of Paul and Barnabas. The image of the half-dead Paul rising up to continue on mission (Acts 14:20) forcefully illustrates the paschal dimension of mission. Paul and Barnabas, like Peter and the apostles before them, discovered that mission is a paschal experience and they shared that insight with those they had evangelised: 'It is through many persecutions (tribulations) that we must enter the kingdom of God' (Acts 14:22). But they also knew that they were not alone on their missionary journey. Their commissioning in Acts 13:1-3 would have reminded them that they had the support of the Spirit and the community which sent them out on mission. In our mission today we too need to draw on that same support.

NOTES

1   Johnson, *The Acts of the Apostles*, 203.
2   The manuscript evidence is divided on whether 'Hellenists' (*Hellenistas*) or 'Greeks' (*Hellenas*) should be read in Acts 11:20. The context favours the latter reading – 'Greeks' presents a better contrast to 'except Jews' (Acts 11:19).
3   'Up to this point in Acts followers in Christ have been called believers, disciples, brothers and saints. They are members of the *koinonia*, followers of "the Way". None of these titles really suggested any difference from Jews. Now that the word has spread beyond Judea (in the broad sense) we are not surprised to learn that a distinctive name for them comes into play: followers of Jesus Christ are called "Christians".' (Fitzmyer, *The Acts of the Apostles*, 474).
4   'Luke gives no indication of how these officials originated in the Christian community or how they might be related to either the apostles or the Seven of 6:3' (Fitzmyer, *ibid.*, 483).
5   There is also the difficulty of reconciling what Paul himself says about only *two* visits to Jerusalem (Gal 1:18 and Gal 2:1-10) with what Luke says about *three* visits to Jerusalem (Acts 9:26-29; Acts 11:29-30; 12:25; Acts 15:1-29) over the same time span. Many would regard the visit in Acts 11:29-30 and 12:25 and that in Acts

15:1-29 as one and the same visit, which Luke has made into two visits for his own purposes. It seems Luke did not have exact information about Paul's visits to Jerusalem. We will return to the matter of these visits in dealing with Acts 15. On the visits of Paul to Jerusalem see Fitzmyer, 'Paul' in *The New Jerome Biblical Commentary*, 1334; Dillon, 'Acts of the Apostles' in *The New Jerome Biblical Commentary*, 747.

[6] The translation of Acts 12:25 in the NRSV is problematic as it speaks of a return *to* Jerusalem (*eis Ierousalēm*), where they are already located! It is better to translate it as follows: 'Having completed their service *at* (or *in*) Jerusalem, Barnabas and Saul returned and brought with them John, whose other name was Mark.'

[7] 'For Luke the episode is important, not only because it reveals the power of Christian faith and prayer, but also the fidelity of God who stands by his chosen agents' (Fitzmyer, *The Acts of the Apostles*, 486). Mullins (*The Acts of the Apostles*, 131) sees Peter's escape and Herod's death as an illustration of the words in Mary's Magnificat: 'He has put down the mighty from their thrones and exalted the lowly' (Lk 1:52).

[8] Dillon ('Acts of the Apostles' in *The New Jerome Biblical Commentary*, 747-748) sees symbolic overtones of Christianity's release from confinement within Judaism in the story of Peter's release from prison.

[9] Johnson, *The Acts of the Apostles*, 218.

[10] Are we to understand Peter's departure and James appearance at this stage in the story in terms of the emergence of new leadership in the Jerusalem church? Fitzmyer (*The Acts of the Apostles*, 485) sees this episode as marking the transition from Peter's importance in the Jerusalem community to that of James, 'who eventually takes over from him as the chief authority in that community'. However we understand it, we should not put the leadership functions of Peter and James on the same level. Kilgallen (*A Brief Commentary on the Acts of the Apostles*, 96-97) says that 'to be one of the Twelve meant to be one of the foundation stones of Jesus' community; it does not seem to have implied that all Twelve are the actual day-to-day leaders of the community. To the Twelve belongs the pre-eminent role of witness *par excellence* and foundation.' Brown (*An Introduction to the New Testament*, 302) says there is no evidence that Peter was ever the local administrator of the Jerusalem church, and thinks James, the brother of the Lord, may have exercised an administrative role for the Hebrew element in the community, as soon as that role was created.

11   For this parallelism see Johnson, *The Acts of the Apostles*, 218; Tannehill, *The Narrative Unity of Luke-Acts*, vol. 2, 152-153. Tannehill (*ibid.*, 153-155) also finds in Acts 12 a number of allusions to the story of the exodus in the Old Testament (Septuagint) and feels Luke is describing what happened to Peter as an exodus experience. Luke has already referred to what happened to Jesus in Jerusalem as his 'exodus' (see Lk 9:31). Kurz (*Acts of the Apostles*, 195) also draws attention to the exodus parallelism.

12   I. Howard Marshall, (*Acts*, Tyndale NT Commentaries [Grand Rapids: Eerdmans 1980], 211-212) summarises Josephus' account: 'Herod celebrated games in Caesarea in honour of the Emperor, which were attended by the leading men of the kingdom. When Herod entered the theatre, clad in a glittering silver garment, his flatterers addressed him as a god: "May you be propitious to us, and if we have hitherto feared you as a man, yet henceforth we agree that you are more than mortal in your being." The king accepted their flattery. Then looking upward he saw an owl perched on a rope and took it as a symbol of ill fortune. At the same time he was seized by violent internal pains and was carried into his palace where he died after five days of illness.'

13   Acts 15:36–18:22 was often taken as the *second* missionary journey and Acts 18:23–21:16 as the *third* missionary journey of Paul. However, many scholars today are somewhat hesitant in dividing Paul's missionary activity into three distinct journeys. For instance, Fitzmyer (*The Acts of the Apostles*, 495) says this of the three missionary journeys: 'It is important to realise, however, that neither the apostle nor Luke has so numbered them. The numbering stems from modern commentators on Acts, who divide up the episodes into three blocks.' It is pointed out that Paul's visit to Jerusalem and Antioch in Acts 18:22-23 is better understood as a pause in the sustained missionary activity in the Aegean region, rather than the end of one missionary journey and the beginning of another. In his 'third missionary journey' in particular, Paul stays for quite some time in Ephesus and when he travels at the end of this period he is making farewell visits to places he had already evangelised, rather than breaking new missionary ground.

14   On the parallelism between Jesus and Paul in Acts 13-14 see Johnson, *The Acts of the Apostles*, 237; Tannehill, *The Narrative Unity of Luke-Acts*, vol. 2, 160-162; Kurz, *Acts of the Apostles*, 201-202.

15   Luke gives us three speeches of Paul during his ministry as a free man. In Acts 13:16-41 Paul speaks to Jews and God-fearers in the synagogue; in Acts 17:22-31 he speaks to cultured Greeks in Athens; in Acts 20:18-35 he delivers a farewell address to the

leaders of a Christian community. These three speeches have the character of model speeches in that they exemplify the different emphases in Paul's missionary preaching, depending on whether he is addressing Jews, Gentiles or Christians.

[16] The 450 years mentioned in Acts 13:20 probably refer to 400 years in Egypt (Gen 15:13) + 40 years in the desert (Num 14:33-34) + 10 years for the conquest of Canaan (Jos 14). Some, however, take it to refer to 450 years of the rule of the judges. On this point see Fitzmyer, *The Acts of the Apostles*, 511.

[17] Acts 4:4, 14 are the only places in the Lukan writings where anyone other than one of the Twelve is called an 'apostle'. 'The designation probably comes from the source he is using, in which the two were so named, and he has not bothered to make the source conform to his otherwise usual practice' (Fitzmyer, *ibid.*, 526).

[18] Many think Luke has embellished his account here with a well-known story about the visit of Zeus and Hermes in human form to an aged couple in the Phrygian hills, who offer the gods hospitality – see Johnson (*The Acts of the Apostles*, 248); Dillon ('Acts of the Apostles' in *The New Jerome Biblical Commentary*, 750); Crowe (*The Acts*, 108); Fitzmyer (*The Acts of the Apostles*, 531). Luke may well be using this story of a positive human response to a divine visitation to convey the remarkable impact the Good News had on these Gentile people.

[19] On the reconstruction of events behind Acts 15, see Fitzmyer, *ibid.*, 125, 544, 552-553, 562-563; Crowe, *The Acts*, 113; Marshall, *Acts*, 243-247; Johnson, *The Acts of the Apostles*, 269-270; Brown, *An Introduction to the New Testament*, 305-309. Johnson (*op. cit.*, 270) has this insightful comment: 'The historian must yield to the literary critic and the theologian, for the value of Luke's narrative is hardly limited to its historical accuracy... We know that, as at every other point in the story, our author is concerned less with "what happened" than with "what should have happened," is indeed constructing a narrative which (no less than the idyllic summaries of the early Church or the speeches of Peter and Paul) is meant to have a paradigmatic character for his readers. Recognising the fundamentally edifying quality of the story, therefore, we are able to engage the author's narrative perspective and thereby engage a quality of narrative "truth" which is not confined to referential accuracy.'

[20] 'He says that "the prophets agree with this" rather than that "this agrees with the prophets" (15:15). In other words, it is the experience of God revealed through narrative which is given priority in this hermeneutical process: the text of Scripture does

not dictate how God should act. Rather, God's action dictates how we should understand the text of Scripture' (Johnson, *ibid.*, 271).

[21] On this point, see Karl Rahner, 'Towards a Fundamental Theological Interpretation of Vatican II,' *Theological Studies* 40 (1979), 716-727; John Fuellenbach, *Church. Community for the Kingdom* (New York: Orbis Books, 2002), 93-107.

[22] 'Indeed, when we open our hearts to those who are different, this enables them, while continuing to be themselves, to develop in new ways. The different cultures that have flourished over the centuries need to be preserved, lest our world be impoverished... we need to communicate with each other, to discover the gifts of each person, to promote that which unites us, and to regard our differences as an opportunity to grow in mutual respect. Patience and trust are called for in such dialogue, permitting individuals, families and communities to hand on the values of their own culture and welcome the good that comes from others' experiences' (Pope Francis, *Fratelli Tutti*, no. 134).

[23] See especially, *Gaudete et Exsultate*, nos 166-175.

[24] 'Today's world is largely a deaf world... At times the frantic pace of the modern world prevents us from listening attentively to what another person is saying. Halfway through, we interrupt him and want to contradict what he has not even finished saying. We must not lose our ability to listen' (Pope Francis, *Fratelli Tutti*, no. 48).

CHAPTER 6

MAJOR MISSIONS
OF PAUL (1)
(ACTS 15:36−18:22)

In treating the mission of Paul and Barnabas above as representatives of the Church in Antioch in Syria (Acts 13-14), I mentioned that many commentators today prefer not to follow the traditional practice of dividing the missionary work of Paul into three distinct journeys (Acts 13:1–14:28; 15:36–18:22; 18:23–21:16).[1] While Acts 13:1–14:28 has a strong claim to be called a 'journey' with the missionaries constantly on the move, much of Paul's missionary activity in Acts 15:36–21:16 involves extended stays in the key cities of Corinth and Ephesus. The purpose of his journeying in Acts 20:1–21:16 is to say farewell to the communities he had evangelised in the Roman provinces of Macedonia, Achaia and Asia, rather than reaching out to new areas. And, as I said, Paul's visit to Jerusalem and Antioch in Acts 18:22-23 is really a break during one long missionary campaign in the Aegean region, rather than the end of one missionary journey and the beginning of another. There are a number of possibilities for sub-dividing Acts 15:36–21:16 in our reading of the story. With these observations just made, and keeping in mind the development of the narrative, I treat the major missions of Paul over the next two chapters, taking Acts 18:22-23 as a pause in one continuous missionary campaign. This present chapter deals mainly with Paul's missionary outreach in the Roman provinces of Macedonia and Achaia. The stand-out event in this part of Acts is surely Paul's mission in Athens (Acts 17:16-24) to which Luke gives particular attention and which is quite relevant today for the important dimension of mission as dialogue with peoples of other religious traditions.

Mission in Macedonia (Acts 15:36–17:15)
On the Way to Macedonia (Acts 15:36–16:10)

The main focus at this point is on mission in the Macedonian cities of Philippi, Thessalonica and Beroea. Acts 15:36–16:10 tells us why and how Paul and his companions got to Macedonia. The new missionary campaign began with Paul's proposal to Barnabas that they visit the places they had earlier evangelised together to see how the new converts were doing (Acts 15:36). However, a sharp quarrel broke out between Paul and Barnabas over the inclusion of John Mark in the missionary team (Acts 15:37-39). Paul did not think John Mark was up to the task as he had previously deserted the team in Pamphylia (Acts 13:13). Seemingly, Barnabas was more understanding of missionary failure, especially on the part of one who was his cousin (see Col 4:10).

Some think the quarrel was symptomatic of a deeper rift between Paul and Barnabas at this time arising from the argument between Peter and Paul in Antioch over the question of Jews and Gentiles sharing meals together in the Christian community (see Gal 2:11-13). Paul was not impressed that Barnabas had allowed himself to be 'led astray' by Peter in this matter. Whatever the real reason for the tension between Paul and Barnabas, it led to the parting of ways between two missionaries who had worked very closely together. Barnabas sails away with John Mark to Cyprus, his place of origin. Did Barnabas just want to distance himself from a situation of tension and seek peace in the friendlier atmosphere of his native land? Did he engage in mission in Cyprus along with John Mark? Luke does not tell us as he is focusing exclusively on the missionary outreach of Paul, who now chooses Silas as a replacement for Barnabas on the missionary team. Silas, the prophetic figure from the Jerusalem church (Acts 15:32), becomes the latest link between Paul and that church. As Paul sets out, the church in Antioch commends him to the grace of God (Acts 15:40), another reminder that Paul is not a maverick missionary but one who is commissioned by a community.

In Acts 15:41–16:10 we read how the journey, which began as a visitation of 'old haunts,' becomes a mission to Gentile Europe. Having strengthened the churches as he passed through Syria and Cilicia, Paul arrives in Lystra where he strengthened his missionary team by co-opting Timothy, a local disciple (Acts 16:1-3). For the remainder of Acts, Timothy becomes a close and trusted co-worker of Paul and that is confirmed by the Pauline letters. Surprise is often expressed that Paul had Timothy circumcised so soon after the Jerusalem Council decided that circumcision was not necessary for salvation. Though Timothy's father was a Greek, his mother was a devout Jew (see 2 Tm 1:5). The child of a Jewish mother was taken to be a Jew. Paul has no difficulty seeing circumcision as an expression of Jewish identity and ancestral commitment to God for *Jewish* Christians. In having Timothy circumcised, Paul is respecting Jewish Christian sensitivities, in line with the instructions of the Jerusalem Council, which Paul shares with the churches he is now visiting (Acts 16:4). But Paul remains adamant that circumcision should not be imposed on *Gentile* Christians as a rite necessary for salvation. Note how in Gal 2:5 Paul resisted pressure to have Titus, his Greek co-worker, circumcised. Acts 16:5 is another short summary to remind us of church growth.

The initiative of God and the direction of the Spirit, as distinct from human plans, are very much emphasised in Acts 16:6-10 as the missionaries begin to break new ground by passing through the Phrygian and (north) Galatian regions. The Holy Spirit steers them clear of the Roman provinces of Asia and Bithynia-Pontus and leads them through Mysia to Troas, a seaport on the Aegean Sea opposite Macedonia. Notice how the Spirit in Acts 16:7 is called the

'Spirit of Jesus,' a reminder to us that the Spirit is the means through which Jesus continues on mission in his disciples. The guidance of God is also highlighted through Paul's vision in Acts 16:9. This is the first of five visions for the Lukan Paul during his missionary career (see also Acts 18:9-10; 22:17-21; 23:11; 27:23-24), all of them to emphasise (usually at critical moments) that the Lord is with him and working in and through his mission. In his vision here Paul sees a Macedonian man pleading with him to come over to Macedonia and help them. As the result of this vision the missionaries lose no time in crossing over to Macedonia, a momentous step which brings the Good News to what is now Europe. So, Paul and his companions got to Macedonia because God wanted them there and got them there. Note the *we* in Acts 16:10. Acts 16:10-17 is the first of the 'we' passages in Acts which lead many to conclude that the author of Acts was a missionary companion of Paul, at least for some time (see also Acts 20:5-15; 21:1-8; 27:1–28:16).

Mission in Philippi (Acts 16:11-40)

Passing by the island of Samothrace and landing at the port of Neapolis, the missionaries come to Philippi, a leading Macedonian city which was some 16 kilometres inland.[2] The Via Egnatia, the great road linking Rome with the East passed through this city which gave it strategic and commercial importance. It had been colonised by veterans of the Roman army from Italy who were very conscious of their identity and privileges as Roman citizens. The administration system of the city was thoroughly Roman. Besides the Roman state religion, some foreign cults were practised in the vicinity. There is no archaeological evidence that the city had a Jewish synagogue. It is estimated that few Jews actually lived in Philippi, but presumably quite a number of Jews and 'God-fearers' came and went on business. We have five scenes for the story of the missionaries' stay of 'some days' (Acts 16:12) in Philippi:

1. *Conversion of Lydia and her Household (Acts 16:13-15).* On the Sabbath day, the missionaries went outside the city to 'a place of prayer' by the river (Acts 16:13). Could it be the place where the small number of Jews assembled for prayer on the Sabbath in the absence of a synagogue? The missionaries spoke to a group of women gathered there, among whom was Lydia, a 'God-fearer' (Acts 16:14a). A native of Thyatira, she was a rather well-to-do dealer in purple cloth which was a lucrative business; purple dress was associated with royalty and the wealthy. She had a house and household in Philippi, another indication of her prosperity. We are told that the Lord opened her heart as she listened eagerly to Paul and she was baptised along with her household (Acts 16:14b-15a). She insisted that the missionaries come and stay at her house (Acts 16:15b). Hospitality is a recurring feature in Luke's story. In his Gospel, he presented Jesus eating meals with all as a sign of God's boundless hospitality. In the Acts, the sharing of hospitality among Christians of different classes and cultures is an expression of Christian *koinōnia*. Most of the first Christian communities were 'household churches'. Luke has already told us of the emergence of a household church with the conversion of a 'God-fearing' man (Acts 10:44-48); now he matches that with the story of the formation of a household church with the conversion of a 'God-fearing' woman. As Peter and his companions accepted the hospitality of Cornelius and his household, so now Paul and his companions accept the hospitality of Lydia and her household. Luke may have had an apologetic interest in pointing out that people of high standing were attracted to the Christian faith (see also Acts 17:4, 12).

2. *Exorcism of the Slave-girl (Acts 16:16-18).* The slave-girl is possessed by a python spirit enabling her to tell fortunes, a power which was a source of handsome profit for her owners (Acts 16:16). This spirit takes its name from

Python, the mythical serpent who was considered to be the guardian of the pagan shrine of Delphi, the source of influential oracles in the Hellenistic world. The spirit's recognition of the missionaries as 'servants of the Most High God' who proclaim 'a way of salvation' could perhaps be taken as a validation of Christianity by a widely respected oracular source. What is uppermost in Luke's mind is probably a parallelism with Jesus whom spirits recognised as the 'Son of the Most High God' before he exorcised them and brought salvation to those they possessed (Lk 4:31-37; 8:26-39). After the slave-girl continued shouting out for many days, Paul exorcises the python spirit with a simple command in the name of Jesus Christ (Acts 16:18). Paul is 'very much annoyed,' perhaps because of the exploitation of the girl by greedy owners who see her just as a way of making profit. The Good News of Jesus cannot tolerate that situation.

3. *Punishment and Imprisonment of the Missionaries (Acts 16:19-24)*. The owners of the slave-girl, who haul Paul and Silas before the authorities, do not mention the real reason why they are against the missionaries, that is, the loss of financial gain. Rather, they play on the racism, anti-Semitism and xenophobia of the local population in accusing the missionaries of disturbing the peace and doing things that are harmful to the Roman way of life. The crowd joined in the attack on the missionaries (Acts 16:22). The charges resemble those levelled against Jesus (Lk 23:2) by the authorities who are joined by the crowds in calling for Jesus' death (Lk 23:21). Without due legal process, the magistrates have the disciples flogged and thrown into prison with instructions that they are to be securely guarded (Acts 16:22-23). The missionaries are put in the innermost cell and their feet are fastened in the stocks (Acts 16:24).

4. *God's Intervention on behalf of the Missionaries (Acts 16:25-34)*. One of Luke's purposes here is to draw a parallel between Peter's release from prison in Acts 12 and Paul's release from his imprisonment. Note how in both stories we have an emphasis on tight security measures (Acts 16:23-24; 12:6), a context of prayer (Acts 16:25; 12:5, 12), and a visit to a Christian house after release (Acts 16:40; 12:12-17). Both stories underline God's powerful protection of his missionaries. God's liberating action comes through an angel in Acts 12 and an earthquake in Acts 16, which shakes the prison to its foundations, opens the doors and unfastens the chains of all. We are reminded how the house in Jerusalem was shaken as the disciples prayed for boldness and a manifestation of God's signs and wonders (Acts 4:31). We have the dramatic scene of Paul preventing the jailer from killing himself in his belief that all his prisoners had escaped and the consequences would be most grave for him (Acts 16:27-28). The focus of the story now switches to the conversion of the jailer and how God saves him and his household (Acts 16:29-34). It becomes a story of their release, rather than the release of the missionaries. Telling the jailer that the way of salvation is belief in the Lord Jesus, the missionaries speak the word of the Lord to him and his household. He washes their wounds and he and his family are washed in the waters of baptism. The jailer brings them into his own house where he serves them food in an atmosphere of joy. Notice again how hospitality and Christian *koinōnia* are closely linked with conversion to the Lord.

5. *Vindication of the Missionaries by the Authorities (Acts 16:35-40)*. We are not told why the magistrates suddenly decided to release the missionaries. Paul, revealing his Roman citizenship and pointing out that they were punished publicly without due process, refuses to be released in secret and insists that the city magistrates themselves come and publicly set them free. This the magistrates do with an

apology. Luke's apologetic motive is evident here. He wants it to be quite clear that Christian mission is not engaged in criminal activity, nor is it against the best interests of Rome. Paul and Silas on their release go back to Lydia's house and encourage the brothers and sisters (Acts 16:40) before they depart for Thessalonica. This reminds us of how Peter, when he was released from prison, immediately headed for a Christian household and spoke with his fellow disciples before he departed for 'another place' (Acts 12:12). From Paul's letter to the Philippians we learn that he left behind him a vibrant church with which he had close and affectionate bonds (see Phil 1:7-8; 4:1). The Philippian church was the only church that supported Paul financially (see Phil 4:16; 2 Cor 11:9).

Mission in Thessalonica (Acts 17:1-9)
Passing through Amphipolis and Apollonia, the missionaries come to Thessalonica (152 kilometres southwest of Philippi) which was the capital city of the Roman province of Macedonia. Luke concentrates on Paul's work among the Jews, though it seems from Paul's first letter to the Thessalonians that the community he founded there was mainly a Gentile community. On three Sabbath days Paul visited the synagogue where he explained that according to the Scriptures the Messiah, whom Paul claims is Jesus, was to suffer and rise from the dead (Acts 17:3; see Lk 9:22; 17:25; 24:26, 46; Acts 3:18). Like Jesus on the road to Emmaus (Lk 24), Paul opens the Scriptures for his hearers and demonstrates that it was necessary (*edei*) for the Messiah to suffer and rise from the dead.

As often happens, the proclamation of the Gospel leads to a division. Some join Paul and Silas, among them God-fearing Gentiles and leading women (Acts 17:4). Others, out of jealousy, organise a mob to create uproar against the missionaries and seek them out to bring them before the city assembly (Acts 17:5). Unable to find Paul and his companions, they attack the house where the missionaries were guests and bring their host, Jason, and some believers before the city authorities (Acts 17:6-7). This time the charge is more political: the missionaries are turning the world (empire) upside down, follow a (rival) king, Jesus, and advocate what is contrary to the decrees of the emperor (compare the charge against Jesus in Lk 23:2). The authorities this time follow legal procedure and release Jason and the believers, having bound them to the peace by taking a surety payment from them. In his first letter to the Thessalonians, Paul speaks of his own tireless work among them (see 1 Th 2:1-16) and of the hostility endured by believers in Thessalonica who became an example to all the believers in Macedonia and Achaia (see 1 Th 1:7).

Mission in Beroea (Acts 17:10-15)

The believers sent Paul and Silas to Beroea (some 80 kilometres south of Thessalonica) for their safety. The pattern of events in Thessalonica was repeated there: the missionaries went to the synagogue; there was discussion on the Scriptures; the preaching found success among women and men of high standing; there was persecution under Jewish instigation. But the response from the Jews in Beroea was much more positive. Note how Luke highlights the positive response and role of women in these chapters (see Acts 16:13-15; 17:4, 12, 34; 18:2, 18). When hostile Jews from Thessalonica came to stir up opposition to Paul in Beroea, the disciples took him away from the place and brought him as far as Athens (Acts 17:14-15). Silas and Timothy remained on in Macedonia and Paul sent them a message to join him as soon as possible. This does not fit easily with 1 Th 3:1-2 where Paul speaks of sending Timothy back to Thessalonica from Athens.

Mission in Achaia (Acts 17:16–18:17)

Achaia was the Roman Province of Greece south of Macedonia with Athens and Corinth as its leading cities. Both were coastal cities open to travellers, both tourists and business people, and home to foreign sojourners who brought with them their many customs, cultures, philosophies and religions.[3]

Mission in Athens (Acts 17:16-34)

Luke's account of Paul's stay in Athens is one of the most impressive episodes in the Acts of the Apostles. Here we read about Paul left alone and in dialogue with the sages of Athens which was regarded as the great centre of Hellenistic religion and culture. For Luke this episode is not just one among many in his story. Paul's speech in Athens, in particular, has an exemplary character. It represents the typical preaching of Paul when faced with people of Greco-Roman culture and religion, just as his speech in Antioch of Pisidia (Acts 13:16-41) represents his typical preaching to those steeped in the Jewish tradition. We can divide the episode in Athens into three parts: (1) Prelude to Paul's Speech (Acts 17:16-21); (2) Paul's Speech at the Areopagus (Acts 17:22-31); (3) Outcome of the Encounter (Acts 17:32-34).

1. *Prelude to Paul's Speech (Acts 17:16-21):* Here Luke is setting the scene for us. Athens had its golden age some five centuries before Paul's arrival. Yet it was the city that most represented the greatness of Greek culture. Besides the brief reference to the fact that Paul debated in the synagogue with Jews and God-fearers (Acts 17:17),[4] Luke concentrates on the Greek world. In depicting the Athenian scene, he tells us of the general populace frequenting the shrines of many gods (Acts 17:16), people who were curious about things different and novel (Acts 17:21), those who had a particular interest in information about new gods (Acts 17:18-20), and philosophers in the marketplace ready to debate with all comers (Acts 17:17-18). Luke notes that Paul is 'deeply distressed' by the widespread idol worship (Acts 17:16). Among the philosophers with whom Paul debated, two schools are

singled out for special attention – the Epicureans and the Stoics (Acts 17:18).[5]

The *Epicureans* (followers of Epicurus, 341-270 BC) said the gods, if they existed at all, had bodies made of an aggregate of very fine atoms, were far removed from the human scene, were uninterested in the lives of humans, and could not be affected by anything humans do. Human bodies and souls were also made up of atoms which came together by chance. Body and soul dissolved at death and there is no afterlife. With gods so distant and no hope of an afterlife, the goal of this life is 'pleasure' – not sensual pleasure, but a happy, tranquil life, characterised by *ataraxia* (peace and freedom from fear) and *aponia* (absence of pain), even in the midst of adversity. The Epicureans were practical atheists who regarded religion as a waste of time and were very critical of the religiosity and superstition that characterised the lives of many Greeks. They saw their philosophy as a way of salvation from the tyranny of the gods and the fear of death. They said people should behave ethically because immoral behaviour will burden them with guilt and take away their peace of mind. They also discouraged people from taking part in public life which is dangerous and gives rise to too much trouble in one's life. They advocated association in small, more private, communities which were open to men and women, and even slaves.

The *Stoics* were followers of Zeno of Cyprus (336-263 BC) and took their name from the *'stoa'* (colonnade) where he taught. They believed in one divinity which is a dynamic thinking breath, an intelligent fire, an immanent cosmic *logos* (reason). This divinity is the mind and soul of the universe (world soul) which pervades and reaches out to all parts of the universe, providing order, harmony, purpose and providence. The Stoics had a pantheistic understanding of God. The human soul is a spark or seed of this universal reason, imprisoned in a body and destined to re-join the great divine soul/fire after physical death. The goal of life is to live in harmony with universal reason (that is, with the divine purpose and order in the universe) and thus attain virtue. Living in harmony with universal reason, one should cultivate indifference to the vicissitudes of fortune, pleasure and pain. For the Stoics, then, God is not removed from the human scene. There is a kinship between God and humans. The Stoics also were critical of popular Greek religion which they said was superstitious and too crude.

We will see that Paul, in facing the Epicureans and Stoics, says things which would resonate with both camps (though more with the Stoics than with the Epicureans), as if he were appealing to what he considered best in both philosophies. Of course, Paul would not agree with everything in these philosophies. For instance, we could not imagine Paul accepting the practical atheism of the Epicureans. And Paul's God, the God revealed in Jesus Christ, is much more personal than the world soul of the Stoics. How did these philosophers see Paul? The first assessment of some is that he is a 'babbler' (Acts 17:18a).[6] Others see him as 'a proclaimer of foreign divinities' (Acts 17:18b). It seems Paul was already speaking of Jesus and the resurrection. They may have understood that as a doctrine about a new god, 'Jesus,' and his female consort, 'Resurrection'. They want to know more about this new and strange teaching, so they take Paul to the Areopagus (Acts 17:19). This should not be understood as an arrest and there is no hint of legal proceedings against Paul.[7] The Areopagus ('Hill of Ares') can be understood as the name of a place or the name of the Athenian council which met at this place. It is better to take it in the latter sense.[8]

2. *Paul's Speech at the Areopagus (Acts 17:22-31):* This is not a word-for-word account of what was said on the occasion. Many commentators speak of the heavy editorial hand of Luke in this speech.[9] It is quite different from the other speeches in Acts. It is, however, similar to Paul's short

speech in Lystra (Acts 14:15-17) where he was also speaking to a non-Jewish audience. The speech in Lystra is probably a conscious prelude to the more developed speech in Acts 17, but it lacks much of the theology of the Areopagus speech. The Athens speech also has similarities to the approaches of Jewish theologians in their encounter with Greek culture and religion. There were two basic approaches. One approach was to engage in polemic against pagan idol worship (see, for instance, Is 40-42; Wis 13-15). A second approach was to speak of the Jewish faith as the fulfilment of what is best in pagan philosophies and poetry (this, for instance, was the approach of Philo of Alexandria, circa 20 BC–AD 50). Paul's speech in Athens combines the two approaches, with more emphasis on the second approach. He is emphasising the common ground between Greek culture and Christian faith, while at the same time challenging the idol worship which pervaded popular Greek religiosity.[10] The speech shows an interweaving of Greek wisdom with Old Testament concepts and ends with reference to Jesus who has been appointed universal Judge by reason of his resurrection. On the basis of its main topics, we can divide the speech itself into five parts, each part comprising two verses in our text:[11]

(a) In *Acts 17:22-23* Paul speaks of the polytheist situation in Athens. We have already been told that this distressed him deeply (Acts 17:16), but here Paul strikes a more positive note. *Deisidaimonesterous* (Acts 17:22) can have a positive meaning ('extremely religious') or a negative meaning ('extremely superstitious'). Both meanings may be intended here. Paul is both affirming the religious spirit of the Athenians and criticising its misguided expression in superstitious idolatry. In the speech we will hear him challenging three notions which are at the basis of idolatry: that God can be confined in a temple (Acts 17:24); that God can be manipulated by human worship

(Acts 17:25); and that God can be portrayed and represented by inanimate objects (Acts 17:29). The philosophers listening to Paul would also be critical of superstitious idolatry. Paul mentions the altar in Athens to the unknown god (Acts 17:23), which becomes his point of departure for what he wants to say about God, human beings, and the relationship between God and human beings. He tells his audience that he is here to reveal something about the God they worship as unknown. No altar or inscription to a single unknown god has ever been discovered, but there are literary references to the practice of erecting altars to unknown deities (plural).

(b) In *Acts 17:24-25* Paul is focusing on the nature and worship of the true God. God is the creator of everything and he cannot be circumscribed in any way by anything, including shrines made by human hands (Acts 17:24). Nor does the God, who gives life to all mortals and breath to all things, have any need of human service and worship (Acts 17:25). In Acts 17:24-25 we hear Paul weaving together Jewish and Greek terms. 'The world and everything in it' is Greek sounding, while 'heaven and earth' (bipartite universe) has a biblical ring to it. Similar terms are found in Acts 4:24; 14:15. The life-giving God of the Bible is the creator of everything (see, for instance, Gn 1:1; 2:7; Ex 20:11; Is 42:5). For the notion that God does not need anything from humans see, for instance, Ps 50:9-12; Am 5:21-23; 2 Mac 14:35. In Stephen's speech (Acts 7:48-50) we have already come across the biblical notion that God cannot be confined in a temple made by human hands (see 1 Kgs 8:27; Is 66:1-2). The idea of a God who cannot be confined to creation and cannot be manipulated by human actions or service would be especially appealing to Epicureans. God as the source of life and breath would strike a positive note in a Stoic's heart.

MAJOR MISSIONS OF PAUL (1)

(c) In *Acts 17:26-27* Paul is focusing on the kinship, relationship and unity between humans due to the way God has created and arranged things. With the Genesis creation story in mind, Paul says that all human beings have a common origin, descending from one ancestor, and God's creative power has separated time and space (Acts 17:26). God has allotted to different nations their historical periods and has set their geographical boundaries. Paul is stressing the unity of all humanity and 'countering the idea that the universe came into being by chance, emphasising rather the divine design and intention that lie behind all human existence.'[12] Acts 17:27 goes on to say that the purpose of human life, as willed by God, is to seek the God who is not far from any one of us. Notice how Paul seems to be saying that this human search can be a groping with no firm guarantee that the God, who is indeed near to us, will actually be found by human effort alone. The Bible gives ample evidence of the human condition as a quest and longing for God (see, for instance, Is 55:6; 65:1; Jer 29:13; Ps 14:2; Prov 8:17). Paul tells philosophers, people who search for the meaning of life, what their search is ultimately all about. The idea of a planned and harmonious human condition with a common origin and destiny would again appeal to the Stoics, as would the notion that God is not far from us.

(d) In *Acts 17:28-29* Paul, developing what he said about the closeness of God (Acts 17:27), goes on to speak about the kinship between God and human beings and its practical consequences. The quotation in Acts 17:28a ('In him we live and move and have our being') is usually attributed to the Cretan poet Epimenides (sixth century BC). It is also reminiscent of a saying of the Stoic philosopher Seneca (4 BC–AD 65): 'He is near, is with you, and is in you.' Paul would most probably have understood the saying in Acts 17:28a to refer to our total dependence on the divine being ('*By him* we live and move and have our being'), rather than the Stoic notion of the human soul as a spark or seed of the world soul/universal reason.[13] It is generally agreed that the saying in Acts 17:28b ('For we too are his offspring') comes from the Stoic poet Aratus (circa 310 BC). The word *genos* (NRSV – 'offspring') can also mean 'family'. The Stoic poet would have understood the saying in the sense of the human soul as the spark/seed of the divine; the Lukan Paul would have understood it in the light of the biblical notion of humans beings created in the *image* of God (Gn 1:26-27). That is the direction Paul's argument takes in Acts 17:29 where Paul draws an essential practical conclusion. God is not an idol depending on the creative imagination of humans; we rather are the ones who are totally dependent on him. The fact that living humans are made in God's image should convince us that God is the living God who cannot be represented by an inanimate object (gold, silver or stone). The Bible often warns against the danger and error of using inanimate things as images of the living God (see, for instance, Deut 5:8; Is 44:9-20; Wis 15:3-17; Rm 1:23). So here Paul is back to his criticism of idolatry (see Acts 17:16, 22).

(d) Paul's speech finishes in *Acts 17:30-31* with an appeal for universal repentance in view of the fact that God has fixed a day on which the world will be judged in righteousness by one man and the assurance of this is that he has raised that man from the dead. The idea that God has overlooked ignorance in the past, but now the time of (excusable) ignorance is ended (Acts 17:30), is also found in earlier speeches of Acts addressed to Jews (see Acts 3:17-19; 13:27). The character of the ignorance is different. The Jews, ignorant of what their Scriptures were really saying, failed to recognise the Messiah; the Greeks' ignorance was a matter of false conceptions of God expressed in idolatry. There is now a new era in God's dealings with humanity. Now is the time for 'all people everywhere' to turn away from this ignorance and turn to God (that is, to repent). We remember Jesus' words about the message of repentance and the forgiveness of sins to be proclaimed to *all* nations (Lk 24:47). The day of God's coming judgement in righteousness is mentioned as a motive for repentance (Acts 17:31; see also Acts 10:42). Belief in a day of judgement, the 'day of the Lord,' is very evident in the Bible (see Am 5:18; Is 2:12; Rm 2:5, 16; 1 Cor 1:8; Phil 1:6, 10; 1 Th 5:2, 4; 2 Th 1:10; 2:2; 2 Tm 1:18; 2 Pt 3:10; for relevant passages in Luke's writings, see Lk 10:12; 12:46; 17:24, 30; Acts 2:20; 10:42).

It is important to remember that, in the biblical understanding, the day of judgement was not just a day when God passed sentence and handed out punishments to those who have not lived according to his ways. It was seen first and foremost as a day of salvation, a day when the faithful God fulfilled his promises. Paul here speaks of judgement in 'righteousness'. The righteousness in question is the righteousness of God. In the Bible God shows his righteousness particularly in his saving activity. So, it would be wrong to interpret Paul's reference to judgement here merely as a threat to his audience; it is more a matter of directing their attention to a tremendous opportunity to experience salvation and forgiveness. In the context of universal judgement/salvation, Paul gets back to speaking about Jesus and the resurrection. That's what he had been talking about when the Athenians took him to the Areopagus (Acts 17:18). Notice he does not mention Jesus' name in Acts 17:31, but it is obvious that he is speaking of Jesus. Paul is here bearing witness to his Christian faith. God has given Jesus the central role in the universal judgement in righteousness and the resurrection of Jesus from the dead is God's 'assurance' to all that this is so. The resurrection here is understood in the sense of Jesus' exaltation to a position of universal Judge/Saviour. As in Acts 10:42-43, reference to Jesus as judge goes hand in hand with reference to the forgiveness of sins.

3. Outcome of the Encounter in Athens (Acts 17:32-34). As so often happens in Luke's story, the preaching leads to a division in the audience. Some reject what is being said (Acts 17:32-33); others accept and believe (Acts 17:34). Among those who reject are the scoffers (those for whom Paul is just a 'babbler') and those who had a genuine interest in what he had to say (see Acts 17:19-20) but could not accept any talk about a resurrection of the body which was foreign to the Greek mind, despite the fact that a lot of what Paul said would have struck a responsive chord in the hearts of some of the Greek philosophers who were present. It is probably better to take the phrase 'We will hear you again about this' as a polite but firm rejection of Paul's message, rather than an expression of interest in pursuing the matter again. We are simply told that Paul left them (Acts 17:33). He bore witness to his Christian belief without forcing it on anyone. Some who heard Paul, on the other hand, became believers and joined him. Luke names two of them – a man and a woman (again Luke is sensitive to the man-woman pairing). It seems Dionysius was a member of the Areopagus council; we get no information about Damaris. So, in Luke's mind, Paul's Athenian mission was not a complete failure, as it is sometimes thought to be.

Mission in Corinth (Acts 18:1-17)

After Athens, Paul moved on to Corinth, the capital of the Roman province of Achaia, where he remained for eighteen months (Acts 18:11). Corinth's strategic, commercial and religious importance was due in large measure to its geographical location.[14] It was situated on the isthmus (of Corinth), the narrow neck of land that connects mainland Greece with the Peloponnese peninsula. Corinth had two ports: Lechaeon (approx. 3 kilometres northwest) on the Gulf of Corinth, leading to the Adriatic Sea; Cenchreae (approx. 10 kilometres southeast) on the Saronic Gulf, leading to the Aegean Sea. Goods and even small ships were transported overland on the Diolkos Road between these two ports.

Corinth controlled trade between Asia Minor and Italy. South of city was the 1,850-foot-high acropolis hill (Acrocorinth). The population of the city was multicultural, multi-religious and multi-ethnic with a majority of hardworking people engaged in the various employments found in a busy manufacturing and commercial centre. The city was full of temples of several deities, as well as having a Jewish synagogue. The Isthmian Games, second only to the Olympic Games in ancient Greece, were held in Corinth every two years. The city had a reputation for immorality and depravity and among its 'industries' was a vibrant sex trade. Paul wrote a number of letters to the Corinthian church, probably the church which gave him most trouble. One only has to read Paul's first letter to the Corinthians to get a sense of the array of difficult challenges that he faced in that city.

In Corinth Paul stayed with a Jewish Christian couple, Aquila and Priscilla (Acts 18:2; see 1 Cor 16:19; 2 Tm 4:19; Rm 16:3), who were among those expelled from Rome by an edict of the emperor Claudius. The ancient historian Suetonius tells us of an expulsion of Jews from that city because of internal strife over a certain 'Chrestus,' probably a misspelling of the Latin 'Christus'. It is reasonable to suppose that the in-fighting was occasioned by Christian missionary work in the Jewish synagogues of Rome. So, Aquila, who originated from Pontus, and his wife Priscilla were refugees who may have engaged in missionary work in Corinth before Paul's arrival. They were tentmakers like Paul and he moved in and worked with them.[15] This trade produced temporary dwellings, canvas awnings, sails and leather goods, for all of which there would have been a good demand in a busy commercial city with many people coming and going. Paul worked with his own hands to support himself and his companions (see Acts 20:34; 1 Cor 4:12; 9:6-12; 1 Th 2:9; 2 Th 3:6-9). He was not like many philosophical and religious teachers who charged for their services.

Every Sabbath Paul went to the synagogue in Corinth to testify that Jesus is the Messiah and, after Silas and Timothy arrived from Macedonia, he engaged in full-time mission among Jews in Corinth (Acts 18:5). When his preaching about Jesus the Messiah was rejected in the synagogue and they reviled him, he shook the dust from his garments in an act of dissociation and solemnly turned from the Jews to the Gentiles a second time (Acts 18:6; see 13:45-46). He makes it quite clear that he is not culpable for their failure to respond to God's word and the effects of this will redound on their own heads (compare Ez 3:17-21; 33:7-9). Again we should not take this as a definitive turning from the Jews. Paul doesn't go very far. He moves into the house of Titius Justus (seemingly a 'God-fearer') next door to the synagogue and makes that the base of his missionary work (Acts 18:7). Crispus, the ruler of the synagogue, was converted along with his household, as well as many Corinthians (Acts 18:8).

At this point in the narrative, Luke inserts a reference to another vision of the risen Lord to Paul (Acts 18:9-10). We have seen that visions are an important way of reminding us of the guiding and empowering presence of God in mission (see Acts 9:3-6, 10-18; 10:3-8, 9-16; 16:9-10). Paul's vision in Corinth makes it clear that the success of the mission (Acts 18:8), and Paul's release when the Jews tried to have him condemned before the proconsul (Acts 18:12-17), are due to the fact that the risen Lord was with Paul. The encouraging words 'Do not be afraid... for I am with you' (Acts 18:9) are similar to those addressed to God's agents and messengers in the past (see Ex 2:12; Num 21:24; Deut 3:2; Jos 8:1; Jer 1:8). They are addressed to the whole people of Israel in Is 41:10. With a promise of protection, the Lord tells Paul that there are many in Corinth who are, or who are about to become, 'my people (*laos*)' (Acts 18:10). We are reminded of James' words at the Council of Jerusalem about God taking from the Gentile 'a people for his name' (Acts 15:14). The vision is like a renewal of Paul's prophetic call and, with the assurance of God's protection, he stayed on in Corinth for a year and six months teaching the word of God (Acts 18:11).

The episode before Gallio the proconsul (Acts 18:12-17) can be dated with a fair degree of accuracy to AD 52.[16] Paul is brought before the proconsul's tribunal by the Jews and the accusation is made that his mission is contrary to the law (Acts 18:12-13). It is not clear whether the Jews are accusing Paul of acting against *Roman* law, or against *Jewish* law. If the former is the case, the Jews would be appealing to Gallio for the protection of their religious community against a disturbing intruder. Judaism was a *religio licita* (legitimate religion) in the eyes of the Roman authorities and enjoyed protection under the law. Gallio refuses to get involved in what he considers an internal Jewish dispute and dismisses the Jews from the tribunal (Acts 18:14-16). The Gallio incident serves two purposes in Luke's narrative. It provides fulfilment of Jesus' promise of protection for Paul in Acts 18:10; it also enables Luke once again to point out that a Roman administrator did not find any reason to condemn Christianity or its missionaries. This is not to say that Luke is presenting Gallio in a completely favourable light. Gallio turns a blind eye to the mistreatment of Sosthenes (Acts 18:17). It's not clear from the text whether Sosthenes is a member of the Jewish community who is the victim of Gentile antisemitism, or a former synagogue official who became a Christian convert and is now set upon by frustrated Jews, or a current synagogue official who incurs the wrath of his own congregation for failing to succeed in the case against Paul.

Paul's Visit to Antioch via Jerusalem (Acts 18:18-22)

As pointed out already, this part of Acts was seen as the end of Paul's second missionary journey and the beginning of the third (see Acts 18:22-23). But it comes across more as a pause in Paul's continuing missionary campaign. Paul's visit to Antioch re-connects him with his 'church of origin,' while the visit to Jerusalem serves Luke's continuity theme. Luke does not want us to forget that Paul the missionary is very much a community person. Paul leaves Corinth with Aquila and Priscilla who go as far as Ephesus with him (Acts 18:18). The mention of Paul's Nazirite vow[17] at Cenchreae (Corinth's eastern port) is meant to stress once again that Paul was not against Jewish practices for Jews. As a Jewish Christian he observed Jewish customs and did not forbid other Jews doing the same. So the charge against Paul in Acts 21:20-24 is false.

The stopover in Ephesus (capital of the Roman province of Asia), where Paul leaves Priscilla and Aquila (Acts 18:19a), may be Luke's way of preparing for Paul's extensive missionary work there at a later stage, or Luke may want to associate Paul with the founding of the Christian community in Ephesus before he tells of Apollos' work there (see Acts 18:24-28). Paul holds discussions in the synagogue at Ephesus with the Jews and they want him to remain, but he departs with a promise to return, if God wills (Act 18:19b-21). Having landed in Caesarea, he goes up (to Jerusalem) to greet the church there before going down to Antioch in Syria (Acts 18:22).[18] Paul wants to strengthen his bonds with the 'mother church,' which was perhaps needed in view of his earlier tensions with Barnabas who was highly respected in Jerusalem. Antioch was Paul's home missionary base where he remains for 'some time' before setting out overland through the regions of Galatia and Phrygia where he strengthened disciples in churches he had previously established (Acts 18:23).

Reflection on Acts 15:36–18:22

It is interesting to note how often new developments in the story of mission in Acts began in the context or aftermath of seemingly unfavourable circumstances. The missionary outreach to Samaria, Judea and farther afield began with the persecution of Hellenist Christians in Jerusalem and their expulsion from that city (Acts 8:1; 11:19). The Gentile mission from Antioch began as the apostles, the great pioneers of Christian mission, were experiencing persecution in Jerusalem and were fading from the scene (Acts 12:1-24; 13:1-3). Paul and Silas set out on a new missionary venture shortly after disagreements in the Jewish Christian community over conditions for entry of new Gentile converts into the Church, and in the wake of a split between Paul and Barnabas who had worked so well together in mission (Acts 15:1-41). So, new developments in mission usually began in the context of external pressures and internal tensions. And the ongoing experience of Paul, Silas and Timothy in the cities of Macedonia and Achaia was one of success in the midst of rejection, persecution and expulsion from one city after another. When things are going well, missionaries can easily forget that, more often than not, mission is carried out in situations of human weakness, vulnerability and limitation. In such situations we are more likely to realise that mission is ultimately the Mission of God and open ourselves to God's guiding and empowering presence.

Once again, in this section of Acts, Luke gives us powerful reminders of the presence of God in mission: the guidance of the Spirit keeping missionaries with other plans on course to Macedonia where God wanted them to be (Acts 16:6-10); the earthquake in Philippi releasing the missionaries from chains that rendered them completely helpless and transforming their hopeless situation into an occasion for preaching the Good News of Jesus (Acts 16:25-34); the vision of Paul in Corinth, encouraging him and assuring him of divine protection in a most difficult situation (Acts 18:9-11). As we go through the experience of transition in mission today, we can feel quite inadequate and confused as we face seemingly insurmountable challenges, grapple with new missionary questions, and try to cope with rapidly decreasing personnel and financial resources. And quite a number of missionaries today find themselves in situations where it is unpopular and even dangerous to bear witness to the Christian message and its values. Others live in situations where morale is low and the Church's credibility is questioned due to serious scandals and failures that contradict its message. At this time of testing we need to rediscover the path of mission in human weakness, humility and vulnerability charged by the power of the Spirit.

Dialogue with people from other religious traditions is an urgent challenge in mission today when cultural and religious differences can easily lead to divisions and conflicts. The Church is in the process of clarifying its theological understanding of dialogue and exploring the paths of genuine dialogue. Paul's mission in Athens is perhaps the New Testament text that is most helpful in this regard. I share some thoughts as I bring my experience of mission in Pakistan to the reading of Acts 17:16-34. Firstly, I feel the experience of living and working in a homeland for Muslims gives me some sense of Paul's state of mind in the centre of Greek culture and religion. One can feel marginalised and vulnerable by the very fact of being in a situation that is completely permeated by a religion different from one's own. The experiences of suffering in Philippi, Thessalonica and Beroea, as well as isolation from his companions, would have intensified Paul's vulnerability. Vulnerability can make one defensive. But, on the other hand, it is a fundamental attitude for entry into dialogue with peoples of other religions, because it can make us more open, humble and willing to listen. One cannot enter dialogue thinking one knows it all and has little to learn from the other. Paul's speech in Athens shows his openness to the religious insights of Greek philosophers and poets. It has been said that the first task for the missionary in approaching peoples of other religious traditions is to take off one's shoes, as one is standing on holy ground.

Secondly, in hearing Paul's warning against confining God in temples of our own making or controlling God in any way (Acts 17:25), I'm reminded that we can't limit God to our understanding and practice. God is always more and God must always remain free to relate to people as he chooses. We are not the ones, for instance, to determine who will be saved or how exactly God will save people. Thirdly, Paul highlights the basic kinship between all human beings (Acts 17:26). The spirit of interreligious dialogue looks for the common ground (common human experiences, aspirations, hopes, fears, concerns) and seeks cooperation in matters of common human concern. In my experience, the best form of dialogue is not the dialogue of theological exchange in which people explore each other's religious doctrines. The dialogue of life (when people live as good neighbours with true humanity) and the dialogue of action (when people of different religions join together in promoting the common good) are often much more productive and enriching forms of dialogue. What Paul says about the way God has ordered nations, and indeed all creation, is a reminder of the need for peoples of different religions to cooperate in working for peace and reconciliation between nations and for the protection of the earth, our common home.

Fourthly, Paul characterises the human condition as a search and groping for God who is not far from any of us (Acts 17:27-28). Dialogue does not take place between religious systems and traditions, but between people who belong to these traditions, who often fall short of the ideals of their own traditions, and who are always on the way to a fuller experience of life lived in truth. We enter dialogue as searchers, wanting to join others in a search for truth (ultimately a search for God), and realising that we don't have all the answers and we are not always models of how God intends life to be lived. Fifthly, Paul speaks of repentance/conversion for everyone without exception (Acts 17:30). Conversion for every dialogue partner means turning to what God is doing in one's own religious experience, in the religious experience of the other, and in the actual experience of the dialogue. The hope is that through the dialogue all will come to a greater understanding of and commitment to God's dream for our world.

Finally, Paul shares his faith in Jesus Christ (Acts 17:31). Dialogue presupposes a commitment to one's own faith and a willingness to bear witness to it. We witness, not as people who have the truth, but as people who are possessed by the

Truth. The Church, in its mission, must always point to Jesus, tell the story of Jesus, make known his values, and bear witness to its experience of Jesus as God's greatest gift to humanity. But we remember the gift can never be imposed. In sending out his missionaries, Jesus told them, 'What you have received as gift, pass on as gift' (Mt 10:8). We bear the gift as fragile, earthen vessels (2 Cor 4:7) and are conscious that we offer the gift with frail, soiled hands. Furthermore, missionary witness to Jesus is not just a matter of talking. It is witness by a way of living and relating that reflects the values of the kingdom proclaimed by Jesus Christ – love, compassion, forgiveness, respect for all as children of God, solidarity with and care for those who are vulnerable and excluded, care for God's creation by living simply and walking lightly on the exploited earth.

One thinks of the words attributed to St Francis of Assisi: 'Preach the Gospel always and, if necessary, use words.' There is a certain tension between proclamation (preaching Jesus Christ in the conviction of his uniqueness) and dialogue (open to being enriched by the other's faith experience). In mission among people of other religious traditions we live with that tension, not wanting to resolve it in one direction at the expense of the other. The Catholic missiologists, Stephen Bevans and Roger Schroeder, understand mission today as 'prophetic dialogue,' a phrase which captures these two indispensable poles of mission.[19] In a similar vein, David Bosch speaks of mission today in 'bold humility'.[20] The joint document from the Pontifical Council for Dialogue and the Congregation for the Evangelisation of Peoples in 1991 also spoke of the need to preserve the close connection between dialogue and proclamation in mission today.[21]

Pope Francis ends his latest encyclical on fraternity and social friendship with a chapter entitled 'Religions at the Service of Fraternity in our World'.[22] He calls for believers belonging to different religions to work together in building universal fraternity, promoting the common good and integral development of all, upholding the innate dignity of every human being, and standing in solidarity with the poor, vulnerable and excluded in our world. The significant and necessary contribution of believers working together is rooted in the transcendent truth that all are children of God, called to live as brothers and sisters in the one human family. Francis, following the teaching of the Second Vatican Council, acknowledges the spiritual sources of other religions and the ways God works in them. He also states clearly that for Christians the wellsprings of human dignity and fraternity are found in the Gospel of Jesus Christ. Dialogue with peoples of other religions does not mean watering down or concealing our deepest Christian convictions. He closes his encyclical by quoting from the declaration he signed with the Grand Imam Ahmad Al-Tayyeb in 2019 in which the two religious leaders, condemning all religiously-motivated violence and terrorism, committed themselves to a culture of dialogue, mutual cooperation and reciprocal understanding as they work together for universal fraternity.

NOTES

[1] In this connection see Dillon, 'Acts of the Apostles' in *The New Jerome Biblical Commentary*, 752-753; Fitzmyer, 'Paul' in *The New Jerome Biblical Commentary*, 1334-1336; Brown, *An Introduction to the New Testament*, 309 (footnote 74) and 432.

[2] For a concise history and description of Philippi see Mullins, *The Acts of the Apostles*, 169-171.

[3] *Ibid.*, 178.

[4] This may be a reminder that the Good News for all nations is first preached to the Jewish people (see Acts 13:46).

[5] On the Epicureans and Stoics see Fitzmyer, *The Acts of the Apostles*, 604-605; Brown, *Introduction to the New Testament*, 89-90; Johnson, *The Acts of the Apostles*, 313; Mullins, *The Acts of the Apostles*, 180-182; Kurz, *Acts of the Apostles*, 269; John Kilgallen, 'Acts 17:22-31: An Example of Interreligious Dialogue,' *Studia Missionalia* 43 (1994), 50.

[6] The literal meaning of *spermologos* ('babbler' in NRSV) in Acts 17:18 is 'one who picks up and drops scraps of information, a peddler in words'. The image is that of a scavenger bird picking up and dropping seeds.

7   'The tone of the proceedings makes us think rather of a discussion than a formal hearing or trial' (Johnson, *The Acts of the Apostles*, 314). Tom Wright (*Paul. A Biography*, SPCK [London, 2018], 193-207), however, understands Paul's appearance before the Areopagus council as a trial in which Paul is defending himself. He thinks it is reminiscent of the trial of Socrates (399 BC) who was accused of corrupting the young and introducing foreign divinities. Whatever the historical situation, Luke is not presenting it as a trial. There is no mention of an arrest, formal accusation and prosecution, or legal judgement on Paul.

8   'The speech fits better if Paul is addressing not only the philosophers but also an official body that has responsibility for the city, including its religious facilities and rites... Paul is telling them that religion in Athens does not live up to the insights of their philosophers and poets' (Tannehill, *The Narrative Unity of Luke-Acts*, vol. 2, 216-217).

9   See, for instance, Johnson, *The Acts of the Apostles*, 318; Marshall, *Acts*, 283.

10 It has been pointed out that Paul's speech in Acts 17:22-31 is much more positive on 'pagan' religions and philosophies than anything that is found in Paul's letters. For instance, in Rm 1:21-32 Paul speaks of the widespread immorality of the non-Jewish world as God's punishment for a refusal to worship him despite clear signs of his presence and power in the created world. However, we should keep in mind the different contexts. Paul in Rm 1 is speaking to Christians and is emphasising that all, whether Jew or Gentile, need the grace of God if they are to experience salvation.

11 Mullins (*The Acts of the Apostles*, 182-183) divides the speech rather along the lines of 'the conventional structure of a public address in the Hellenistic world, beginning with an *exordium* or introduction, including a *captatio benevolentiae* or a winning over of the audience, a *propositio* or setting out of the topic to be discussed, a *probatio* or persuasive discussion of the topic and a *peroratio* or winding up of the speech with a clinching argument and exhortation to the audience to accept the proposition and its implication for their lives'. It seems these elements are clearer in Paul's later defence speeches in Jerusalem and Caesarea.

12 Fitzmyer, *The Acts of the Apostles*, 609.

13 Fitzmyer, *ibid.*, 610; Johnson, *The Acts of the Apostles*, 316.

14 For a short description of Corinth's history and life see Brown, *Introduction to the New Testament*, 511-513; Mullins, *The Acts of the Apostles*, 188-189.

15 Aquila and Priscilla were co-workers with Paul in mission, at least on some occasions (see Acts 18:18-19; Rm 16:3-5; 2 Tm 4:19).

16 See Fitzmyer, *The Acts of the Apostles*, 620-623. The dating is based on an inscription discovered in Delphi in the first decade of the twentieth century.

17 The Nazirite vow (see Num 6:1-21) was a form of consecration to God, often for a set period of time. It involved abstention from alcohol and refraining from cutting one's hair. Shaving the hair was part of the ritual on conclusion of the period of consecration, so it seems Paul is now completing his vow.

18 Jerusalem is not mentioned in the Greek text of Act 18:22, but the verbs 'to go up' and 'to go down' were traditionally used in speaking of journeys to and from Jerusalem, especially pilgrimages.

19 Stephen B. Bevans and Roger P. Schroeder, *Prophetic Dialogue. Reflections on Christian Mission Today* (New York: Orbis Books, 2011).

20 Talk about the tension between missionary witness and dialogue 'boils down to an admission that we do not have all the answers and are prepared to live within the framework of penultimate knowledge, that we regard our involvement in dialogue and mission as an adventure, are prepared to take risks, and are anticipating surprises as the Spirit guides us into fuller understanding. This is not opting for agnosticism, but for humility. It is, however, a bold humility – or a humble boldness. We know only in part, but we do know. And we believe that the faith we profess is both true and just, and should be proclaimed. We do this, however, not as judges or lawyers, but as witnesses; not as soldiers, but as envoys of peace; not as high-pressure sales-persons, but as ambassadors of the Servant Lord' (Bosch, *Transforming Mission*, 489).

21 'Interreligious dialogue and proclamation, though not on the same level, are both authentic elements of the Church's evangelising mission. Both are legitimate and necessary. They are intimately related, but not interchangeable; true interreligious dialogue on the part of the Christian supposes the desire to make Jesus Christ better known, recognised and loved; proclaiming Jesus Christ is to be carried out in the Gospel spirit of dialogue. These two activities remain distinct but, as experience shows, one and the same local Church, one and the same person, can be diversely engaged in both' (Pontifical Council on Interreligious Dialogue and Congregation for the Evangelisation of Peoples, *Dialogue and Proclamation* [Rome: L'Osservatore Romano on July 1, 1991], no. 77).

22 See *Fratelli Tutti*, nos 271-285.

CHAPTER 7

MAJOR MISSIONS OF PAUL (2)
(ACTS 18:24–21:16)

In this chapter we continue with the story of Paul's mission in the Aegean region. Firstly, we hear of Paul's missionary work during his long stay in the city of Ephesus (Acts 18:24–19:41). Then we have the account of Paul's farewell journey as he visits the Christian communities he had evangelised in the Aegean region, a journey which marks his departure from that region and brings him to Jerusalem (Acts 20:1–21:16).

Mission in Ephesus (Acts 18:24–19:41)

In Acts 18:24–19:41 we have a series of episodes united by the Ephesus locale. All these episodes (with the exception of the mission of Apollos in Acts 18:24-28) are focused on Paul and his missionary work. Luke intends the events in Ephesus to be the climax of Paul's missionary work as a free man. His mission in this city, addressed to all, both Jews and Greeks (see Acts 19:10, 17; 20:21), is presented by Luke as a lasting model for the Church after Paul's departure (see Acts 20:18-35). The picture of Paul in Ephesus is that of a missionary at the height of his power, one who has responded in an exemplary way to the mission the Lord had entrusted to him. We will see that the later attack on Paul in Jerusalem results from his work in Ephesus (see Acts 21:27-29; 24:19). Ephesus, the capital of the Roman province of Asia, was the hub of one of the most thickly populated areas in Asia Minor. It is estimated that close on a quarter of a million people lived in the city at that time. Its importance as a wealthy commercial centre was due to the fact that it was on major trade routes between East and West. Its magnificent Temple of Artemis (the protector of young girls and one of the primary goddesses of childbirth and midwifery) was the centre of a widespread cult.[1] It also had temples for an assortment of other deities and was well known as a centre for the practice of magic.

Mission of Apollos (Acts 18:24-28)

By way of prelude to Paul's mission in Ephesus, Luke tells us about the mission of Apollos in Ephesus and Corinth. Historically, Apollos' involvement in the founding of the Ephesian church may have been greater than that of Paul. Apollos also became a very influential teacher in the Christian community in Corinth. We are told that Apollos was a learned man from Alexandria who was well versed in the scriptures (Acts 18:24). This Egyptian city, which was ranked second in importance in the Roman Empire, was a great centre of Hellenistic culture and erudition. It had a large and influential Jewish community where scholars explored ways of expressing their Jewish faith in the categories of Hellenistic culture. Here the Hebrew Scriptures were translated into Greek (the Septuagint). In the Acts of the Apostles Luke does not tell us anything about the foundation and growth of the Christian community in Alexandria which became a most important Christian centre within a few centuries. We are left to speculate where and how the learned Apollos became a Christian and why his Christian education (instruction in the 'Way of the Lord') was somewhat incomplete. Though he taught accurately and boldly about Jesus in the Ephesian synagogue, he was aware only of the baptism of John and seemingly ignorant of baptism in the name of Jesus (Acts 18:25). Paul's associates, Priscilla and Aquila, took him aside and gave him more accurate instruction in the 'Way of God' (Acts 18:26). The believers in Ephesus encouraged and facilitated Apollos in his wish to do missionary work in Achaia where he helped those who had become believers by the grace of God and also publically debated with Jews to demonstrate from the scriptures that Jesus is the Messiah (Acts 18:27-28).

How did Luke regard Apollos and why did he introduce him at this stage of his narrative? Many would say that Luke saw Apollos in a favourable light and had quite a high opinion of his missionary endeavours. The remarks about Apollos have a very positive ring about them.[2] Luke may well have introduced him here because he knew Apollos had a role in the foundation of the Ephesian church and Luke wanted to acknowledge the contribution of this celebrated missionary. But he wants to offset any conclusion that Apollos' mission was in competition with the mission of Paul which continued the mission of Jesus and the apostles. He does this especially by showing Priscilla and Aquila, Paul's close associates, instructing Apollos and leading him into a more accurate understanding of the mystery of Jesus. There is evidence that in the Corinthian church there was some rivalry and competition between the disciples of Paul and the disciples of Apollos (see 1 Cor 1:12; 3:4-11, 22; 4:6; 16:12).

Meeting with Baptist's Disciples (Acts 19:1-7)
In Acts 18:21 we heard Paul saying that he would return to Ephesus 'if God wills'. Now Luke marks Paul's return with an episode that has been called the 'Ephesian Pentecost'. Paul meets disciples who have been baptised into John's baptism of repentance, but who had never heard about the Holy Spirit, even though they had become believers (in Jesus) (Acts 19:1-3). Their situation is somewhat similar to that of Apollos who had not been fully initiated into the community of Jesus' disciples. Paul teaches them that John's baptism of repentance was a preparation for belief in Jesus, the one who was to come after John (Acts 19:4). This led to their baptism 'in the name of the Lord Jesus' and the descent of the Holy Spirit when Paul laid his hands on them (Acts 19:5-6). The presence of the Spirit is manifested in the disciples' speaking in tongues and prophesying. The number of disciples who

received the Spirit is put at twelve (Acts 19:7), recalling the twelve tribes of Israel and the twelve apostles.

One could mention a number of reasons for Luke's interest in this story. Its references to conversion, baptism, the laying on of hands and the outpouring of the Spirit, make it a suitable episode for opening Paul's mission in Ephesus. It reminds us of the beginning of the Christian community in Jerusalem when on the day of Pentecost many were baptised in the name of Jesus Christ and received the Holy Spirit (Acts 2:37-41). It provides another parallel between Paul and Peter (see Acts 8:14-17), both of whom laid hands on people as the Holy Spirit came upon them. This episode gives Luke another opportunity to mention the presence and activity of the Spirit in mission. At the time Luke when was writing, there may still have been pockets of John the Baptist's disciples around and he wants to clarify their relationship to the Christian community and perhaps appeal to them to accept Jesus, the one to whom the Baptist pointed. Luke, in his Gospel, shows quite a bit of interest in the relationship between John and Jesus. This is the fifth reference in Acts to John, the precursor of Jesus (see Acts 1:5; 11:16; 13:25; 18:25).

Success of Mission to Jews and Greeks in Ephesus (Acts 19:8-20)

This section underlines the remarkable success of Paul's powerful mission in word and deed among Jews and Gentiles in Ephesus. As was his custom, Paul begins his mission in a Jewish synagogue, preaching boldly and persuasively about the kingdom of God (Acts 19:8). He meets stubborn resistance from people who spoke badly about 'the Way,' though, as the story progresses, there are indications that some Jews responded positively (Acts 19:10, 17). As in Corinth, Paul moves away from the synagogue and sets up his base of operation elsewhere, this time in the lecture hall of Tyrannus (Acts 19:9). From there he carried out a successful mission for two years among Jews and Gentiles of the Roman province of Asia (Acts 19:10).[3] Note the hyperbole: 'all the residents of Asia, both Jews and Greeks, heard the word of the Lord.' It is quite probable that from Ephesus a larger area was evangelised (for instance, Colossae, Laodicea, Hieropolis) by Paul himself or his co-workers.[4]

Luke goes on to underline this great success story with a generalising statement about the 'extraordinary miracles' that God worked through Paul (Acts 19:11-12). This parallels the summaries about the miracle-working ministries of Jesus (Lk 4:40-41; 6:17-19; 7:21-22), of the Twelve (Acts 2:43), and of Peter (Acts 5:15-16). Paul's successful ministry is further highlighted by the episode of the Jewish exorcists, and in particular the seven sons of Sceva, which provides a contrast to the exorcism ministry of Jesus and Paul (Acts 19:13-16). Whereas God performed miracles through Jesus (see Acts 10:38) and Paul, the Jewish exorcists think they themselves can engineer exorcisms if they repeat the magic formula Paul is using! One is reminded of Simon the magician who tried to buy a formula from Peter which would enable him to dispense the Holy Spirit (see Acts 8:18-19).

Whereas the evil spirits recognised Jesus as the 'Holy One of God' (Lk 4:34) or 'Son of the Most High God' (Lk 8:29), and Paul as one through whom the divine power was at work, they recognised the Jewish exorcists as charlatans whom they attacked and put to flight. Jesus and Paul were victorious over the evil spirits; the evil spirits were victorious over the Jewish exorcists. This became known to all the residents of Ephesus, both Jews and Greeks, and the name of the Lord Jesus was praised (Acts 19:17). Finally, the great success of the Ephesian mission is illustrated by the report that many who practised magic became believers and in a public display of their new faith burned their very expensive books of magic (Acts 19:18-19). In doing this they would also have lost the regular income from their 'profession' as magicians. This section, which opened with a summary of Paul's ministry of healing and exorcism, ends with a short summary about the word of the Lord growing mightily (Acts 19:20).[5]

Paul's Future Plans (Acts 19:21-22)

Acts 19:21-22 is important, not only in its immediate context, but also as a programmatic statement for the remainder of the story of Acts. Paul decides to move on – to visit once more the churches in Macedonia and Achaia, and then to move toward Jerusalem and Rome. It is quite clear that Paul is doing this in accordance with God's plan for his mission. We are told that Paul 'resolved in the Spirit' (NRSV)[6] and said that he 'must' (*dei*) see Rome (Acts 19:21; see also 23:11). The little word *dei* is always a signal that the working out of God's plan is in view. There is parallelism between Acts 19:21-22 and Lk 9:51-52 where we are told that Jesus set his face to go to Jerusalem and sent messengers ahead of him. Notice how Paul sends Timothy and Erastus on ahead to Macedonia (Acts 19:22). It is important to note that these two important verses are placed before the report of the silversmiths' riot in Ephesus. Luke is making it clear that Paul leaves Ephesus in response to God's plan for him, not because he was forced out by those who opposed him. In Acts 20:1 Paul will begin to put the plan into effect. In Paul's letters the visit to Achaia (Corinth) seems to be motivated by trouble there (1 Cor 16:5-7) and the reason for moving in the direction of Jerusalem is to deliver the collection which Paul had taken up among the churches for Jerusalem (see 1 Cor 16:1-4; 2 Cor 8-9; Rm 15:25-32). But Luke downplays those 'human' motivations here, probably because he wants to highlight that God was moving things forward in his unfolding plan.

Riot of the Silversmiths in Ephesus (Acts 19:23-41)

We gather from Paul's letters that his mission in Ephesus involved quite a bit of hardship and difficulty (see 1 Cor 15:32; 2 Cor 1:8-9), which Luke seemingly downplays in his eagerness to highlight the extraordinary success of the mission. In telling us about the riot of the Ephesian silversmiths, it would seem that Luke's main purpose is not to illustrate the sufferings Paul endured. Paul remains in the wings during the riot and has some local officials on his side! Luke's principal emphases are probably to be detected in the two short speeches which are found in this episode (Acts 19: 25-27, 35-40).

Demetrius, a silversmith in the lucrative business of making silver shrines of Artemis, gathered together his fellow artisans to make them aware of the detrimental impact Paul's preaching about 'the Way' is having on their business (Acts 19:24-27). Paul's persuasive preaching against 'gods made with hands' has influenced people in Ephesus and 'in almost the whole of Asia,' and was leading to an alarming drop in demand for representations and shrines of Artemis. That seems to be Demetrius' main concern, though he does add that he is concerned about the reputation of the great goddess Artemis who is worshipped by 'all Asia and the world' (Acts 19:27). Obviously, the more her reputation suffers, the more their business will decrease! So economic considerations and provincialism were important factors in the opposition to Paul (compare Acts 16:19). Luke wants us to realise what an extraordinary impact the successful mission of Paul had on the economic, civic and religious life of Ephesus.[7]

Acts 19:28-32 describes the chaotic riot with enraged people shouting, 'Great is Artemis of the Ephesians'. It develops into a situation of utter confusion with people shouting different things and some not even knowing why they had come together. Riots are often joined by people with all kinds of agendas and even by people who just want to vent pent-up frustrations, anger and grievances. The mob drags Gaius and Aristarchus, two of Paul's travelling companions, into the city theatre. We are not told why they did not get their hands on Paul himself. Paul wants to go into the crowd but is prevented by disciples and friendly officials of the province (asiarchs), obviously concerned for his safety. Here we have another indication that Paul's mission influenced upper-class people.

Jews who were present pushed Alexander forward to speak. It is not clear what they want him to say and we can only speculate. Perhaps they want to disassociate themselves from the Christian 'troublemakers'. Is it beyond the bounds of possibility that the Jews wanted to be supportive of Paul's stance against idol worship? Alexander was shouted down in a blast of antisemitism by a crowd who continued yelling their slogans for about two hours (Acts 19:33-34). Luke wants us to pay particular attention to the speech of the town clerk who succeeded in calming the situation (Acts 19:35-41). With a clever rhetorical question about the special position of Ephesus as the temple-keeper of the great Artemis and of her image that fell from heaven, he first gets the crowd on his side (Acts 19:35).[8] He goes on to say that the missionaries are not criminals ('temple-robbers' or 'blasphemers of our goddess'), so one should avoid doing anything rash in proceeding against them (Acts 19:37). If Demetrius and the artisans wish to pursue the matter, they should do so through the courts (Acts 19:38-39). Finally, he points out that the crowd is leaving itself open to the charge of rioting and disturbing the peace without any justification (Acts 19:40). We are told that the clerk was successful in dispersing the crowd (Acts 19:41). The speech of the town clerk (Acts 19:35-40) serves Luke's interest in emphasising that Christians are not perpetrators of criminal acts and this has been acknowledged by the appropriate authorities. So, in one and the same episode, Luke succeeds in portraying Christian missionaries as those who challenge idol worship without being involved in criminal activity.

Paul's Farewell Journey and Orientation towards Jerusalem (Acts 20:1–21:16)

There are two threads running through Acts 20:1–21:16. Firstly, Paul the missionary is saying farewell to the communities he had established, encouraging them to remain steadfast in their Christian commitment. Secondly, Paul, facing himself in the direction of Jerusalem, is putting into effect the plan which was mentioned in Acts 19:21-22. The interweaving of these two threads gives Acts 20:1–21:16

the character of a transition between the missionary campaigns of Paul and his arrest and imprisonment in Jerusalem. In this transition passage Luke is consciously drawing a parallel between Jesus and Paul. Paul is reliving Jesus' experience of journeying to Jerusalem to face suffering and rejection.

> Luke has so obviously structured it to mirror the great journey of the prophet Jesus to his death and triumph in Jerusalem (Luke 9:51–19:44). Paul announces his intention, sends out delegates ahead of him, and then proceeds to move steadily towards a destiny that is ever more clearly enunciated as he approaches the city of Jerusalem.[9]

As Paul takes leave of the churches, we sense the very close relationship between him and those he had evangelised (see Acts 20:36-38; 21:5-6, 12-13). The atmosphere is not unlike that in the upper room when Jesus took leave of his own disciples (see Lk 22:7-38). On that occasion, Jesus shared a meal with his friends and addressed a farewell discourse to them. In Acts 20:1–21:16 we will hear of Paul breaking bread with some disciples (Acts 20:7-12) and shortly afterwards giving a farewell discourse to other disciples (Acts 20:17-38). As a final introductory comment on this section, we note the three 'we' passages in which the author of Acts speaks as a participant in the events narrated (Acts 20:5-8, 13-15; 21:1-18).

From Ephesus to Macedonia and on to Troas (Acts 20:1-6)

In Acts 20:1, Paul begins the journey which is God's plan for him (see Acts 19:21-22). The themes of farewell and encouragement are sounded immediately, as Paul takes his leave of the Christians in Ephesus. He heads for Macedonia and Greece (Achaia), where he stayed three months (probably the winter of AD 57-58). Because of a conspiracy of the Jews against him, Paul decides to return overland to Macedonia, rather than set sail to Syria from Greece (Acts 20:3). Luke names seven travelling companions of Paul, indicating their churches of origin (Acts 20:4).[10] They are representatives of churches Paul had evangelised. Historically, their gathering at this time may have something to do with the collection Paul was taking up from these churches to bring to Jerusalem (see 1 Cor 16:1-4; 2 Cor 8-9; Rm 15:25-32). But here Luke does not mention these companions of Paul as collectors or bearers of the collection, though he was aware of the collection (see Acts 24:17). He probably has in mind the parallelism with Jesus who was accompanied by disciples on his journey to Jerusalem. Some went ahead to Troas, while Paul and others seem to have waited in Philippi to celebrate the feast of Unleavened Bread/Passover before moving on to Troas.[11] Luke may once again be presenting Paul as one faithful to his Jewish traditions (see also Acts 20:16 which speaks of Paul's desire to celebrate Pentecost in Jerusalem).

Farewell Visit to Troas (Acts 20:7-12)

During a seven-day stay in Troas Paul breaks bread with disciples on the first day of the week (Acts 20:7). While this meal parallels Jesus' farewell meal with his own disciples (see Lk 22:14-23), there is little doubt that the breaking of bread on the 'first day of the week' refers to the Christian Eucharist (see Acts 2:42, 46) on the day which commemorates the Lord's resurrection. Paul seemingly was into long homilies, which is given as the reason why young Eutychus fell asleep (Acts 20:9)! He fell out of the window and was picked up dead three floors below. Paul went down, bent over the boy, took him in his arms, and pronounced that he was alive (Acts 20:10).[12] What Luke is doing by this story is drawing a parallel between Paul and other prophetic figures – Elijah (1 Kgs 17:21); Elisha (2 Kgs 4:34), Jesus (Lk 8:54), and Peter (Acts 9:39-41) – all of whom restored life to people who were dead. Paul, like Peter before him, continues the life-giving mission of Jesus, who in Luke's Gospel is seen as an Elijah-like prophet. Acts 20:10 shows the power of the resurrection at work in Paul.

From Troas to Miletus (Acts 20:13-16)

Luke gets us from Troas to Miletus in double-quick time by a series of one-day journeys along the west coast of Asia Minor and offshore islands. In Acts 20:16 we read that Paul intended to sail past Ephesus, perhaps because it was not a safe place for him after the experience of the riot. Luke gives us the impression of a man in a hurry. He may be comparing Paul to Jesus as a prophet with a sense of urgency to complete his task. The eagerness of Paul to be in Jerusalem to celebrate Pentecost is another reminder of his fidelity to his Jewish ethos.

Farewell Discourse to the Ephesian Elders (Acts 20:17-38)

Despite his hurry, Paul summons the elders of the church in Ephesus to meet him in the seaport of Miletus (some 60 kilometres south of Ephesus) where he delivers a most significant address (Acts 20:17). The 'elders' (*presbyteroi*) were the local church leaders (see Acts 11:30; 14:23; 15:2, 4, 6, 22, 23; 16:4); in Acts 20:28 they are called 'overseers' (*episkopoi*), but at the time Luke was writing the terms seemed to be interchangeable. At Miletus Paul delivers a moving address to these leaders. It is the only speech delivered by the Lukan Paul to Christians. Luke probably intends it to be taken, not only as an address to a particular local church, but as an example of what Paul said when preaching to Christians and indeed as his last will and testament for all the churches he has evangelised (see Acts 20:25). In Acts the speech is an interpretative hinge between the ministry of Paul and his suffering in Jerusalem. It gives us an insight into how Paul looked on his mission, which is now coming to an end, and how he saw the prospect of suffering in Jerusalem. But it also marks the end of the founding period for the churches Paul established and the transition to the next phase when they will have to cope without his visible presence. Paul is preparing these churches for the future.

The speech is a farewell discourse, similar in form to the final instructions of great biblical figures for the generation they were leaving behind as they depart the scene – compare the farewell discourses of Jacob (Gn 49), Moses (Deut 31-34), Joshua (Jos 23-24), Samuel (1 Sm 12), David (1 Chr 28-29) and Mattathias (1 Mac 2:49-70). Among common elements in these discourses are: the speaker's announcement of his imminent departure; recalling how he has been with his family/community/followers in the past and asking to be remembered; appealing for unity among those he is leaving behind; exhorting them to serve God and keep God's commandments; giving practical instructions for the present and warnings about future difficulties; appointing a successor or speaking about those who will replace him; defending his integrity and calling them to imitate him; praying for God's blessing on those he is leaving. In particular, Luke wants us to see a parallel between Paul's farewell discourse in Acts 20:18-35 and Jesus' farewell discourse to his disciples in Lk 22:14-38 on the occasion of the last supper. Among the Synoptics, Luke is the only one to present Jesus giving a farewell discourse. Both speeches have similar themes: the prediction of death (*passim* in Lk 22:14-38; Acts 20:22-24); predictions of attacks on the disciples (Lk 22:31-32, 35-38; Acts 20:29-30); ideal behaviour urged, especially service (*diakonia*) in imitation of the one giving the speech (Lk 22:24-27; Acts 20:35); watchfulness and fidelity (Lk 22:31-32; Acts 20:31); succession of leadership (Lk 22:29-30, 31-32; Acts 20:28).[13] Finally, we should not overlook similarities of terms and concepts between the farewell discourse in Acts 20:18-35 and the Pauline letters. All of the commentaries on the speech give extensive cross references to Paul's letters.[14]

Most would hold that the speech is a Lukan composition. Dillon draws attention to the repetition of the phrase 'and now'.[15] On that basis we are given the following fourfold division: (a) *Acts 20:18-21* – Paul looks back; (b) *Acts 20:22-24* – Paul reflects on his present situation and immediate future; (c) *Acts 20:25-31* – Paul reflects on the future of the community and passes on his testament; (d) *Acts 20:32-35* – Paul's concluding commendation and exhortation.

In *Acts 20:18-21* Paul looks back on his missionary work. He emphasises his manner of life and attitude when he was among those he evangelised: humble service, endurance in trials, frankness in preaching and teaching, testimony to all human beings without distinction. Paul often referred to himself as a servant in his letters (see, for instance, Rm 1:1; Gal 1:10; Phil 1:1). It is as if Paul is repeating the words of Jesus in his farewell discourse: 'I am among you as one who serves' (Lk 22:27). The emphasis on complete and public proclamation is probably meant to offset the claims of future teachers in presenting something new (see Acts 20:30). Paul sums up the content of his preaching: 'repentance towards God and faith towards our Lord Jesus' (Acts 20:21). Paul's past record is meant to be a model for the elders and this will be spelled out more clearly as the speech progresses.

In *Acts 20:22-24* Paul turns his thoughts to his present situation and immediate future. He describes himself as 'bound by the Spirit' (Acts 20:22), which most probably means (in view of Acts 20:23) the constraint he experiences as one whose destiny is in the hands of the Spirit. The Holy Spirit testifies to him in every city that suffering awaits him in Jerusalem. This anticipates Acts 21:4, 10-11 and as such is the first of three predictions of Paul's 'passion' in Jerusalem (probably to be taken as parallels to the three predictions of Jesus' passion in Luke's Gospel – see Lk 9:21-22; 9:44; 18:31-33). Paul's deepest desire is to finish his course (see 1 Cor 9:24; Phil 3:14; 2 Tm 4:7) and fulfil the ministry entrusted to him (see 2 Cor 5:18-19). In doing this he does not count the cost to himself (see Lk 9:24). In Acts 20:24 he speaks of his ministry in terms of 'testifying to the good news of God's grace,' which is an apt summary of Paul's proclamation, though the phrase does not occur in his own writings. So, in these verses we see Paul walking in the footsteps of Jesus in his fidelity to God's plan and his willingness to face suffering and possible death in Jerusalem.

In *Acts 20:25-31* Paul focuses on the situation of the local church leaders who are listening to him. Their circumstances are about to change and the departing Paul gives them instructions. Paul will no longer be present with them and they will not be able to entertain the hope of seeing him again (Acts 20:25). Note that Paul here speaks of his ministry as 'proclaiming the kingdom' – the same ministry Jesus had (see Lk 4:43). In Acts 20:26-27 Paul says that he has done his part faithfully. Note the emphasis once again on completeness with the reference to 'the *whole* purpose (*boulē*) of God' (see Lk 7:30; Acts 2:23; 4:28; 5:38; 13:36). Now it is over to them; they are accountable for what happens from now on. For the blood metaphor, see Ez 18:13; 33:1-6; Acts 18:6. As mentioned above, Paul's reference to his own behaviour in the early part of the discourse is meant to be an implicit exhortation to leaders who are being asked to imitate him. Now in Acts 20:28-31 we have explicit and direct exhortation. The leaders are exhorted to be watchful (Acts 20:28) and alert (Acts 20:31) (see Lk 12:35-39; 1 Cor 16:13; Col 4:2; 1 Th 5:6). They are to watch over themselves and the flock, a reminder that they too are not immune from going astray.

For the flock as a metaphor for God's people, see Is 40:11; Jer 13:17; Ez 34; Lk 12:32; 15:3-7; Jn 10:1-30; 21:15-17; 1 Pt 5:2. The Holy Spirit (not Paul) has appointed them as overseers (*episkopoi*) to shepherd the flock. The flock is said to be 'the church of God which he obtained (acquired, bought) with the blood of his own Son' (Acts 20:28, NRSV). The 'church of God' is a very Pauline phrase (see 1 Cor 1:2; 10:32; 11:16, 22; 15:9; 2 Cor 1:1; Gal 1:13; 1 Th 2:14; 2 Th 1:4; 1 Tm 3:5, 15). The Greek text has 'the blood of his own' and the NRSV translation supplies 'Son' for clarity and that is certainly an acceptable meaning of the text. This is one of the rare occurrences of expiation theology in Luke's writings. The blood which acquires God's Church reminds us of the blood of the covenant in Lk 22:20. Paul warns against dangers to the flock from without (Acts 20:29) and within (Acts 20:30). Those who will come from outside are called 'savage wolves' that will not spare the flock (see Lk 10:3).

False teachers will also arise from within the community, who will distort the truth and lead disciples astray. The antidote to these dangers is a vigilant Church leadership which draws inspiration from remembering the example of Paul who ceaselessly warned everyone (Acts 20:31).

Finally, in *Acts 20:32-35* Paul commends the leaders to God and makes a final appeal to them to be selfless in their service of others, especially the weak. He gives the leaders over to the care of God (Acts 20:32). He knows that the source of their strength and inspiration will have to be God and 'the word of his grace'. Church office is not above the word, but in service of the word, a word which not only enlightens, but also empowers. It is a word which builds up the community and leads the community to its destiny and goal, its 'inheritance among all who are sanctified' (Acts 20:32). Again we have language with a strong Pauline ring: 'build up' (see, for instance, Rm 14:19; 1 Cor 3:9; 2 Cor 10:8; 1 Th 5:11; Eph 4:12); 'inheritance' (1 Cor 6:9-10; Gal 3:18; Eph 1:14; Col 3:24; Ti 3:7); 'those who are sanctified' (Rm 15:16; 1 Cor 1:2; 6:11; 7:14). Paul again presents his practice of selfless, disinterested service as an example for these leaders (Acts 20:33-35). He did not covet anyone's possessions and he worked to support himself and his companions (see Acts 18:3; 1 Cor 4:12; 9:15-18; 1 Th 4:11; 2 Th 3:6-10). Leadership and ministry are not for one's own benefit and aggrandisement, but are meant to be a service and support for others, especially the weak. To reinforce his instruction about selfless service, Paul finishes with a saying of the Lord Jesus which we do not find in any of the canonical gospels: 'It is more blessed to give than to receive' (Acts 20:35). Detachment from possessions and special concern for the poor are prominent Lukan themes (see Lk 6:30, 38; 11:41; 12:33; 18:22 for injunctions to give to others).

Acts 20:36-38 is a touching departure scene after the discourse. Paul knelt down to pray with the elders before they brought him to the ship. Jesus, shortly after his farewell discourse, also knelt down in prayer (Lk 22:41). Important moments in Luke's writings are always in a context of prayer. In Acts 20:37-38 we sense the strong emotional bonds which united Paul and those he evangelised.

From Miletus to Jerusalem (Acts 21:1-16)

The 'we narrative' resumes and Luke quickly gets the travelling group to Tyre in Phoenicia, via Cos, Rhodes and Patara, and passing Cyprus on their left (Acts 21:1-3). At Tyre, Paul and his companions seek out the Christian community and stay with them for seven days. In the story of Acts to date, we have heard already of the initial preaching of the gospel in Phoenicia (Act 11:19). Paul may have known some of the Christians there from the time he and Barnabas passed through on their way to the Council of Jerusalem (Acts 15:3). What happens at Tyre reminds us once more of the two threads running through this section of Acts: the journey to Jerusalem and Paul's farewell to the churches. In Tyre we have the second intimation that suffering awaits Paul in Jerusalem (Acts 21:4; see also 20:22-23 and 21:10-14). The city-by-city testimony that Paul spoke of in Acts 20:23 is now coming to pass. The Christians at Tyre were led by the Spirit to foresee suffering for Paul at Jerusalem and of their own accord they urged him not to go. It is a case of well-intentioned disciples trying to deflect Paul from a path leading to suffering, as in Acts 21:12 (see Mt 16:22-23 where Peter tries to turn Jesus away from the path of suffering). The touching farewell scene in Acts 21:5-6 is very similar to Acts 20:36-38. All knelt down on the beach and prayed together before saying their farewells.

After one day in Ptolemais to greet the disciples there (Acts 21:7), the party arrives in Caesarea where they stay with Philip, whose presence in Caesarea we have already heard about in Acts 8:40. We are reminded that he was 'one of the seven' who were chosen for the service at tables on the occasion of the dispute between the Hebrews and the Hellenists in the Jerusalem community (see Acts 6:1-6). He is also called 'the evangelist,' perhaps a reminder of his evangelising work in Samaria and Judea (Acts 8:4-40). We are told that he now has four virgin daughters who have the gift of prophecy. Luke may be alluding to the fulfilment of Joel's prophecy about 'your sons and your daughters' prophesying, mentioned by Peter on the occasion of the first Christian Pentecost (see Acts 2:17). Philip's daughters play no special role in the narrative at this point. That's left to Agabus, a prophet from Judea (Acts 21:10). We heard of him in Acts 11:28, but he is introduced here as someone we are hearing about for the first time. Like some of the Old Testament prophets, he not only prophesies in word, but also enacts his prophecy in deed (see, for instance, Is 20:1-6; Jer 13:1-14; Ez 4:1-3). He takes Paul's belt and binds his own feet and hands to signify that Paul will be bound in Jerusalem (Acts 21:10). The words in Acts 21:11 interpret the action. They are introduced by 'thus says the Holy Spirit', which reminds us of the very common introduction to prophecy in the prophetical books, 'thus says the Lord'. The words are similar to Jesus' third prediction of his passion in Lk 18:32. Reference to being handed over to the Gentiles is found in both texts. The Jews, however, did not in fact hand Paul over to the Romans; the Romans rescued Paul from the Jews! The Jews did not bind Paul; the Romans did (see Acts 21:33).

A high emotional level is again evident in Acts 21:12-14 – people, including Paul's travelling companions, weeping and urging him not to go to Jerusalem and Paul feeling his heart breaking. In the midst of all this, we hear Paul saying he is willing to face what has to be faced in Jerusalem and even to die there for the name of the Lord Jesus. Paul can't be persuaded to desist from following the path before him. The resolve of Paul to go to Jerusalem parallels Jesus' resolve in Lk 9:51. There is silence and the people say 'The Lord's will be done'. This reminds us of what Jesus says in Gethsemane on the eve of his passion in Jerusalem (see Lk 22:42). It's the final word that's uttered before Luke tells us in Acts 21:15-16 that Paul headed for his destiny in Jerusalem. Paul and his travelling companions stayed in the house of Mnason of Cyprus (probably a Hellenistic Jewish Christian), which may have been somewhere between Caesarea and Jerusalem. We are again reminded of the network of hospitality which was so important in the early Christian mission (see Acts 9:43; 10:6; 16:15, 40; 21:4, 8).

Reflection on Acts 18:24–21:16

During his missionary work in the Aegean region Paul spent extended periods in the megacities of his day. Some would see this as a change from his previous strategy of moving relatively quickly from place to place, though this movement was often forced on him by his opponents. We have seen that evangelisation in the great economic, political, cultural and religious centres brought new challenges for Paul. In Paul's world, religion, politics, economics and culture were very much interconnected. The gospel preached by Paul had ramifications for all dimensions of societal life and this inevitably brought him into conflict with economic, political and cultural self-interests. Paul was a threat to the status quo. In speaking of areas for mission today, Pope John Paul II spoke not just of geographical areas, but also of some new challenging situations: the world of the big cities, the world of youth, the world of migrants and refugees, situations of degrading poverty, the world of modern communications, the world of scientific research, the world of international relations, etc.[16] In more recent years, we have become increasingly aware of the challenge that environmental degradation poses for Christian mission today, a challenge which Pope Francis highlighted in his encyclical letter on care for our common home (*Laudato Si'*). All of these global issues are massive challenges for mission today and we can easily feel quite inadequate in addressing them. Furthermore, promoting such issues as the rights of the unborn, justice for workers, fair treatment of migrants, and protection of the environment, will get us into conflict with economic, political and cultural interests not in keeping with Christian

MAJOR MISSIONS OF PAUL (2)

values. Luke is holding up Paul as a model and inspiration for missionaries of all generations. Reflecting on the story of Paul's courageous commitment to mission in the circumstances of his day helps us to clarify our faith-inspired vision and discover where we get strength as we face the daunting challenges of mission today.

Paul's speech to the elders of the church of Ephesus can get us thinking about leadership at a time of transition in mission. As he departs the scene, Paul is encouraging the leaders of the churches he evangelised as they are entering a new era without his presence. It is difficult to be a leader in changing circumstances when new situations arise for which there are few precedents, when the road ahead is not clear, when people are discouraged and grow tired on the journey. Today we look for leaders who are decisive and also invite the participation of all in the decision-making process, who are open and honest in sharing their own views and also listen to the views of others, who are prudent and also not afraid to take risks, who wisely manage current affairs and also have the foresight to plan for the future, who can keep a community focused on its mission to others and also be attentive to good internal relations, who can challenge the wayward and also be a source of support and encouragement for the weak and those who fail.

The call to leadership can be quite intimidating. What can we learn about leadership for mission as we listen to Paul the leader instructing local leaders in a church he had built up? Paul is a leader with a vision. His vision is no less than the 'whole plan of God,' that is, God's plan of universal and all-inclusive salvation in and through Jesus Christ. Paul calls that plan 'the good news of God's grace' and 'the word of God's grace' to which people must turn in faith. Paul's mission was directed and driven by that vision and master plan. It has been said that the good leader is the 'keeper of the vision,' the one who keeps the community focused on its fundamental aim and nature. Paul reminds every Christian leader about the vision they are to foster and the master plan which is the fundamental point of reference for all decisions and planning.

Paul is a servant leader. He speaks of his role in terms of 'serving the Lord with all humility'. For him, leadership meant putting himself at the service of the dynamic, saving word of God which is able to build up people and give them an inheritance among all who are sanctified. In short summary statements, Luke has reminded us about the powerful word of God at work in mission (see Acts 6:7; 9:31; 12:24; 19:20). He told us of apostles who were servants of the word (Acts 6:4; see also Lk 1:2). The true Christian leader does not control the word of God, but is rather guided and controlled by that word. Note how Paul commends the elders of Ephesus to the word of God's grace which is to be the source of energy for their leadership ministry. Paul, the servant leader, also served the community of believers. He is at pains to tell us that he never sought prestige, position or wealth. He did not seek financial support from the community; rather, he worked with his own hands to support himself and his companions. These words of Paul are a clear echo of what Jesus said about the leader in his community taking the lowest place in humble service, rather than the place of honour with a desire to be served (see Lk 22:24-27; Mk 10:42-45; Mt 20:25-28; Jn 13:12-17). It is a teaching that is all too often overlooked in our Church today.

Furthermore, Paul reminds the elders of the church in Ephesus that they are called to be overseers and shepherds of the precious flock that is entrusted to their care by the Holy Spirit. The flock is not their own; it is 'the Church of God that he obtained with the blood of his own Son'. Christian leaders should be careful about using words like 'my' and 'mine' in speaking about those committed to their care. Paul was a shepherd leader who was close to the flock and whose presence to them was both supportive and challenging. Luke has told us how Paul visited churches to encourage and strengthen them, particularly at times of difficulty (see Acts 14:22; 15:41; 18:23; 20:1). As Paul makes his farewell visits to churches, we hear of the close bonds of affection between Paul and these churches (Acts 20:36-38; 21:5-6, 12-13). He was very conscious of the need to support his fellow Christians, especially the weak. On the other hand, Paul was not slow in challenging people to live up to their Christian commitment. At Miletus we hear Paul challenging local leaders to be watchful and warning them of future dangers inside and outside the community.

Paul was a faithful and steadfast leader in time of trial. In city after city the Holy Spirit is making him increasingly aware that trials await him in Jerusalem. Yet he presses on, anxious to complete the course that the Lord had set out before him. He speaks as a 'captive to the Spirit,' knowing that his life and destiny are in the hands of the Spirit. We can be sure that the Spirit who enlightened him was also the Spirit who empowered him to stay the course. One is reminded of Paul's words in his letter to the Philippians about reaching the goal set before him: 'I press on to make it my own, because Jesus Christ has made me his own' (Phil 3:12). Anyone who is called to leadership in mission today can expect difficulties and trials of one kind or another. Looking at the experience of Paul, and the experience of Jesus who made Paul his own, we realise that leadership involves going through a paschal experience.

Finally, Paul's leadership is marked by coherence between what he says and what he does. If he presents high and challenging ideals to the elders at Miletus, he does so as one who embodies those ideals in his own leadership style and practice. Today the Church is blessed with the leadership of Pope Francis, who in many respects is a leader in the mould of Paul at a time when there is dearth of good leadership on the world stage. He is a leader with a clear vision for mission today that is thoroughly rooted in the Gospel of Jesus Christ (see, for instance, his vision in *Evangelii Gaudium, Laudato Si'* and *Fratelli Tutti*). He is constantly bringing us back to the centre of our missionary call which is a lived relationship with Jesus Christ. Francis is a servant leader who speaks out against clericalism as an abuse of power and is shifting the focus in leadership from the authority of power to the authority of service. As a leader who listens and takes advice, he is building a more listening, discerning Church as it tries to bear faithful witness to the message of Jesus for today's world. As a humble leader, he is in touch with his own humanity and vulnerability and constantly reminds us to open ourselves in trust to the love and compassion of God. He is a shepherd leader who encourages and supports all and has a special concern for the poor, the excluded people, and the exploited earth. He moves easily among people and speaks of the Church's need for pastors who can smell the sheep of God's flock. Like Paul, Francis is an authentic leader whose deeds and way of life match his teaching.

NOTES

1   'Artemis, known in Latin as Diana, was a huntress in Greco-Roman mythology, and she is portrayed in some statues as a mother goddess with multiple breasts' (Kurtz, *The Acts of the Apostles*, 298-299).

2   The Greek phrase *zeōn tō pneumati* (Acts 18:25) refers to Apollos' enthusiastic spirit and not the Holy Spirit.

3   The two years mentioned in Acts 19:10 may not include the three months Paul spent preaching in the synagogue (Acts 19:8). In Acts 20:31 he speaks of his work 'for three years' among the Ephesian Christian community.

4   'Some would detect a deliberate change of missionary style – radiating out from a steady base of operations rather than frenetically moving on after a few weeks in each place' (Brown, *An Introduction to the New Testament*, 312, footnote 79).

5   'The refrain that "the word of the Lord grew" (Acts 19:20; cf. 6:7; 12:24) signals that, alongside Jerusalem and Antioch, Christianity now has another major centre, Ephesus, and that Paul's ministry has been blessed even as was the ministry of the Twelve' (Brown, *ibid.*, 312).

6   Some say the phrase 'decided in the spirit' refers merely to an internal personal decision on Paul's part (for instance, Fitzmyer, *The Acts of the Apostles*, 652). But another reference to the role of the Holy Spirit at this critical point cannot be ruled out.

MAJOR MISSIONS OF PAUL (2)

7   Tannehill (*The Narrative Unity of Luke-Acts*, vol. 2, 201-204) draws attention to four type-scenes in Acts 16-19 which feature accusations against Christians: in *Philippi*, the Gentile owners of the slave girl accuse Paul and Silas before the city magistrates of disturbing the city and promoting Jewish customs contrary to the Roman way of life (Acts 16:19-24); in *Thessalonica*, Jews, having dragged Jason and others before the magistrates, accuse Paul and Silas of disturbing the world and being troublemakers who reject Caesar's rule and support another king (Acts 17:5-9); in *Corinth*, Jews accuse Paul before the proconsul of promoting a worship which is contrary to the law (Acts 18:12-17); in *Ephesus*, Gentiles drag companions of Paul into a public arena, having been incited by Demetrius the silversmith who says that Paul is promoting a message which is a threat to the silversmiths' trade, to Ephesus' position as a cult centre, and to the goddess Artemis herself, (Acts 19:23-41). 'Caught between two suspicious communities, Paul is a troublesome outsider to both, for he advocates teachings and behaviour that threaten their ways of life... Both Jews and Gentiles view the mission as a threat to the customs that provide social cohesion, to the religious basis of their cultures, and to the political stability through Caesar's rule' (Tannehill, *ibid.*, 203). In relating his story, Luke presents Paul and the missionaries as people who challenge the status quo, but who are not engaged in criminal activity. The opposition to them is often motivated by economic self-interest (see Acts 16:19; 19:25, 27) and jealousy (see Acts 17:5).

8   The phrase *kai tou diopetous* in Acts 19:35 literally means 'and of that which fell from heaven'. Most English translations take it to refer to a statue or image of Artemis which was believed to have fallen from heaven. Is the town clerk saying that since Artemis' image fell from heaven it cannot be classified as an idol made by human hands? One can't imagine Paul or Luke agreeing with that argument. Perhaps what is in mind is a statue of Artemis sculptured from a piece of meteorite which fell from the sky. That would certainly be an idol made by human hands.

9   Johnson, *The Acts of the Apostles*, 357.

10 Three of these (Aristarchus, Gaius and Timothy) have already appeared in the story of Acts and another (Trophimus) will appear in Acts 21:29. Timothy often appears in the Pauline letters as one of Paul's foremost co-workers. These letters also mention Tychicus (2 Tm 4:12; Ti 3:12; Eph 6:21; Col 4:7) and Trophimus (2 Tm 4:10). Perhaps Sopater (Acts 20:4) and Sosipater (Rm 16:21) are one and the same person.

11 The 'they' who went ahead to Troas (Acts 20:5) could be taken to include Paul, which would mean that the narrator is included in the 'we' group which later re-joined Paul and the others in Troas.

12 Is the narrator saying that Eutychus was actually dead or that those who saw Paul picking him up thought he was dead? It seems 'Luke's intent is to tell of a miraculous effect produced by Paul' (Fitzmyer, *The Acts of the Apostles*, 669).

13 For a comparison between the two speeches, see Jerome Neyrey, *The Passion According to Luke. A Redaction Study of Luke's Soteriology* (New York: Paulist Press, 1985), 43-46.

14 'The speech has overtones of Paul's own preaching. Many are the allusions in it to ideas that one finds in his letters. In fact, it is the Pauline speech in Acts with the greatest number of such echoes... The echoes of Pauline teaching in the speech are not an indication, however, that Luke had read any of Paul's letters. He shows here at least that he was not wholly unfamiliar with Pauline phraseology' (Fitzmyer, *The Acts of the Apostles*, 675).

15 'Acts of the Apostles' in *The New Jerome Biblical Commentary*, 758.

16 *Redemptoris Missio* (1990), nos 37-38.

CHAPTER 8

WITNESS IN JERUSALEM
(ACTS 21:17–23:35)

Overview

We have journeyed with Paul as he bade farewell to the Christian communities in the Aegean region and, in fidelity to God's plan, moved in the direction of Jerusalem. Paul's 'passion' is about to begin. Jesus in Paul relives his passion. For the remainder of the Book of Acts we hear the story of Paul, the prisoner in Jerusalem, Caesarea and finally in Rome. Formal speeches take up approximately one third of Acts 21:17–28:31. If we add the dialogue material, then in almost half of what remains in Luke's story we have someone speaking! In our present chapter we focus on Paul's imprisonment and trials in Jerusalem, and in the following chapter we consider Paul's imprisonment and trials in Caesarea. Our final chapter deals with the climax of Luke's story – Paul's journey to Rome and his witness to Jesus at the centre of the known world.

Before considering what happens to Paul in Jerusalem and Caesarea (Acts 21:17–26:32), it may be helpful to outline Luke's main emphases in relating the story of Paul's passion. *Firstly*, Luke is conscious that prophecies made earlier in his story are now being fulfilled. Jesus told his disciples that they will be arrested, handed over to synagogues and prisons, and brought before kings and governors (Lk 21:12). In speaking to Ananias, Jesus said that Paul will suffer much in fulfilling his role as the chosen vessel to carry the name of Jesus to Gentiles and the people of Israel (Acts 9:15-16). The prophet

Agabus foretold that Paul would be bound and handed over to the Gentiles (Acts 21:11).

Secondly, the parallelism between Jesus and Paul continues to be strongly accentuated by Luke. Paul, like Jesus, appears before the Jewish Sanhedrin, Roman governors and a Herodian prince. There are many similarities between Lk 23:1-25 (appearance of Jesus before Pilate and Herod Antipas) and Acts 25-26 (appearance of Paul before Festus and Herod Agrippa II). As in Jesus' case (see Lk 23:4, 14-15, 22), Paul's innocence is declared three times by Roman authorities (Acts 23:29; 25:25; 26:31-32) and once by a Herodian prince (Acts 26:31-32).

Thirdly, while Jesus spoke very little during his passion, Paul does not remain silent. We have three major defence speeches in Acts 22-26 (in the Temple in 22:3-21; before Felix in 24:10-21; before Festus and Herod Agrippa in 26:2-23). However, Paul is not just defending himself against the charges brought against him. More importantly, for him the trials are opportunities for bearing witness (as Jesus had predicted in Lk 21:13). We hear Paul switching the focus from the charges presented by his accusers to what he considers to be the real reason why he is on trial, that is, his belief that in the resurrection of Jesus the hopes of Israel have been fulfilled (see Acts 23:6 [before the Sanhedrin]; 24:21 [before Felix]; 26:6-8, 22-23 [before Festus and Agrippa]).

Fourthly, in these chapters, Luke is focusing on Paul's identity and mission (see the tribune's inquiry in Acts 21:33 about *who* Paul is and *what* he had done). With regard to his identity, Paul is a faithful Israelite, rooted in the traditions, hopes and promises of Israel which are fulfilled in Jesus. With regard to his mission, Paul has been sent by the risen Christ to all, including the Gentiles. Paul's Damascus experience is recounted twice more (Acts 22:6-16 and 26:12-18) with the emphasis going on the call, rather than the conversion, aspect of that experience. In Acts 22:17-21, we hear of a vision of the Lord to Paul in the Temple (heart of Judaism), when the Lord sends him to the Gentiles. In Acts 23:11, the

Lord encourages Paul during a night vision, saying he must also bear witness in Rome, as he did in Jerusalem. Jesus' mission to be 'a light for revelation to the Gentiles and for glory to your people Israel' (Lk 2:32) is finding fulfilment in Paul's mission (see especially Acts 26:23). *Finally*, Luke does not portray Paul as a helpless victim during his confinement and trials, but as one who keeps the initiative and takes positive steps to respond to God's plan for him (see Acts 21:39; 22:25; 23:17; 25:10-12).

Paul's Reception by the Jerusalem Church (Acts 21:17-26)

We have seen that Paul went up to Jerusalem with his travelling companions and also some disciples from Caesarea (Acts 21:15-16). The warm welcome by the Jerusalem community (Acts 21:17) reminds us of the welcome Paul and Barnabas received when they attended the Council of Jerusalem (Acts 15:4). The next day the party went to visit James and the elders (Acts 21:18). James was the one who played a prominent role at the meeting in Acts 15 and at this time (approx. AD 58) he may well have been the voice of moderation amid rising Jewish fundamentalism. The purpose of the visit in Luke's mind is to deliver a report on what *God* has been doing among the Gentiles through the mission of Paul (Acts 21:19; compare 14:27; 15:3-4; 15:12). We are reminded of Peter's report to the Jerusalem community after the Cornelius episode (Acts 11:1-18). The initial response is one of praise (Acts 21:20a) – a typical Lukan response to the visitation of God (see Lk 2:20; 5:25-26; 7:16; 13:13; 17:15; 18:43; 23:47; Acts 4:21; 11:18).[1]

From their side, the leaders of the Jerusalem community report to Paul that 'thousands' of Jews have become believers (Acts 21:20b). They go on to speak of Jewish Christians, zealous for the law, who are concerned about reports of Paul teaching the Jews living among the Gentiles to disregard the law of Moses and Jewish customs, and not to have their children circumcised (Acts 21:20b-21). These charges are similar to the ones made against Stephen (Acts 6:13-14) and it is ironic that Paul was probably among those who made such charges at that time. The reader of Luke's narrative knows that the charges now made against Paul are totally unfounded. Paul has gone out of his way to observe Jewish customs and practices (see Acts 16:3; 18:18; 20:6, 16). For him, circumcision is a practice which expresses *Jewish* cultural identity and is appropriate for the *Jewish* expression of Christian faith, but it is not to be imposed on Gentiles as a necessity for salvation. The leaders have a suggestion to avoid tension and trouble from the wing of their community which was concerned about Paul's missionary approach (Acts 21:22-24). They ask Paul to join four men who are under a Nazirite vow (Num 6:1-21; see Acts 18:18), to go through a rite of purification with them, and to pay for their expenses at that time, which would include the expenses of the animal sacrifices and other offerings (see Num 6:14-15).

This public display of Jewish piety would be a clear sign that Paul is a devout *Jewish* Christian and that the charges against him are false. After making the request to Paul, the leaders immediately mention the letter of the Jerusalem Council concerning what is required of Gentile Christians living in mixed communities of Jews and Gentiles (Acts 21:25; see 15:20, 29).[2] Perhaps Luke's main reason for repeating the Jerusalem decree here is to remind the reader that what is being asked of Paul by the leaders in Acts 21 is not to be misunderstood in any way as a compromise or retreat from what has already been decided with regard to Gentiles who want to become Christians (compare the reference to the Council decree in Acts 16:4 after Timothy had been circumcised). Paul begins the purification rites with the four men and enters the Temple to make arrangements for the sacrifice concluding the period of the men's vow (Acts 21:26). Luke now has Paul in the Temple area where he will be arrested and where he will address the people. In a sense, this parallels Jesus' entry into the Temple after his journey to Jerusalem and his teaching there.

Paul's Arrest in the Temple (Acts 21:27-39)

Trouble erupts near the end of the seven-day period of purification (Acts 21:27). Jews from Asia (Ephesus area) see Paul in the Temple and stir up the crowd against him. He is charged with *teaching* everyone everywhere against the Israelite people, the law and the Temple (see Acts 21:21). These charges parallel the charges against Stephen in Acts 6:13.[3] He is also accused of *acting* against the law by bringing a Gentile into the Temple area forbidden to Gentiles (Acts 21:28). So Paul's accusers see his mission as an anti-Jewish movement, which threatens the defining characteristics of Judaism. Luke makes it quite clear that these accusers unjustly jumped to conclusions because they saw Paul in the streets with Trophimus the Ephesian (Acts 21:29; see 20:4). There is archaeological evidence of the inscription in the Temple which warns Gentiles from entering the inner Temple under penalty of death. The riot scene in Jerusalem (Acts 21:30-36) is similar to the earlier riot in Ephesus (Acts 19:28-30) – compare, for instance, 21:30 with 19:29; 21:34 with 19:32. The involvement of 'all the city' (Acts 21:30) is probably an exaggeration. Paul is seized, dragged outside the (inner) Temple and the gates are shut (probably by the Temple police to contain the riot outside). There may be some symbolism in shutting the doors on Paul – he is excluded from the cultic life of Judaism. Perhaps we are also meant to remember Jesus' crucifixion outside the wall and Stephen's stoning outside the city.

The mob was about to lynch Paul when he is rescued by the Roman tribune and soldiers (Acts 21:31-33). The Roman garrison was stationed in the Fortress Antonia at the northwest corner of the Temple area. The fortress overlooked the Temple and was connected to the Temple area (courtyard of the Gentiles) by two flights of stairs. A Roman cohort was made up of 1,000 soldiers (760 infantry and 240 cavalry). Paul is arrested and bound with two chains (Acts 21:33). It seems the Romans thought Paul was some kind of revolutionary leading an uprising in the Temple (see Acts

21:38). In Luke's mind, the binding of Paul fulfils the prophecy of Agabus (Acts 21:11), though not in exact detail, and the 'two' chains recall the experience of Peter (Acts 12:6). For the rest of Luke's story, Paul is a prisoner. The tribune wants to know *who* Paul is and *what* he has done (Acts 21:33). This raises the question of Paul's *identity* and *mission*, which he will answer in his Temple discourse (Acts 22:1-21). The murderous rage and violence of the mob is so great that the tribune gives orders that Paul be brought into the barracks in the Fortress Antonia (Acts 21:34). Paul has to be carried by the soldiers perhaps to shield him (Acts 21:25). The shout of the crowd is the shout that was directed against Jesus during his passion: 'Away with him ' (Acts 21:36; see Lk 23:18; Acts 22:22).

Paul takes the initiative and speaks to the tribune when he was about to be brought into the barracks (Acts 21:37). Seemingly Paul spoke in Greek which surprised the tribune and led him to conclude that Paul was not the Egyptian revolutionary the tribune supposed him to be (Acts 21:38). The Jewish historian Josephus tells us of an Egyptian charlatan who claimed to be a prophet during this period and led some 30,000 men to the Mount of Olives on the promise that the walls of Jerusalem would fall at his command. The Romans killed or captured most of his followers, though he escaped. This may be the revolutionary Luke has in mind, though the number of followers (4,000) is smaller and there is no mention of the Mount of Olives. In Palestine at that time resistance groups were springing up. Paul denies he is an Egyptian by saying that he is a Jew and a citizen of Tarsus (Acts 21:39). The question of Paul's identity and mission (who he is and what he is about) is already raised in this conversation between Paul and the tribune in the context of suspicion that he is a dangerous revolutionary. It will be taken up again in the second conversation between them after Paul has delivered his Temple speech (see Acts 21:24-29). At this point Paul is more interested in clarifying his identity and mission at a deeper level in speaking to his fellow Jews, rather than clarifying further his identity as a Roman citizen.

Paul's Speech in the Temple (Acts 21:40–22:29)
Having received permission from the tribune to address the crowd, Paul stood on the steps (obviously not rendered incapacitated by the beating) and waved his hand for silence like an ancient orator. A great hush descends on the crowd and they become quieter still when he begins to address them in Hebrew (Aramaic) (Acts 21:40; 22:2). Luke may have in mind a parallel between Paul and Peter who addressed the Jerusalem people in the Temple in Acts 3:12-26.

Paul calls his speech a 'defence' (*apologia*) in Acts 22:1 (the cognate verb *apologeomai*, 'to defend oneself,' is found in Acts 24:10; 25:8; 26:1-2, 24).[4] This is the first defence speech in a series that will dominate the rest of Acts (see also Acts 24:10-21; 26:2-23). As mentioned above, these speeches are not just legal defences. They are opportunities to bear witness to the risen Jesus, and in that respect they are not completely different from the missionary discourses in the early part of Acts. Dillon points out that Paul in this speech is not answering the charge against him in Acts 21:28-29. Luke, he says, is more concerned to augment 'the reader's understanding of Paul's vocation, building on the account in 9:1-19 ... Luke supplies his own perspective to the Damascus event in this speech and chap. 26, steadily remodelling the conversion story as a vocation story.'[5] In this defence speech the question of Paul's identity and mission is being answered at a deep level. Paul's identity as a faithful Jew is underscored and his mission to the Gentiles is rooted, we shall see, in his experience of the risen Lord.

In the opening part of his speech (Acts 22:1, 3-5) Paul is introducing himself and is stressing what he shares with his audience in the hope of bonding with them and winning them over (this aspect of a speech is often called the *captatio benevolentiae* which means 'winning of goodwill'). He speaks in the everyday language of his audience and addresses them as 'brothers and fathers' (family members) – compare the opening of Stephen's speech in Acts 7:2. Referring to his birth, early upbringing and education, he stresses the fact that he *is* (and remains) a loyal Jew (Acts 22:3). The implication is that he sees no contradiction between being a Jew and being a follower of Jesus. Speaking to the inhabitants of Jerusalem, Paul is saying something like this: 'Though I was born in Tarsus, I'm not just a "blow-in"; I was brought up in this city.' The phrase 'at the feet of Gamaliel' should probably go with 'educated strictly according to our ancestral law', rather than with 'brought up in this city' (as in NRSV). Gamaliel was one of the most prominent and respected rabbis of his day (see Acts 5:34). Note Paul's use of *our* (Acts 22:3) to stress his relationship with his audience.

He also talks of 'being zealous for God, just as all of you are today' – again stressing his solidarity with the Jewish people. He goes on to say that his zeal for God found expression in his persecution (even to the point of death!) of the followers of Jesus (Acts 22:4-5; see Acts 8:3; 9:1-2). This not only builds up the picture of Paul the committed Jew, but also resonates with the state of mind of the audience which at that time wants to persecute Paul, a follower of Jesus, because of their zeal for the law. The appeal to witnesses in Acts 22:5 is part of the genre of defence speeches. What Paul says about his life before his conversion fits in with what we know about Paul from Rm 10:2; 1 Cor 15:9; Gal 1:13-14; Phil 3:6.

In Acts 22:6-16 we get the second account in Acts of Paul's experience on the road to Damascus, this time on the lips of Paul. The first account is in Acts 9:3-19 and the third account, also on the lips of Paul in a defence speech, is found in Acts 26:12-18. The fact that Luke gives the story of Paul's conversion/vocation experience three times is in itself an indication of its great importance for Luke. Note the differences between the account in Acts 9 and our present account in Acts 22. To some extent, these differences are due to a writer's desire to give a little variety and to the fact that the story is now being told from the perspective of the one who had the experience. We are now told that the event happened at noon (Acts 22:6; see 26:13). 'Jesus the Nazorean' (Acts 22:8) has a more Jewish flavour than just plain 'Jesus' (Acts 9:6). Notice how Ananias' Jewish pedigree is also stressed in Acts 22:12 (in Acts 9:10 he is simply called a 'disciple'). Paul is doing all he can to highlight the Jewish dimension in all that has happened to him.[6] Acts 22:9 is the opposite of what is said in the first version (Acts 9:7). The main point is that, while all the travelling companions had some experience, there was something personal and unique about Paul's experience. Paul speaks of the effect of the 'brightness' (*doxa*) of the light on him (Acts 22:11). *Doxa* ('glory') is often used in the Bible as a technical term for God's effective presence in the world (see, for instance, Lk 2:9, 14, 32; 9:31-32). In 2 Cor 4:6, where Paul may well be thinking of his conversion experience, 'glory' and 'light' also appear together. The blindness and healing dimension (Acts 22:11, 13) are not as pronounced here as in Acts 9:8-9, 17-19.

As mentioned above, the account in Acts 9 is mainly a conversion story, while the two other accounts emphasise progressively the vocation dimension of the experience. In comparison with Acts 9, Jesus says more to Paul on the road, adding that he will be told in Damascus 'everything that has been assigned' to him to do (Acts 22:10), and Ananias indicates to him what his vocation is to be (Acts 22:14-15; contrast Acts 9:17 where Ananias says nothing to Paul about his future mission, though he had already been told about it in Acts 9:15-16). The experience of Paul and the commission delivered by Ananias (Acts 22:14-15) are couched in Jewish terms: 'God of our fathers' (see Acts 3:13; 5:30; 7:32; 13:23); 'Righteous One' (see Lk 23:47; Acts 3:14; 7:52). Paul has been chosen to experience the risen Jesus and to be his witness to 'all the world,' testifying to what he has 'seen and heard'. Like the apostles (Acts 1:8, 22; 2:32; 3:15; 5:32; 10:39; 13:31), Paul is a witness to the resurrection. He is stressing the universal dimension of his commission before an audience which is objecting to his presence and work among the

Gentiles; the apostles in Acts 13:31 are said to be 'witnesses to the people (Israel)'. In his defence Paul is already bearing witness to what he has experienced. His experience of the risen Lord is the very foundation of his identity and mission. Acts 22:16 expands the simple statement in Acts 9:18 that Paul was baptised – here his baptism is seen as a cleansing from sin (see Acts 2:38) as he calls on the Lord's name (see Acts 2:21). There is no mention of the Spirit (see Acts 9:17). 'Why do you delay' may be meant to highlight that the initiative was the Lord's, not Paul's.

Paul diplomatically says nothing about his conflicts with the Jews in Damascus and Jerusalem after his experience of the risen Lord (see Acts 9:19-30). Instead he tells us about his vision in the Temple at the heart of Judaism (Acts 22:17-21). We hear of this vision for the first time. As in the experience on the road to Damascus, Paul experiences the risen Lord and is commissioned by him to universal mission. Johnson says that Luke achieves four things by this additional vision: (a) he shows Paul's long standing devotion to the ethos of Judaism; (b) he highlights Paul's piety and recognition of the Temple as a place of prayer; (c) he parallels Paul's experience and the experience of Peter who also had a vision in connection with the Gentile mission (see Acts 10:11; 11:5); (d) he presents Paul as a prophetic figure – Isaiah also had a vision in the Temple during which he was commissioned by God (see Is 6:1-10).[7]

When Jesus tells Paul to leave Jerusalem because of the Jewish refusal to accept his message (Acts 22:17), Paul hesitates and objects. What Paul seems to be saying in Acts 22:19-20 is something like this: 'Surely they will not continue to refuse to listen to one they know to have been an ardent persecutor of Christians, even to the extent of wholeheartedly approving of the death of Stephen; surely they will realise that something very significant must have happened to Saul to change him so radically.' But the Lord gives the command to Paul to go to the Gentiles (Acts 22:21; in Acts 9:30 it was the 'brothers' who sent Paul out of

Jerusalem). Paul is emphasising for his Jewish audience that he went to the Gentiles, not by personal choice, but in obedience to the Lord's will. At this stage we have become very familiar with the pattern in Acts of rejection by Jews followed by a turning to the Gentiles. The commission of Paul in Acts 22:21 should be taken in the sense of an extension, rather than a restriction, of his mission to the Gentiles, a universal mission which directed him to Jews *and* Gentiles.

Paul's speech ends abruptly in Acts 22:22 with the silent crowd once again becoming an angry mob. The shout of Acts 21:36 is repeated and reinforced with the call for Paul's death. What incites them is the mention of an extension of God's blessings to the hated Gentiles. One is immediately reminded of the rejection of Jesus in his hometown of Nazareth when he spoke of his mission beyond Israel (Lk 4:24-29). The crowd's actions in Acts 22:23 symbolise their rejection of Paul and complete disassociation from him (see Acts 14:14; 13:51; 18:6). This also reminds us of the strong reaction to Stephen when he had spoken of his vision of the risen Lord standing at the right hand of God (Acts 7:57).

The tribune, still not knowing who Paul is and what he is about, directs that he be brought inside the barracks and information extracted from him by torture, a common practice (Acts 22:24). The question of Paul's identity and mission is once more being explored in a Roman context. At the last moment Paul reveals his Roman citizenship and points out that his torture is illegal (Acts 22:25; see Acts 16:19-39).[8] The centurion reports this to the tribune (Acts 22:26) who questions Paul directly about his citizenship (Acts 22:27). The contrast between one who had to buy his citizenship (perhaps by bribery) and one who was born a citizen serves to underline the status of Paul (Acts 22:28). Immediately those who were about to torture him draw back in respect and the tribune himself is fearful because he has mistreated a Roman citizen in having him bound (Acts 22:29). The initiative has passed to Paul and he is the one who is influencing what is happening. Paul's emphasis on his citizenship of Tarsus (Acts 21:39) and Rome (Acts 22:25) reaches its climax in Acts 25:10 when Paul appeals to Caesar. Paul is a member of the Jewish and Greco-Roman worlds to which he is sent.

Paul before the Sanhedrin (Acts 22:30–23:11)

In his ongoing attempt to find out what Paul was being accused of by the Jews, the tribune brings Paul before the Jewish Sanhedrin (Acts 22:30).[9] What is reported in Acts 22:30–23:10 is hardly a trial. There are no charges brought against Paul and he starts speaking immediately. For Luke, Paul is reliving the experience of those before him who witnessed before the Sanhedrin – see Lk 22:63-71 (Jesus); Acts 4:5-22 (Peter and John); Acts 5:26-40 (the apostles); Acts 6:12-7, 60 (Stephen). This scene also gives Luke the opportunity to explore more deeply the reason for the strong reaction to Paul on the part of the Jewish leaders. It is becoming increasingly clear that the basic reason for his rejection and persecution by his Jewish accusers is his proclamation that Jesus is risen and alive and is the one through whom God's salvation is now experienced.

The scene before the Sanhedrin falls into two parts of equal length, each part beginning with a statement of Paul (Acts 23:1-5 and Acts 23:6-10). The initiative rests with Paul and others can only react to him with anger and frustration. Addressing the Sanhedrin as 'brothers', Paul testifies to a 'clear conscience before God' up to this day (Acts 23:1). 'Conscience' (*suneidēsis*) is a very Pauline word (see Rm 2:15; 9:1; 13:5; 1 Cor 8:7, 10, 12; 10:25, 27, 28, 29; 2 Cor 1:12; 4:2; 5:11). His statement amounts to a rejection of any charges against him and a request for recognition of his sincerity and uprightness. The high priest unexpectedly orders that Paul be struck on the mouth (Acts 23:2). The motivation for this is not clear and Luke may have in mind the striking of Jesus when he stood before the Sanhedrin (a detail which Luke omits in his Gospel; see Jn 18:22-23). The high priest Ananias held office from AD 47 till AD 58/59 and was assassinated as a Roman sympathiser by Jewish guerrillas in AD 66. Luke may have his unhappy end in mind with Paul's remark that God will strike the high priest (Acts 23:3).

Paul points out in strong terms that those who are accusing him of having no regard for the law are breaking the law themselves (see Lev 19:15 which forbids judges rendering unjust judgement). This retort is similar to Stephen's in Acts 7:53. 'Whitewashed wall' reminds us that Jesus called the Pharisees 'whitewashed tombs,' that is, hypocrites (see Mt 23:27). When Paul was taken to task by the bystanders for insulting the high priest (Acts 23:4-5; see Jn 18:22-23), he answers that he did not know that the man was the high priest. It is almost unbelievable that Paul would not recognise the high priest. Some suggest that Paul had poor eyesight or that he was unfamiliar with the high priest due to his long absence from Jerusalem. So they understand Paul's words as an apology for his mistake. But it may be better to see here further criticism of the high priest: 'I did not think that a man who acts in such a way could possibly be a high priest.' Paul quotes Ex 22:27 to show that he knows the law and desires to live by it.

Paul, noticing that some in the Sanhedrin are Sadducees and others Pharisees, made a statement which divided the assembly and got them arguing with one another, rather than accusing him (Acts 23:6). However, in Acts 23:6-10 Luke's main interest in not to tell us about Paul's clever ploy, but to reveal the real reason why Paul is being rejected and accused with such vehemence. Here the focus shifts from accusations about general disregard for the Mosaic law and cherished Jewish practices to the fact that Paul is preaching 'the hope of the resurrection of the dead' (Acts 23:6). In the subsequent defence speeches, Paul comes back to this point with greater insistence (see Acts 24:15, 21; 26:6-8, 23; 28:20). The general resurrection of the dead is in view in Acts 23:6, but, in developing this theme in his speeches, Paul eventually puts the focus on Jesus as 'the first to rise from the dead' (see Acts 26:23). Paul says he is a true Pharisee; there is continuity in what he believed as a Pharisee and what he now believes and proclaims as a Christian. As Luke tells us in Acts 23:8, the Pharisees acknowledged the possibility of resurrection in the future. They accepted the hope of resurrection which developed in late Judaism (see, for instance, Dn 12:2-3; 2 Mac 7:9, 11, 14). The Sadducees, on the other hand, denied that there will be a resurrection and also disagreed with the Pharisees on the question of angels and spirits. The Sadducees appear only once in Luke's Gospel in a context of controversy with Jesus over the resurrection of the dead (Lk 20:27-38). In Acts 4:1-2 and 5:17 we have heard them resisting the apostles who proclaimed the resurrection in Jesus. The Sadducees were more conservative than the Pharisees in theology, accepting only the written Torah and rejecting a living tradition. The Pharisees' statement that they find nothing wrong with Paul (Acts 23:9) should probably be understood in the context of a desire to score points in the theological argument with the Sadducees, rather than as an acceptance of Paul and his message. Their question ('What if a spirit or an angel has spoken to him?') seems more an expression of theoretical possibility than a judgement on what actually happened to Paul on the road to Damascus. The 'dignified' members of the Sanhedrin turn into a mob (not unlike the mob in the Temple) shouting and fighting among themselves, with Paul caught in the crossfire. The tribune once more has to rescue Paul from Jews who were in danger of killing him (Acts 23:10).

In Acts 23:11 we have another appearance of the risen Lord to Paul in a vision (see Acts 9:4; 16:9; 18:9-10; 22:17-21). This is Luke's way of reminding us that Paul's destiny is not determined by unruly forces and the decisions of Jews or Romans in his regard. In Paul's life, things are working out according to God's plan and initiative. Notice the 'must' (*dei*) in Acts 23:11, always a sign that God's plan is in view (see also Acts 19:21; 27:24). The one who has witnessed in Jerusalem, the centre of Judaism, will also witness in Rome, the centre of the Gentile world. The fact that Paul is now in the custody of the Romans is in fact the working out of God's plan in his regard. Paul's transfer to Caesarea, the seat of Roman power in Palestine, will be a step closer to his God-given destiny.

Paul's Transfer to Caesarea (Acts 23:12-35)

The reader knows from Acts 23:11 that Paul's transfer to Caesarea (96 kilometres from Jerusalem) is part of the working out of God's plan for him. At the human level the transfer is due to a combination of a plot on the part of Jewish fanatics (with the approval of the authorities) to assassinate Paul and a desire on the part of the Roman tribune to hand over a potentially troublesome case to higher authorities. This is quite a dramatic section, where we see Luke's gifts as a storyteller.

More than forty Jews vowed they would neither eat nor drink until they had done away with Paul (Acts 23:12-13, 14, 21). This fits in with the fanatical elements within Judaism at this time. The growing resistance to Paul has now hardened into a plot to kill him. They go to the chief priests and the elders (Pharisees not mentioned!) to tell them about their oath and ask their assistance in getting Paul into a vulnerable position (Acts 23:14-15). One is reminded of Judas going to the religious leaders to discuss with them the matter of doing away with Jesus (Lk 22:3-6). The plan is to have Paul brought again to the Sanhedrin on the pretext of examining his case more closely and to assassinate him on the way. It is highly unlikely that the tribute would be willing to grant such a request after what happened the previous day. Paul's nephew hears of the plot and informs his uncle (Acts 23:16). We notice that the nephew has easy access to Paul, which may not have been unusual for relatives and close friends. In Acts 23:17-18 we have the unusual situation of Paul the prisoner calling the centurion and sending him on an errand to the tribune! Is this another instance of the initiative remaining with Paul? The tribune receives Paul's nephew with kindness and openness, taking him aside by the hand (Acts 23:19). The behaviour of the Romans is better in every respect than that of the Jewish leadership. The nephew repeats what he knows to the tribune and tells him not to grant the Jews their request to have Paul brought out again (Acts 23:20-21). The tribune is being told what he must not do! He dismisses the young man and orders him to keep quiet, because, as we will see from what follows, the tribune has now decided to get Paul out of the dangerous situation in Jerusalem and transfer him to the custody of the Roman governor in Caesarea.

The preparations the tribune made for Paul's escape under cover of darkness (9 p.m.) seem excessive (Acts 23:23-24). The four hundred and seventy soldiers amount to almost half the entire garrison in Jerusalem! This may be to highlight the importance of Paul (the one who will witness to the Good News in Rome) or the special care given to Paul by the empire. In Acts 23:25-30 we have the letter of the tribune (Claudius Lysias) to the governor in Caesarea (Antonius Felix, who was governor from AD 52 to AD 60). It follows the standard Hellenistic pattern for letters (and is most probably a Lukan composition addressed to his readers). It summarises succinctly what has transpired to date. But notice how Lysias tells the story in such a way that he will appear in a good light! He passes over the fact that he ordered Paul to be flogged and he says that he immediately intervened and rescued Paul from the Jews when he discovered that he was a Roman citizen! Lysias' opinion about Paul (Acts 23:29) coincides with that of Gallio in Acts 18:15 – the whole matter is about internal disputes on Jewish religious matters, not a criminal matter deserving death (see also Acts 25:19; 26:3). The innocence of Paul is a major theme in his 'passion,' as it was during the passion of Jesus (see Acts 25:18; 26:31-32; Lk 23:4, 12, 22). The tribune says he is sending Paul to Caesarea for his own safety and to ensure that due process is followed. Paul's accusers are to be informed (obviously when Paul is safely out of reach) that they can go to Caesarea to pursue their case against Paul in a proper way (Acts 23:30).

Acts 23:31-35 tell us how the soldiers carried out Lysias' orders and delivered Paul and the letter safely to Felix in Caesarea. They travelled via Antipatris (60 kilometres from Jerusalem), where the foot soldiers turned back to Jerusalem (perhaps because the party was far enough away from the danger in Jerusalem and the remainder of the journey would be quicker without them). Felix acted according to proper legal procedure by establishing where Paul came from and deciding that he would hear the case when Paul's accusers arrived from Jerusalem. Though Tarsus was not in the province governed by Felix, he was within his rights to hear Paul's case. A governor could hear a case of one who came from a distant province. We are reminded of Pilate's question in Lk 23:6-7 with regard to the matter of legal jurisdiction in Jesus' trial.

Reflection on Acts 21:17–23:35

One cannot read about Paul's imprisonment and trials without thinking of the many people today who are falsely accused and detained in prison for a long time without justice. I think in particular of Asia Bibi, an illiterate Christian woman in Pakistan who in 2009 was falsely accused of blasphemy and detained for over nine years during a prolonged legal process. In some respects her case was similar to that of Paul. Her family was the only Christian family in a small village. She worked as a farmhand and had experienced pressure from some Muslim women to convert to Islam which she resisted. When she drank from a cup that Muslims used, an argument ensued and she was reported to the local religious authorities for having insulted the prophet Mohammed. She was arrested for violating the country's strict blasphemy laws and imprisoned for one year without being formally charged. In 2010 she was sentenced to death by a local court. The Lahore High Court upheld the death sentence four years later. The case was appealed to the Pakistan Supreme Court which took another four years to hear the case and give its verdict. Asia Bibi was acquitted of the blasphemy charges in late 2018. She was not released because a petition was immediately lodged for a review of the Supreme Court's verdict. Eventually, after another six months, she was allowed to leave the country.

So, like Paul, Asia Bibi was falsely accused of speaking against a nation's religion and dragged from court to court over an extended period. She too was severely beaten by a mob before she was arrested. She too had to listen to shouts calling for her death. She too faced threats of being assassinated. She too stood before judges who were unwilling to acquit her because they wanted to protect themselves and avoid the reaction of extremists. But, while many remained silent, some courageous people in Pakistan supported her and spoke out against the country's unjust blasphemy laws, among them Salmaan Taseer (the Muslim Governor of the Punjab Province) and Shahbaz Bhatti (the only Christian minster in Pakistan's government at that time). Both of these were assassinated by extremists in 2011. For four years Muslim fundamentalists succeeded in blocking the hearing of Asia Bibi's appeal in the Supreme Court. On eventually acquitting her, the Muslim judges pointed out that the charges against her had been fabricated and she had been persecuted because of her belief in Jesus Christ. They also said that the Muslim faith requires people to respect Jesus Christ as a prophet and the Bible as a holy book. Paul likewise was persecuted for his faith in Jesus and during his trial he tried to point out to his accusers that acceptance of Jesus was very much in line with their Jewish religious tradition. Along with Paul, Asia Bibi relived the passion of Jesus Christ.

In the synagogue in Nazareth, Jesus said that the Spirit of God has sent him to proclaim release to captives and to let the oppressed go free (Lk 4:18). Being on mission today in the way of Jesus means working tirelessly for the release of those held in bondage or oppressed in any way. During his trials Paul spoke repeatedly of the hope of resurrection, of a God who wants people to experience real life. While the full experience of that life comes in the future, the resurrection of Jesus means that it has already broken into our world and God wants all to begin experiencing it in the present. When people are deprived of their rights and dignity as human beings or are oppressed in any way, they are denied the life that God wishes for all.[10] Christians must be to the fore in promoting the basic human rights of all, regardless of their race, culture, religion, social status or gender. We must join in coalitions with adherents of other religions and all people of goodwill to promote universal justice. The way the Muslim Salmaan Taseer and the Christian Shahbaz Bhatti courageously stood together and paid the ultimate price in supporting Asia Bibi, and speaking out against unjust blasphemy laws is a powerful inspiration for such cooperation. And it is a magnificent example of Muslim-Christian dialogue in action.

And in our work for justice we cannot overlook the exploited earth. In his letter to the Romans, St Paul himself spoke of creation subjected to futility and in bondage to decay, longing eagerly for release and a share in the salvation of the children of God (Rm 8:18-23). For too long God's creation has been exploited by human greed, kept in bondage, abused in many ways and denied its God-given rights. We saw how Paul in his trials cried out to remind his fellow Jews of the close bond between them and those who follow Jesus Christ. Similarly, creation cries out to remind us of its indispensable bond with us in the marvellous web of life designed by God. Pope Francis reminds us of our relationship with all creation and of the vital link between social and ecological justice:

> Peace, justice and the preservation of creation are three absolutely interconnected themes, which cannot be separated and treated individually without once again falling into reductionism. Everything is related, and we human beings are united as brothers and sisters on a wonderful pilgrimage, woven together by the love God

has for each of his creatures and which also unites us in fond affection with brother sun, sister moon, brother river and mother earth.[11]

NOTES

[1] Most commentators mention the surprising fact that Paul here says nothing to James and the elders about the collection which he had taken up among the predominantly Gentile churches for the Jerusalem church (see 1 Cor 16:1-4; 2 Cor 8-9; Rm 15:22-32), though Luke seems to know of the collection (see Acts 24:17; see also 21:24; 24:26). From Rm 15:31 we pick up Paul's concern that the collection might not be accepted by the Jerusalem church. What could have given rise to such a concern? One suggestion is that Jewish nationalism was growing stronger in Jerusalem at that time and Jewish Christians did not want to give any impression that they were not thoroughly Jewish. Accepting financial help from Gentile churches by the hand of a Jew, who was said to de-emphasise Jewish customs and way of life, may well give rise to suspicions about the loyalty of Jewish Christians to the nation. Luke, who likes to emphasise unity and harmony in the Christian community, may well have decided to say as little as possible about such tensions. One wonders why Luke did not tell us of any Christian support for Paul during his imprisonment in Jerusalem, the type of support Peter experienced when he was in prison there (Acts 12:5, 12). On this matter see Johnson, *The Acts of the Apostles*, 377-379.

[2] One gets the impression that Paul is being told about the letter for the first time here, which lends weight to the view that Paul was not present at the Jerusalem meeting which decided this and had left Antioch when the delegates came from Jerusalem to promulgate it. But one could ask did Paul not hear about the decree during his short visit to Jerusalem in Acts 18:22. Clarifying points of historical accuracy is not Luke's main concern.

[3] For other parallels with the Stephen episode, see Tannehill, *The Narrative Unity of Luke-Acts*, vol. 2, 273.

[4] A defence speech is designed to persuade its audience of the innocence of the one accused. Johnson (*The Acts of the Apostles*, 392-393) says Luke is familiar with the formal elements of the defence speech in Hellenistic oratory: *exordium* in which the speaker introduces himself and bonds with his hearers; *narratio* which provides the speaker an opportunity to give his version of

the events at issue; *probatio* which outlines proofs and mentions witnesses on one's behalf; *refutatio* in which the speaker refutes the charges against him; *peroratio* which concludes the speech. Luke uses these conventions but is not constrained by them in his speeches, which are marked by spontaneity.

5 'Acts of the Apostles,' in *The New Jerome Biblical Commentary*, 760.

6 'The principal characters of Paul's narrative – himself, the Lord, Ananias – are all characterised in ways that emphasise their roots in the tradition that zealous Jews know and honour. In this way Paul attempts to speak persuasively to his Jewish audience, helping them to understand his mission as a fitting development within their own heritage' (Tannehill, *The Narrative Unity of Luke-Acts*, vol. 2, 279).

7 Johnson, *The Acts of the Apostles*, 390.

8 The Valerian Law (509 BC) and Porcian Laws (second century BC) exempted Roman citizens from degrading forms of punishment.

9 Many point out historical improbabilities here: that a Roman tribune would use a Jewish court to pursue his own investigations; that the tribune had the competence to convene a meeting of the Sanhedrin and set its agenda; that a Roman tribune would have been present at a meeting of the Sanhedrin; that Paul would be struck for simply saying that his conscience is clear; that Paul would curse the high priest publicly; that Paul would not recognise the high priest; that Paul could manipulate so easily the divisions within the Sanhedrin to his own advantage (See, for instance, Dillon, 'Acts of the Apostles,' in *The New Jerome Biblical Commentary*, 760). Some say that it is not historically improbable that the tribune, who was anxious to have a clearer idea of what is going on before he reported to his superior, had some kind of unofficial consultation with the Jewish leaders (see, for instance, Fitzmyer, *The Acts of the Apostles*, 715-716; Marshall, *Acts*, 360). As we have said, Luke's main interest in Acts is not to give exact historical information, but to present a theological message.

10 Emphasising the God-given dignity of every human person, Pope Francis calls for a penal justice system, which is not driven by a spirit of vindictive punishment, but by a desire for the healing and reintegration of wrongdoers into society. This entails the abolition of the death penalty in all its forms, the elimination of sentences which are disproportionate to the crimes committed, and the improvement of prison conditions (*Fratelli Tutti*, nos 263-270).

11 Pope Francis, *Laudato Si'*, no. 92.

CHAPTER 9

WITNESS IN CAESAREA
(ACTS 24:1–26:32)

At this stage you may be wondering why Luke is giving us such a lengthy account of Paul's trials before various authorities. Earlier, when considering the communities for which Luke wrote, we proposed that they were communities undergoing crises of identity, missionary motivation and faith. Many of Luke's original readers came from Gentile churches where Paul was the great hero and even the founding father. But these churches had a weak sense of identity. They did not feel firmly rooted in the history of God's dealings with Israel, nor even in the events of Jesus' life and the life of the early Church. Luke is writing to give them 'assurance' (*asphaleia*, see Lk 1:4) by stressing the continuity between their own faith experience and God's dealings with his people in the past. Paul and his mission represent a vital link in that chain of continuity. In relating Paul's trials in Jerusalem and Caesarea, Luke is at pains to portray Paul as one who insists on the continuity between Christian faith (in particular faith in the resurrection) and the faith of Israel. The resurrection of Jesus, the central event for Christian faith, is presented as the fulfilment of the promises and hopes of Israel. Furthermore, the strong parallelism between the passion of Jesus and the passion of Paul throughout Luke's account of the latter's trials is aimed at helping the communities to see that their faith experience, like Paul's, is rooted in the experience of Jesus Christ.

Secondly, by portraying Paul on trial as the bold and steadfast witness to Jesus, Luke is addressing the crisis of missionary motivation in the communities for which he wrote. Mission must continue even in unfavourable circumstances. In fact, in such circumstances of human weakness, the power at work in mission breaks through most strongly. Paul, the prisoner on trial, is the great missionary model who continues to bear witness to Jesus despite opposition and imprisonment. Thirdly, by showing how God's plan of salvation is unfolding in the adverse situation of Paul's trials and through events that threaten to bring God's plan to an end, Luke is reinforcing the wavering faith of communities which are tempted to think that God will not be with them in their tribulations.

Finally, we should also remember that at the time Luke was writing, Paul was probably still seen as a very controversial figure. Christians had to listen to Jews speaking about Paul as the main culprit in the propagation of the Christian 'heresy'. Perhaps even in Jewish Christian circles there were ambiguous feelings about Paul and his contribution. So, in this part of his narrative, Luke wants to stress the integrity of Paul by showing that his mission among the Gentiles was in response to the divine call and by having the Roman authorities, and even a Jewish King, state that Paul was innocent of the charges brought against him.[1]

Paul before Felix (Acts 24:1-27)

In relating the story of Paul's trial here, Luke is conscious that Paul is reliving the experience of Jesus in his trial (see Lk 22:66–23:25). In both cases there is a hearing before a Roman governor after a hearing before the Sanhedrin; in both cases Jewish spokesmen press a combination of religious and political charges (see Acts 24:5-6; Lk 23:2); in both cases the accusers fail to convince the governor of the validity of the charges (Acts 24:22; Lk 23:14).

Of all the appearances of Paul before the authorities, the appearance before Felix is the one that most looks like a trial. We have a lawyer, Tertullus, who on behalf of the Jewish accusers puts the case for the prosecution (Acts 24:2-8). This is followed by Paul's defence speech (Acts 24:10-21) which corresponds to the prosecution speech and is structured in the same way: *captatio benevolentiae*, the 'winning of goodwill' (v. 10 corresponds to vv. 2-4); rebuttal of charges (vv. 11-18 correspond to vv. 5-6); invitation to the governor to pursue the evidence (vv. 19-21 correspond to v. 8). In his defence, Paul skilfully answers what Tertullus has said and builds his own case.

The Jewish authorities brought along Tertullus, a professional attorney, to prosecute the case against Paul (Acts 24:1). His *captatio benevolentiae* (Acts 24:2-4) is long-winded and makes up half of what he says, which in itself is a sign of a very weak case. What Tertullus says about Felix is not true. Josephus, the Jewish historian, tells us that Felix was a bad administrator and during his time as governor (AD 52-60) there was quite a bit of unrest, with relations between Rome and the Jews deteriorating. In fact, the Jews complained to Rome about the way Felix was handling affairs. Tertullus presents three general charges against Paul in Acts 24:5: (i) he is a pest; (ii) he stirs up trouble among the Jews all over the Empire; (iii) he is the ringleader of the sect of the Nazarenes. 'Sect' (*hairesis*) has a pejorative sense here, though it was used by ancient authors in a neutral sense to refer to parties within Judaism.

These charges are aimed at presenting Paul as a dangerous person in the eyes of the Romans, particularly at a time when revolutionary groups were springing up among the Jews. Having praised Felix for the peace he provided (Acts 24:2), Tertullus is saying that Paul is a threat to that very peace. After these general charges, there is the specific religious charge of profaning the Temple (Acts 24:6). Tertullus gives an air of legality to the mob action against Paul: 'we arrested him.' Note that Tertullus does not bring forward any witnesses or cite any evidence to prove the charges, a fact that Paul will not be slow to point out (see Acts 24:13, 19). The brief prosecution speech ends on the confident and fawning remark that the governor himself on examining

Paul will be able to verify the charges (Acts 24:8). The Jewish accusers just support what Tertullus said without strengthening the case against Paul in any way (Acts 24:9). We are reminded of the accusing voices from the leaders and the crowd during the trial of Jesus (see Lk 23:10, 18, 21, 23).

Paul has no attorney to speak on his behalf, but Luke would not want us to forget Jesus' promise that he and the Holy Spirit would be at hand to support disciples on trial (see Lk 12:11-12; 21:12-15). Paul's *captatio benevolentiae* (Acts 24:10) is very brief and subdued in comparison with that of Tertullus. He simply appeals to Felix's long experience as a judge in Judea.[2] He then moves on to refute the charges brought against him (Acts 24:11-18). The reference to the twelve days since he came to Jerusalem (Acts 24:11) is probably meant to indicate a short time which could easily be investigated (or a time which is too short to organise a revolution). Paul also makes it clear that his purpose in coming to Jerusalem was not to cause disturbance but to worship as a pious Jew (Acts 24:11-12). The charge of being someone who causes disturbance cannot be proved (Acts 24:13). In Acts 24:14-15 Paul refutes the claim that Christianity is a 'sect' in the pejorative sense.[3] That is the name hostile outsiders use of it, but Paul (and the insiders) prefer to call it the 'Way' (see Acts 9:2; 16:17; 18:25-26; 19:9, 23; 22:4). The Christian faith is not a sectarian distortion. It is, rather, a legitimate, and indeed the authentic, form of Judaism – the fulfilment of what is contained in the law and the prophets. In Acts 24:15 Paul specifies the Christian belief and hope in the resurrection, the event which is the fulfilment of the hopes of Israel (see Dn 12:2).

Note that Paul speaks of a resurrection of the righteous and unrighteous (as in the text from Daniel). Josephus says that the Pharisees believed only in a resurrection for the righteous. Paul once again speaks of his clear conscience with regard to God and all the people (Acts 24:16; see 23:1). He returns in Acts 24:17-18 to his purpose for coming to Jerusalem. Behind Acts 24:17 may well be the memory of the collection taken up among the Gentile churches for the Jerusalem church, which Luke prefers not to highlight in his narrative (see 1 Cor 16:1-4; 2 Cor 8-9; Rm 15:25-32). It seems to be mentioned here to reinforce the impression of Paul as a dutiful member of the Jewish community, one who is loyal to his nation.[4]

Paul was apprehended in the Temple, not when he was making a disturbance, but when he was engaged in a rite of purification. Paul next draws attention to a legal point which seriously weakens the prosecution's case. Those who accused him in the Temple, some Jews from Asia (see Acts 21:27), are not in court to accuse or present evidence (Acts 24:19). The accusers who are present, if they want to proceed, should bring forward what came up during the hearing before the Sanhedrin; that's what they know about (Acts 24:20; see Acts 22:30–23:10). That gets Paul back to the point he wants to highlight, the hope in the resurrection which became the focal point during the Sanhedrin hearing (when Paul's accusers became violent and created a disturbance!). Paul says that his hope in the resurrection is the real issue between himself and his Jewish accusers (Acts 24:21; see also 23:6).[5] Note that Paul's speech ends (or is brought to an end) when Paul makes a key point (compare Acts 22:21-22).

On the basis of what came up during this trial, Felix should have released Paul. Luke says that Felix was already 'rather well informed about the Way' (Acts 24:22). But he adjourns the hearing, saying he wants to wait till Lysias comes to Caesarea before deciding the case. The picture we get of Felix is that of a man not committed to following the course of justice. In Acts 24:27 Luke says Felix kept Paul in prison for two years (AD 58-60) because he wanted to do the Jews a favour. Josephus tells us that the Jewish authorities were complaining to Rome because Felix was not dealing with the emergence of revolutionary groups. Perhaps Felix did not release Paul because he was afraid that would be used against him in such complaints. We are reminded of Pilate who should have released Jesus when he found that he was innocent, but did not because of Jewish pressure (Lk 23:24). Felix, however, allowed Paul some liberties in his imprisonment (Acts 24:23). Paul had friends in Caesarea who could visit him (see Acts 21:8-14).

What Luke highlights during Paul's two-year imprisonment is his contact with Felix and his Jewish wife, Drusilla. She was daughter of Herod Agrippa I, whose death was related in Acts 12. She had been married to the King of Emesa (in Syria), but she left him for Felix. She was the sister of Herod Agrippa II, who will shortly appear in the story of Acts along with their other sister Bernice. The scene here recalls how another member of the Herodian family (Herod Antipas), whose marriage was also unlawful, used to converse with John the Baptist in prison (see Mk 6:18, 20). Luke wants to underline that Paul continues to witness to Jesus Christ, even while in chains, thus fulfilling Jesus' prophecy in Lk 21:12-13.

What Paul speaks about to Felix (and Drusilla) is righteousness, self-control and the coming judgement (Acts 24:25) – perhaps what the couple needed to hear, given their adulterous union. This would explain the discomfort and fright of Felix (Acts 24:25). Felix seems to be more interested in getting a bribe from Paul than in opening himself to the word of God (Acts 24:26). He may have recognised Paul as a man of means who had brought money to Jerusalem or he may have in mind a bribe coming from Paul's network of friends in Caesarea. This puts him among those in Luke's story who are motivated by greed and consequently do not have the proper disposition to receive the Good News (see Acts 8:18-20; 16:16-20; 19:23-27). Felix departs without having followed up on his stated intention of giving a judgement when Lysias arrives. He was succeeded by Festus in AD 60, who has a short reign of two years.

Paul before Festus (Acts 25:1-12)
Shortly after he arrives in the province, Festus goes to Jerusalem where the Jewish leadership brings up Paul's case with the request, by way of a favour, that Paul be transferred

to Jerusalem (Acts 25:1-3). It's not clear whether a trial before the Sanhedrin or a trial before the governor in the place where the alleged crime took place is in mind here at this point. We are told that the real reason for their request was to get another opportunity to assassinate Paul (see Acts 23:12-15; now the leaders are the instigators of the plot!). Festus refuses but invites them to accompany him to Caesarea, if they have any accusation against Paul, and he will try the case there (Acts 25:4-5).

On his return to Caesarea he did not delay in following up on his intention (Acts 25:6). The Jews, who had come down from Jerusalem, surrounded Paul bringing many serious charges against him (Acts 25:7). Luke does not go into the charges again, as the reader already knows them. He merely notes once again that they could not prove the charges. Once again he paints the picture of Paul surrounded by a hostile crowd. Paul's defence amounts to a brief denial of charges and he adds that he has not committed any crime against the emperor (Acts 25:8). Festus, who had refused in Jerusalem to grant the Jews the favour in having Paul transferred there, now asks Paul if he is willing to go to Jerusalem to be tried there before him (Acts 25:9). We are told he is doing this, not for Paul's benefit, but to grant the Jews a favour.

This is the third time the question of granting the Jews a favour is mentioned in the narrative (see Acts 24:27; 25:3). Obviously it is a dynamic that is operating against Paul and preventing him from getting justice. Paul is a victim of political expediency. This latest manoeuvre by Festus becomes the occasion for a decisive turn in Luke's story. Paul expresses his unwillingness to be turned over to the hostile Jews and appeals to a higher court – the emperor's tribunal in Rome (Acts 25:10-11). In doing this Paul says he is prepared to face death if it is proved that he is guilty of wrongdoing. He is not running away in fear. Festus, having consulted his council, grants Paul's request to be transferred to Rome. Luke is presenting Paul as the one who takes the decisive step in going to Rome. We are meant to see this as the working out of God's plan in Paul's regard (see Acts 19:21; 23:11; see also Acts 1:8). We are left with the impression that Festus and his council just 'rubber-stamp' a decision *Paul* has taken.[6]

Paul before Herod Agrippa II and Festus (Acts 25:13–26:32)

While we might expect that Paul would now be put on a ship for Rome, Luke again lingers to tell us of another appearance and speech of Paul – this time before a Roman governor (Festus) and a Jewish king (Herod Agrippa II), along with their entourage. This fulfils Jesus' prophecy in Lk 21:12-15 about his disciples being brought before governors and kings because of his name, which will be an opportunity to testify, and also the prophecy Jesus made to Ananias about Paul bringing the name of Jesus before Gentiles and kings (see Acts 9:15). It also gives Luke another opportunity to reinforce the parallelism between Jesus and Paul. Right to the end, Paul is reliving the experience of Jesus, which is another way of saying that Jesus is present and active in Paul's mission – this latter point becomes explicit in Acts 26:23.[7]

Prelude to the Hearing (Acts 25:13-22)

Herod Agrippa II was the son of Herod Agrippa I (about whom we heard in Acts 12) and great grandson of Herod the Great. He was brought up in Rome and had influential connections there. The emperor Nero gave him his father's kingdom and some other principalities in Palestine. He lived with his sister, Bernice, in what was regarded as an incestuous union. She was previously married to her uncle; she later had an affair with Titus before he became emperor! They pay a courtesy call to welcome the new governor (Acts 25:13) and Festus takes the opportunity to speak of Paul's case to Agrippa (Acts 25:14-21).

In telling the story, Festus is not slow to make himself appear in a good light; he emphasises his own correctness and steadfastness and does not mention that he was willing to send Paul to Jerusalem as a favour to the Jews (see Acts

25:9). There are a few new elements: the Jews asked for a sentence against Paul when Festus was in Jerusalem (Acts 25:15); Festus states a principle of Roman law about the accused being given an opportunity to answer charges (Acts 25:16); Festus gives his opinion that the case is about an internal dispute among Jews over religious matters, with specific reference to Paul's claim that Jesus was alive (Acts 25:19); Festus says that he was at a loss how to investigate such questions and that is why he suggested to Paul that he go to Jerusalem to be tried there (Acts 25:20 – hard to imagine a Roman governor handing over his judicial responsibility). Acts 25:18-19 (which reminds us of the opinion of the proconsul Gallio in Acts 18:14-15) amounts to a declaration that Paul is innocent of crime.[8] Agrippa expresses a wish to see Paul (Acts 25:22) and Festus complies. We recall Herod Antipas' interest in seeing Jesus (Lk 9:9; 23:8). So, in this private conversion between Festus and Agrippa (which Luke could not have heard!), Luke prepares for Paul's last appearance in the long sequence of appearances before authorities. Despite his hypocrisy, Festus says things Luke would want him to say – he declares Paul's innocence and indicates that the real point at issue is the resurrection.

Proceedings at the Hearing (Acts 25:23–26:29)

Acts 25:23-27 can be seen as the setting of the scene which includes Festus' summary of the state of the question from his viewpoint. Paul, at Agrippa's invitation, then states his case (Acts 26:1-23). When Paul's speech is interrupted by Festus, an exchange ensues between Paul and Agrippa in which those present are challenged to be open to the Christian message (Acts 26:24-29).

Setting the Scene (Acts 25:23-27)

We have an impressive ceremonial setting for Paul's last appearance (Acts 25:23). This may be to highlight the importance of Paul and what he is about to say on this occasion. In the midst of all these important people, Paul is the main actor in Luke's eyes. Johnson thinks that we have here a 'show trial' that is part entertainment for the guests, part a subtle political manoeuvre by Festus.[9] Festus again sums up the case to date, this time in public (Acts 25:24-27). Saying that 'the whole Jewish community' (Acts 25:24) sought Paul's death is an exaggeration. In Acts 25:25 we have another important declaration of Paul's innocence, as well as a reminder of Paul's appeal to the emperor. The impression Festus wants to create is that he upheld Paul's innocence, despite the fact that he was under severe pressure, and that Paul's appeal to the emperor was irrational and unnecessary. Festus in Acts 25:26-27 gives a reason for the present hearing. He feels he has nothing definite to go on in Paul's case and he wants something to put in writing for the emperor. This is a surprising statement in view of everything that has gone before and many would say that it is unimaginable that Festus would make such a statement or admit to such ignorance and incompetence in public. Some, however, see historical plausibility in Festus' reason for holding the hearing; he wants Agrippa on his side, should he be accused of incompetence in Rome. It may be Luke's way of saying again that up to now there is no case against Paul, while at the same time giving a reason within the narrative for the appearance of Paul before Agrippa during which Luke can continue to press home his emphasis. What follows in the hearing is not aimed at clarifying Festus' mind.

Paul's Speech before Agrippa and Festus (Acts 26:1-23)
This speech is by and large the work of Luke. It is the climax and conclusion of Paul's defence and his *apologia pro vita sua* before a Jewish king, Gentile governor and a mainly Gentile audience. It is also a defence of Christianity which emphasises its relationship to Judaism. And it gives Luke the opportunity to sum up major points in his work as a whole: the continuity of Christianity with Judaism (Christianity is the fulfilment of the hopes and promises which Israel cherished, particularly the hope of the resurrection); the

nature and legitimacy of Paul's mission to both Jews and Gentiles. As with all of Luke's speeches, what is said here is mainly for the benefit of the reader. Luke is giving us a summary of Paul's mission as a model for our mission. The Paul we see in this speech is not a helpless victim trying to defend himself, but a courageous witness to the Lord. We can divide Paul's speech into three parts: (a) Paul and the Hope of Israel (Acts 26:4-8); (b) Paul's Experience of Christ (Acts 26:9-18); (c) Paul's Witness to Christ (Acts 26:19-23).

In customary oratorical style Paul stretches out his hand and begins with the *captatio benevolentiae* (Acts 26:2-3), saying he is fortunate to make his defence before King Agrippa, a man acquainted with Jewish beliefs and customs. He then immediately establishes his credentials as an authentic Jew (Acts 26:4-5). His Jewish way of life from youth is a matter of public knowledge and there are people who can testify to it. In fact he belonged to the strict Pharisee sect (see Acts 22:3; Phil 3:4-9). Paul goes on to pinpoint the central issue in the Jewish case against him, his hope of the resurrection (Acts 26:6-8; see Acts 23:6; 24:15; 25:19). He speaks of that hope in terms of a promise which the twelve tribes of Israel hope to attain, as they earnestly worship day and night. The mention of the twelve tribes evokes the image of the whole people of Israel. In Luke's work, the 'twelve' is symbolically related to the restoration of the people of Israel (see Lk 6:13; 22:30; Acts 1:15-26). Israel is spoken of as a worshipping people, waiting in hope for the fulfilment of God's promise. The language used here reminds us of the prophetess Anna worshipping night and day in the Temple (Lk 2:36-38). She is a model for the Israel Paul is speaking about here. Paul is accused because he claims that in the resurrection of Jesus the promise has found fulfilment. In his first major speech in Antioch of Pisidia, Paul focused on the resurrection of Jesus as the fulfilment of the promise to David (see Acts 13:26-27); in his last major speech in Acts 26, he again emphasises that the 'promise that our twelve tribes hope to attain' is fulfilled in the resurrection of Jesus.[10]

Paul goes on in the second part of the speech to speak of his personal experience of Christ (Acts 26:9-18). When he first became aware of Christ and his community, he did 'many things against the name of Jesus of Nazareth' by fiercely persecuting his followers (Acts 26:9-11). Paul says that he was convinced that he 'ought to' do this (infinitive *dein* in v. 9). This verb is usually used in Luke-Acts to speak of the will and plan of God. Paul thought he was doing God's will in persecuting Christians. This would mean that Paul's persecution of Christians was a (mistaken) expression of his Jewish zeal (see Gal 1:13-14; Phil 3:5-6). The persecutor's portrait is intensified here (compare Acts 8:1, 3; 9:1-2; 22:4-5). Paul is speaking from the perspective of his later Christian faith: he did many things against the name (person) of Jesus (Acts 26:9); he tried to force the followers of Jesus to blaspheme against him (Acts 26:11); he cast his vote against Christians when they were condemned to death (Acts 26:10).[11]

In Acts 26:12-18 we have the third account in Acts of what happened to Paul on the road to Damascus (see Acts 9:1-19; 22:6-16). Notice that Ananias does not appear in this account, there is no blindness and healing, and Paul receives his call and commission on the road directly from the risen Christ. The emphasis has shifted now almost exclusively to the experience as a call and commission, rather than a conversion. The part played by Paul's companions is almost suppressed (see Acts 26:13-14). Though they fall to the ground with Paul (contrast Acts 9:4; 22:7), it seems that he is the only one who sees the light and hears the voice (contrast Acts 9:7; 22:9). Paul hears the voice in the 'Hebrew (Aramaic) language'. The main words in the dialogue remain the same in all accounts: 'Saul, Saul, why are you persecuting me? ... Who are you, Lord? ... I am Jesus (of Nazareth in Acts 22:8) whom you are persecuting.' We have an additional saying in Acts 26:14: 'It hurts you (it is hard for you) to kick against the goads.' The 'goad' is to be understood as a sharp pointed stick used to drive livestock in the direction required. This proverb was widely used in Greek and Jewish literature to highlight the futility of resisting divine guidance.[12]

The most notable expansion in this account of Paul's experience on the road is his direct and immediate commissioning as a minister and witness by the risen Lord (Acts 26:16-18). Paul stands in the line of authentic ministers of the word and witnesses to Jesus Christ along with the Twelve (Acts 1:22; 2:32; 10:39, 41) and Stephen (Acts 22:20). The second account of Paul's Damascus experience also highlights his role as witness (see Acts 22:15). The language that is used in these verses also reminds us of the call and ministry of the prophets (see Ez 2:1-3; Jer 1:7-8; Is 42:6-7, 16). So Paul also stands in the long prophetic line of Israel. He is told in Acts 26:16 that he is to witness to what he has seen (the Damascus experience of the risen Lord) and what he will see (the future experiences of the risen Lord, which we already know about from the narrative in Acts [see Acts 18:9-10; 22:17-21; 23:11; see also 2 Cor 12:1-4]). Paul is to witness to his personal experience of the risen Lord. There is the promise of protection (Acts 26:17). Having read the narrative of Acts up to this point, we know that Jesus has been faithful to this promise to Paul (see, for instance, Acts 16:25-40; 18:12-16; 19:23-41). Acts 26:18 explains the purpose and outcome of Paul's mission with a number of favourite Lukan concepts: opening of eyes (see Lk 4:18); repentance and forgiveness (see Lk 24:47; Acts 2:38; 3:19); a place among those who are sanctified (see Acts 20:32).

In the third part of the speech (Acts 26:19-23) Paul tells of his witness to Jesus Christ which eventually led to his arrest and imprisonment. The mention of Paul's obedience to the heavenly vision (Acts 26:19) underlines once more Paul's character as a loyal and obedient Jew and the divine origin of his mission to Jews and Gentiles. Paul's mission in Damascus and Jerusalem (Acts 26:20) recalls Acts 9:19-30, but Luke has not told us about a mission of Paul 'throughout the countryside of Judea' (unless Acts 15:3-4 can be taken in that sense). It is probably best to take Acts 26:20 as one of those

Lukan verses which give a broad sweep of the Christian mission – Damascus; Jerusalem; Judea; Gentiles (compare Acts 1:8). Acts 26:20 also indicates what is needed in the response to the mission of Paul: *metanoein* ('turning from' sin), *epistrephein* ('turning to' God) and a repentance (*metanoia*) which finds expression in deeds (see Lk 3:8). Paul goes on to say that the Jews seized him in the temple and an attempt was made on his life (Acts 26:21). But God protected him (Acts 26:22), as he had promised (see Acts 26:17). Note that Paul does not proceed to defend himself. He keeps the focus on his witness 'before small and great' to the one who is the fulfilment of what the prophets and Moses said.

Acts 26:23 is the climactic verse in the speech. The mention of a Messiah who suffers and rises reminds us of what transpired when Jesus met the two disciples on the road to Emmaus and told them how 'Moses and all the prophets' spoke of a Messiah who was to suffer and enter into his glory (see Lk 24:26). The resurrection of Jesus is spoken of as the first in a series (see 1 Cor 15:20-21 where the resurrection of Jesus is seen as the first fruits). The figure of the suffering Messiah is combined here with that of the Suffering Servant, whose vocation is to be a light to Israel and the nations (see Is 42:9; 49:6). What is important to note about Acts 26:23 is that *Jesus himself* is said to be the one who proclaims light to the people (Israel) and the nations. When did Jesus proclaim light to the nations? The only answer can be that Jesus does this in and through the mission of Paul (see also Acts 13:47). Thus, in and through Paul's mission the universal mission of Jesus which Simeon proclaimed finds fulfilment (see Lk 2:29-32).

Paul's Exchange with Agrippa (Acts 26:24-29)
The planned interruption of Paul's speech in Acts 26:24 is a Lukan device to indicate that something of great importance has just been said (compare Acts 17:32; 22:22). Festus, obviously concluding Paul is speaking gibberish, says he is crazy. Paul calmly claims that he is speaking the sober truth

(Acts 26:25). He then turns his attention to Agrippa who as a Jew should know what Paul is talking about (Acts 26:26). He feels he can talk freely (and boldly) to Agrippa. Paul also emphasises the public character of the Christian movement; it is not secret and subversive. This is also a reason why Agrippa should know about it. He puts a question to Agrippa which expects him as a Jew to acknowledge the prophetic principle in Judaism (Acts 26:27). The question implies a challenge to Agrippa to become a Christian. Even in his chains Paul's continues to proclaim Christ. Agrippa side-steps the question, sensing that Paul is leading him to accept the logic of what he is saying (Acts 26:28). Paul expresses a longing and a prayer that all who are listening to him would become Christians, though he would not wish them to be persecuted for it, as he is being persecuted (Acts 26:29).

Result of the Hearing (Acts 26:30-32)
The hearing ends with strong emphasis on the innocence of Paul. On retiring, the distinguished people agree among themselves that Paul is innocent (Acts 26:30-31). Luke highlights in particular the Herodian king Agrippa's declaration of innocence (Act 26:32). This corresponds with Herod Antipas' opinion that Jesus is innocent (see Lk 23:15). The reason why Paul cannot now be set free is that he has appealed to the emperor. We are reminded again that the story is taking the direction towards Rome where Paul will witness. And Paul is the one who, under the guidance of the Lord (see Acts 23:11), has given it this direction.

Reflection on Acts 24:1–26:32
As he relates the story of Paul's imprisonment and trials, Luke is holding him up to us as the model missionary. We are being told who Paul really is and what he is about. We hear Paul saying that his identity is rooted in the faith tradition of God's people. He is a disciple of Jesus Christ who fulfils the hopes and the promises of this tradition, especially the hope of resurrection. Like the prophets of old, Paul has a deep

sense of being called by God and given a special mission. What do we say when we are asked today about who we are and what we are about? Is our missionary identity shaped by strong faith convictions centred on Jesus Christ who is alive and present among us and who wants all to experience authentic life? Have we got a deep sense of being called by the Lord to share in his life-giving mission? At a time of major transition in mission, missionaries can be troubled with questions about identity and purpose. Like Paul, we need to seek answers to these questions in our faith tradition and in our relationship to Jesus Christ, the one who calls us and fulfils his promises to us.

We have noted that Luke, in telling the story of Paul the missionary, devotes a lot of attention to the period of his imprisonment and trials when it would seem that his missionary career had been abruptly halted. For Luke, Paul the prisoner is still on mission and indeed has arrived at the high point of his missionary career. In his suffering he is now the Lord's chosen instrument, witnessing openly before Jews and Gentiles, governors and kings, in fidelity to the commission he received from the Lord (see Acts 9:15-16). He witnesses not only in word but also in deed, reliving the passion of his beloved Lord. Paradoxically, his witness in weakness and vulnerability is a powerful witness. Paul was very conscious of that. In his second letter to the Corinthians, at a time when many were saying that he was not a true apostle, he says that Christian missionaries are 'clay jars' filled with the extraordinary power of God (2 Cor 4:7).

He was probably thinking of the small clay oil-lamps which were used widely in the world of his day to give light to a darkened room, particularly in the houses of the poor who could not afford metal oil-lamps. These clay lamps were inexpensive, very fragile and easily broken. What Paul is saying is that the Christian missionary is a fragile, vulnerable person, who is called to carry the light of Jesus Christ into situations of human darkness, confusion and suffering. The power to do that comes from God, not from us. Our vulnerability and weakness are the entry points through which the power of God breaks into our ministry. In the same letter to the Corinthians Paul goes on to say, 'I will boast all the more gladly of my weaknesses, so that the power of Christ may dwell in me. Therefore I am content with weaknesses, insults, hardships, persecutions, and calamities for the sake of Christ; for whenever I am weak, then I am strong' (2 Cor 12:9-10).

Are you weak enough to be a missionary? That's the surprising question I once read in the vocations brochure of a missionary congregation at a time when all such brochures had a list of the qualifications needed to become a missionary – for instance, be within a specified age range, enjoy good health, come from a good Catholic family, be well-educated, have a good moral character. Over the years missionaries were encouraged to avail of ongoing training to acquire new human skills and resources which would enable them to engage in mission more effectively. And they should continue to do that. But they must also give time to getting in touch with their own vulnerabilities and develop a missionary spirituality based on the power of God working in human weakness. Feelings of weakness, vulnerability and inadequacy can come from experiencing the limitations of ageing, poor health, scarcity of personnel and financial resources, the enormity of the missionary challenges facing us today, opposition, unexpected tragedies and setbacks, individual and institutional failures. Like Paul, who endured tribulations of all kinds and faced powers which threatened to overwhelm him, we need to open ourselves to God's Spirit who works in and through human weakness and enables us to continue witnessing to Jesus in our actual circumstances, no matter how unfavourable they may seem to be. And like him we must keep our focus on the hope of the resurrection.

NOTES

1 See Johnson, *The Acts of the Apostles*, 451-416, for a treatment of Luke's reasons for the lengthy narration of Paul's trials.

2 Before becoming governor, Felix had been involved in the administration of his predecessor Cumanus (AD 48-52).

3 'From 24:14 on Paul is speaking as much to his Jewish accusers as to the Roman governor. He is arguing that he is a faithful Jew. Although the charges of Tertullus have a political slant, Paul's defence is still influenced by the charge in 21:28 that he denies the fundamentals of Judaism, the chosen people, the law, and the temple' (Tannehill, *The Narrative Unity of Luke-Acts*, vol. 2, 299).

4 Some understand the alms in Acts 24:17 as customary Temple offerings made by a Jewish pilgrim (see, for instance, Tannehill, *ibid.*, 300; Mullins, *The Acts of the Apostles*, 242).

5 '"The resurrection of the dead" thus echoes like a refrain in these latter chapters of Acts. Directly *anastasis nekrōn* refers to the specific Pharisaic belief, but implied in Paul's statement is his own belief in "the resurrection of the Dead (One)," i.e., of Jesus Christ, his risen Lord. That idea, however, would scarcely be understood by a Roman governor and will not surface until 25:19' (Fitzmyer, *The Acts of the Apostles*, 737).

6 The right of a Roman citizen to appeal to the Emperor was based on an ancient Roman law. Seemingly, it could be an appeal before a decision is given by a local court (*provocatio*) or an appeal against such a decision (*appellatio*). Luke obviously wants us to understand the former in Paul's case. Perhaps the historical core is that Paul just got fed up with having justice delayed by governors who were unwilling to condemn him, but were using his case to keep themselves on side with the Jewish leadership in a tricky political situation.

7 For a detailed list of the similarities and parallels between Lk 23:1-25 and Acts 25-26, see O'Toole, *The Unity of Luke's Theology: An Analysis of Luke-Acts*, 67-81. Some think that the part played by Herod Agrippa in Paul's case is a Lukan creation with little or no historical basis (see, for instance, O'Toole, *ibid.*, 70; Dillon 'Acts of the Apostles' in *The New Jerome Biblical Commentary*, 762). Johnson (*The Acts of the Apostles*, 427-428) thinks that Festus' consultation with a Jewish royal couple would not be out of place with what we know of politics in Palestine in the first century.

8 This is probably to be taken as the first of three declarations by Festus that Paul is innocent (see also Acts 25:25; 26:31), which correspond to Pilate's three declarations of Jesus' innocence in Lk 23:4, 14-15, 22. In speaking of the three declarations of Paul's

innocence by a Roman authority, Johnson (*The Acts of the Apostles*, 427) mentions the following: Acts 23:29 (Lysias); Acts 25:25 (Festus); Acts 26:31 (Festus).

[9] Johnson, *ibid.*, 428.

[10] It is not clear to whom Paul addresses the question in Acts 26:8: to Jews, who do not accept the resurrection as the fulfilment of their ancient promises; to Gentiles, who find it hard to accept any talk of resurrection (see Acts 17:32); to the readers of Luke's narrative? Perhaps all these are in mind.

[11] All of this raises some interesting historical questions: Was Paul a member of the Sanhedrin? Were more Christians put to death besides Stephen? Had the Jews the right to put people to death? Perhaps it is best to allow for some rhetorical exaggeration.

[12] On the basis of this proverb, some (for instance, Dillon, 'Acts of the Apostles' in *The New Jerome Biblical Commentary*, 763; Johnson, *The Acts of the Apostles*, 435) say that Paul, even before he met Jesus on the road to Damascus, had been resisting a growing conviction that Jesus fulfilled the hopes of Israel and this resistance found expression in his hostile actions against Christians.

CHAPTER 10

TOWARDS ROME
(ACTS 27:1–28:31)

We recall that Luke's whole work is the story of one great journey – the journey of Jesus from Galilee to Jerusalem which continues in the journey of his disciples (especially Paul) towards the ends of the earth. It is the story of God's saving word reaching out to all. Jesus asked his disciples to be servants of and witnesses to that word 'in Jerusalem, in all Judea and Samaria, and to the ends of the earth' (Acts 1:8). In the story of Acts we have followed how the journey of the word of God progressed, particularly in the ministries of Peter and Paul. Now we have come to the last stage of Luke's narrative which culminates in the arrival of Paul in Rome where he bears witness to the word openly and without hindrance. Having the saving word of God proclaimed at the centre of the known world is a powerful demonstration of its universal significance and dynamism. As we read this section of Acts, we keep in mind that we are hearing about a most important moment in the unfolding of God's plan of salvation for all. It was God's plan that Paul should bear witness to him in Rome and Paul resolutely took steps to carry out God's plan for him (see Acts 19:21; 23:11; 25:10-11). In this chapter we first consider Paul's last journey and arrival in Rome (Acts 27:1–28:16) and then focus on his witness in the capital of the empire (Acts 28:17-31).

Paul's Journey to Rome (Acts 27:1–28:16)

We divide the journey into three main sections: (a) Paul's Sea Voyage and Shipwreck (Acts 27:1-44); (b) Paul in Malta (Acts 28:1-10); (c) Paul's Arrival in Rome (Acts 28:11-16).

Paul's Sea Voyage and Shipwreck (Acts 27:1-44)

This is perhaps the most dramatic episode in Acts. Many draw attention to the strong influence of Hellenistic literature on the story of Paul's sea voyage and shipwreck.[1] Epic literature (like the Odyssey of Homer and the Aeneid of Virgil) has stories of adventures and sea voyages which illustrate such Greco-Roman cultural ideals as philosophical calmness in the face of adversity, loyalty and friendship. One finds similar stories in popular Hellenistic romances which were written to entertain and perhaps edify the reader. On the other hand, some argue that Luke's story of Paul's sea journey is fundamentally a factual account of what happened.[2] They take the use of 'we' throughout the narrative as evidence of an eyewitness account. They point to the accuracy of references to places, time and nautical information. And they appeal to what Paul says in 2 Cor 11:25 about being shipwrecked three times. While acknowledging the basic historicity of Paul's sea journey and shipwreck, we should keep in mind that Luke's main purpose is not to give us accurate, detailed information about what happened, but to convey a theological message and in doing this he uses narrative techniques which were found in Hellenistic literature.[3]

Acts 27:1-8 tells us what happened on the journey between Caesarea and Crete. Notice that in Acts 27 the 'we narrative' is again resumed (see vv.13, 17, 19, 28, 29, 38, 39-44). We are told that Paul had at least one of his companions with him – Aristarchus (Acts 27:2). The journey to Italy began in the month of October. In Acts 27:9 Paul says that the Fast had already gone by when they got to Crete; he is referring to the Jewish feast of Atonement, which fell on the 10th day of the Jewish month of Tishri (lunar calendar which is

September/October in our calendar). This was right in the middle of one of the risky times for sailing in the Mediterranean. Paul and some other prisoners were entrusted to the keeping of Julius, a centurion of the Augustan Cohort (Acts 27:1).[4] The relationship between Paul and Julius throughout the narrative is positive and cooperative. Julius treats Paul kindly (Acts 27:3) and even saves him from death when the soldiers in a panic wanted to kill the prisoners (Acts 27:43). He allows Paul the freedom to visit groups of Christians along the way (Acts 27:3; 28:14). Paul, for his part, is seen to help out the centurion and give advice in difficult situations (the centurion did not heed the advice in Acts 27:10-11, but he seems to have acted on Paul's suggestion in Acts 27:31-32).

They set sail from Caesarea on a ship of Adramyttium (a port near Troas on the coast of Asia Minor).[5] During a short stopover in Sidon Paul makes contact with some friends, probably the Christian community in that place (Acts 27:3). Seemingly, Luke does not want to overlook Paul's contact with Christian communities (see also Acts 28:13, 15). Could that be to offset any suspicion of Paul as a maverick who wasn't in the mainstream of the Christian movement? During the journey from Sidon to Myra in Lycia (Acts 27:4-5), the ship hugged the shore rather than risking the open sea in unfavourable winds. Remaining sheltered from the wind, they headed between the north coast of Cyprus and the coasts of Cicilia and Pamphylia. At Myra they transferred to an Alexandrian ship headed for Italy (Acts 27:6). They made slow progress in difficult conditions, passing by Cnidus (a port at the southwest extreme of the province of Asia Minor), sailing by the east coast of Crete to avail of the shelter of the land, and finally arriving at a place called Fair Havens on the south coast of Crete (Acts 27:7-8).

Paul intervenes four times in the narrative of Acts 27 (vv. 9-11; vv. 21-26; vv. 31-32; vv. 33-38). The narrative shifts between scenes which heighten the danger and scenes in which Paul responds to this danger with a view to the salvation of all. Through these interventions, Luke builds up a picture of Paul as the one who advises, exhorts, comforts, strengthens and challenges in crisis situations, as well as predicting the future and speaking on behalf of God. Like the prophets of old, Paul speaks of God's saving presence and sustains people's hope. He also displays the calmness, prudence and insight expected of heroes in Hellenistic epic literature. We have the first intervention of Paul in Acts 27:9-11. It is strange that Paul the prisoner would have such a say in deliberations about what is to be done. Paul advises against continuing the voyage in such bad conditions, warning of the loss of the cargo, the ship and even lives. This time the centurion prefers to follow the advice of the 'experts', the captain of the ship and the owner.

The majority want to attempt to reach Phoenix, another port on the southern coast of Crete which would be a safer place to spend the winter. Acts 27:12-20 tells us how this foolhardy attempt lands them in a hopeless situation. A violent wind of hurricane proportions (called the 'northeaster') swept down from Crete and they could do nothing but give way to the force of the wind. The ship was out of control and at the mercy of the elements (Acts 27:14-15). As they drifted for a short while under the shelter of the island of Cauda, they secured the ship's small lifeboat to the deck (it would normally be towed behind the ship), and took measures to strengthen the hull of the ship (Acts 27:16-17). Their big fear was that they would be blown towards the Syrtis, a treacherous area of shallows and quicksand off the coast of Cyrenaica. To prevent this they lowered the anchor (Acts 27:17).[6] Luke builds up the picture of the steadily deteriorating situation by telling us of the ship being pounded by the storm and of the crew throwing first the cargo and then the ship's tackle overboard, in order to lighten the ship (Acts 27:18-19). With the sun and the stars hidden, there is no way of calculating their course. They reach the point when all hope of being saved was abandoned (Acts 27:20).

At this most critical juncture we have Paul's second intervention (Acts 27:21-26). He begins with a mild rebuke ('I told you so') because people did not listen to the sound advice he had given in Crete (Acts 27:21). But his main reason for intervening now is to encourage people in a hopeless situation. He predicts that there will be no loss of life, only loss of the ship (Acts 27:22). This is a revision of what he expected in Acts 27:10. He even predicts that the ship will be lost by running aground on some island (Acts 27:26). The source of Paul's confident foresight is not common-sense or prudence (which was the basis of Paul's advice in Acts 27:10), but a vision of the angel of God in which Paul was reassured of God's plan for him to bear witness in Rome (Acts 27:23-24; compare Acts 23:11). Paul has faith that things will turn out as he has been told and that he will arrive safely in Rome (Acts 27:25). And he is also confident that the protection of his God will extend to *all* those who are with him (Acts 27:24). Once again the note of universal salvation is sounded in Luke's writings. The emphasis on the salvation of all will be the major factor as the story of the life-threatening situation unfolds.[7]

In Acts 27:27-32 we hear what happened on the fourteenth night of drifting aimlessly across the Adriatic Sea (between Crete and Sicily). The crew, perhaps hearing the sound of breakers, suspect they are approaching land. They take soundings (probably by lowering a line weighted with lead) and discover that the depth of water beneath was rapidly becoming more shallow (Acts 27:28). Their fear is that they will run aground and they lower four anchors from the stern to keep the ship from drifting onto the rocks in the middle of the night. With no visibility, they prayed for day to come (Acts 27:29). The sailors must have been in a desperate state, because they plan to save their own skins by abandoning the ship in the lifeboat and leaving the others to their fate in a ship they cannot handle. They lower the lifeboat on the pretext of putting out anchors from the bow to make the ship more secure (Acts 27:30). Paul again intervenes (Acts 27:31). The sailors have not taken heart from Paul's words in Acts 27:21-26 and what they are now doing runs counter to God's plan to save all together. Their self-centred act is in contrast to Paul's concern for others. Paul tells the centurion that it is necessary for the sailors to stay in the ship, so that all can be saved (that is, so that God's plan can be realised). This time the centurion listens to Paul. The soldiers cut the ropes and let the lifeboat drift away (Acts 27:32). So Paul has been instrumental in keeping on course God's plan to save all together.

In this situation, where people are fearful, desperate and thinking only of their own skins, Paul again sets about encouraging them. In Acts 27:33-38 we have Paul's fourth intervention (Acts 27:33-36) and its immediate result (Acts 27:38).[8] Note the repeated references to *all* in Acts 27:33-37. Paul's intervention shows his concern for all and is again aimed at the realisation of God's plan to save all together. The people haven't eaten food for a long time (Acts 27:33; see also Acts 27:21). This was probably due to seasickness rather than shortage of food (Acts 27:38 presupposes that they still had grain on board). Paul encourages them to eat so that they can gain strength to face the ordeal of reaching the land and so survive (Acts 27:34). In words reminiscent of Lk 21:18 ('not a hair of your head will perish'), Paul again assures the people that all will be saved. He not only urges them in word, but leads by example in eating food before them (Acts 27:35). *All* of them were encouraged and took food for themselves (Acts 27:36).

It is not said that Paul distributed food or that they shared in his meal. We are told that Paul *took* bread, *gave thanks* and *broke* it before eating. Some say this merely means Paul ate the bread in the way any pious Jew would do (a Jewish 'grace before meals'). Johnson sees Paul's action of breaking bread and giving thanks as a witness to God whose power and unseen presence was truly at work.[9] Tannehill takes Paul's prayer of thanksgiving as an act of trust in God's promise to rescue all in the face of the immediate danger.[10] The words used in Acts 27:35 remind us of words associated with the Christian Eucharist (see Lk 22:19; 24:30). From elsewhere in Acts we know that the meal the community celebrated when they gathered for worship is called the 'breaking of bread' (see Acts 2:42, 46; 20:7, 11). But Luke most probably is not referring to the celebration of the Eucharist on a ship full of non-Christians. Perhaps he is drawing a parallel with what Jesus did in the presence of a hungry crowd, which led to all eating and satisfying their hunger (see Lk 9:16-17). Furthermore, Luke may have shaped his narrative in this way in order to remind Christians that they can draw strength from the Eucharist in facing the ordeals of life. After all had eaten food, the remaining cargo (wheat) is cast overboard so that that ship will have a better chance of reaching land in the shallow waters (Acts 27:38).

Acts 27:39-44 describes the dramatic shipwreck. The plan is to run the ship unto a beach which they can now see in the morning light. Acts 27:40 tells us of three further steps taken to achieve that end: the four anchors they had used to prevent the ship ending up on the rocks are now cast off; the rudder is freed from the cables that secured it so that the ship can be steered towards the beach; a sail is raised in the hope that the ship would be blown in the right direction. But they strike a reef, leaving the bow firmly stuck and immovable, with the stern being pounded and broken up by the force of the waves (Acts 27:41). Now the soldiers think of saving their own skins at the expense of others. They plan to kill the prisoners lest they escape in the confusion. If this happened, the soldiers would be punished afterwards for neglect of duty (see Acts 12:19; 16:27). In the crisis, it is now the soldiers' turn to forget that God's plan is to save all. However, the centurion intervenes to stop them carrying out what they plan and we are told that he does this because he wished to save Paul (Acts 27:43). Luke would see this in the context of God's plan to bring Paul to Rome and to save all who are associated with Paul in the present ordeal. The centurion orders those who could swim to jump overboard and make for the land, to be followed by the rest holding on to planks and pieces of the ship. In this way *all* were brought safely to land (Acts 27:44). God's purpose to save all has been achieved, not without the cooperation of quite a number of human agents.

At this stage, it may be helpful to summarise the main points of Luke's message in giving us the long and detailed account of the perilous sea voyage. (1) Luke wants to show how the faithful God is acting to bring Paul safely to Rome in fulfilment of the promise in Acts 23:11. This is stated explicitly in Acts 27:24. Nothing, including natural disasters, can hinder God's plan. God achieves his plan, not through miraculous intervention, but through the cooperation and concerted efforts of human agents.[11] (2) Luke emphasises that God is acting to bring salvation to all. There are a number of references to being *saved* from the sea (see Acts 27:20, 31, 43, 44; see also 28:1, 4) and, as we have seen, the focus is put on the salvation of *all* in the ship (Acts 27:24). Moves by some to save themselves at the expense of others are thwarted (Acts 27:31, 43). The salvation of all on this voyage is symbolic of God's plan of salvation for all flesh, which is the central theme in Luke's work (see Luke 2:32; 3:6). (3) Paul, the prisoner, plays the central role in the story, which is symbolic of his central role in Luke's drama of the unfolding of God's plan of salvation for all (Jews and Gentiles). Paul advises, exhorts, comforts, strengthens and challenges his fellow travellers in crisis situations. He leads by example (for instance, by eating bread in Acts 27:35). To a mainly Gentile group, he presents himself as a prophet predicting the future and speaking on behalf of God. (4) During the drama of the sea voyage we see Christians and non-Christians in the ship cooperating together to ensure salvation for all. It has been suggested that Luke sees the ship as a symbol of the situation in which Christians of his day find themselves – a small minority in Greco-Roman society who are challenged to enter into cooperation with others for the good of all.[12]

Paul in Malta (Acts 28:1-10)

Malta is identified as the island on which Paul had been shipwrecked (Acts 28:1). The inhabitants of the island are called 'barbarians' (*barbaroi*) (Acts 28:2), which in this context is a neutral term for those who do not speak Greek or share the dominant culture of the Greco-Roman world. The Maltese language and culture were Phoenician/Punic. The unusual kindness to the shipwrecked strangers is in line with the friendly treatment of Paul by Julius in Acts 27:3 and the hospitable treatment by Publius in Acts 28:7. Luke wants to convey an atmosphere of friendliness, hospitality and cooperation throughout Paul's journey to Rome. The kindling of the fire and the welcome to gather around it (Acts 28:2) is an outward expression of that kindness. Paul helps in gathering firewood (Acts 28:3) – a touch which fits in with the picture of Paul who was more than willing to get his hands dirty (see Acts 18:3; 20:34; 1 Cor 4:12; 1 Th 2:9; 2 Th 3:7-8). This sets the scene for the incident with the viper which attaches itself to Paul's hand and presumably bites him (Acts 28:3-6). On seeing this, the locals first conclude that Paul the prisoner must be a murderer who is being pursued by 'Justice' (*Dikē*), the goddess of retribution and vengeance. He may have escaped from the sea, but 'Justice' always settles scores. When they see that no harm comes to Paul, they change their minds and regard him as a god. Notice that Paul does nothing to correct the false notions of the locals, as he and Barnabas did at Lystra (Acts 14:11-18). What seems to be uppermost in Luke's mind in this episode is to portray Paul once again as an innocent man, which had been emphasised during the various hearings in Jerusalem and Caesarea. The story may also serve to highlight the divine power and protection that accompanies Paul. One is reminded of the Lord's sayings in Lk 10:18-19 and Mk 16:18.

Luke goes on to tell us of Paul's contact with the leading man on the island, Publius, who shows hospitality to them for three days (Acts 28:7). Luke characteristically associates Paul with leading figures of a locality (see Acts 13:7; 16:22;

17:19; 18:12; 19:31), probably a way of indicating that the Christian message is credible and blameless. In Acts 28:8 we hear that Paul prays and lays his hands on Publius' father, curing him from fever and dysentery (*dysenterion* – the only reference to this word in the New Testament and the Septuagint!). This leads to the healing of the rest of the sick on the island (Acts 28:9). We are reminded of the healing ministry of Jesus in Capernaum at the beginning of his ministry (Luke 4:38-40). In each case the healing of one person suffering from a fever is followed by the healing of all the sick in a region. The parallelism between Jesus and Paul continues in Luke's story of mission. The ending of the account of Paul's stay in Malta repeats the positive note on which it began. The locals continue to show kindness by bestowing honours on Paul and his companions, and giving provisions for the onward journey (Acts 28:10).

Luke does not mention any direct preaching of the Christian message in Malta, nor are we told that any of the locals became Christians. Historically, it is highly likely that this happened. We could say that Paul's healing ministry was a witness through deeds to the power of the kingdom of God. Johnson feels that the sharing of possessions on the part of the people in Malta is, according to Luke's way of thinking, an indication of their openness to the visitation of our hospitable God which prepares for Paul's statement in Acts 28:28 about the openness of the Gentiles to hear the Christian message.[13] Tannehill feels that what is uppermost in Luke's mind in telling us about Paul's stay in Malta is not missionary preaching but the cooperative relationships between Christians and non-Christians.[14]

Paul's Arrival in Rome (Acts 28:11-16)

After a three-month stay in Malta, the journey to Rome continues on an Alexandrian ship which had wintered in that island (Acts 28:11). Luke reminds us of Gentile religiosity by telling us that images of Castor and Pollux (sons of Zeus and astral deities who were regarded as protectors of sailors) were on the ship's figurehead. Of course, at this stage Luke's reader knows that the real protector on the voyage is Paul's God. After a three-day stopover at Syracuse in Sicily, they move on to Rhegium on the toe of Italy, where they stay only one day before sailing to Puteoli (on the Bay of Naples). At that time Puteoli was the most important port in Italy where both passengers and cargo for Rome were offloaded. There Paul stays with Christians for seven days (Acts 28:14). Note that, before Paul's arrival, there are already Christian communities in Italy, including Rome (see Acts 28:15). In giving the story of the Christian outreach to the Gentiles, Luke has concentrated on Paul's missionary activities, but he has not given us the full story of Christian missionary expansion.[15] The phrase in Acts 28:14 'And so we came to Rome' has a climactic ring to it.

In this section Luke mentions Paul's arrival in Rome twice (Acts 28:14, 16), probably for emphasis. His narrative has been moving in this direction for a long time. God's plan in Paul's regard (Acts 19:21; 23:11; 27:24) reaches fulfilment. Paul's entrance into Rome is like a triumphant procession. He is greeted by Christians from Rome at two main stopping places on the way, the Forum of Appius (70 kilometres from Rome) and Three Taverns (53 kilometres from Rome). By having Paul met by Christians at these two places, and also at Puteoli, Luke is underlining the links of Paul with the Christian community after his isolation during his imprisonment and trial. Paul is no maverick; he is accepted and welcomed by a Christian community at the heart of the empire. This contact with the Christian community is a source of encouragement for Paul, for which he thanks God (Acts 28:15). Acts 28:16 indicates that Paul was under some kind of house arrest in Rome; from Acts 28:30-31 we gather that this afforded him quite a bit of freedom. At this point the 'we passages' end; attention is focused exclusively on Paul.

Paul's Witness in Rome (Acts 28:17-31)

In this last section of Acts we don't hear anything about Paul's trial before the emperor and its outcome, as we might expect, nor is there anything about Paul's relationship to the Christian community in Rome. It focuses on Paul's message to the Roman Jews and explores dimensions and implications of the fact that the Jews, for the most part, did not respond positively to the Good News of Jesus Christ, while not forgetting that the Good News is a universal message meant for all. The conclusion that Luke wants us to take away from the final part of his work is that God has fulfilled his promise to Israel and is carrying out his plan of extending salvation to all peoples. This final part of Acts has accounts of two meetings with Jews in Rome (Acts 28:17-22 and 28:23-28) and a concluding statement about Paul's witness to all comers (Acts 28:30-31).[16]

First Meeting with Jews in Rome (Acts 28:17-22)

Acts 28:17-22 tells of the first meeting with the leaders of the Roman Jews three days after Paul arrived in the city. Throughout the story of Luke, the opposition to the Good News has come from Jewish leaders. In the story of Acts we have seen that Paul always headed for the Jewish synagogue whenever he arrived in a new place. He cannot do that now because of his house arrest, but he invites the Jewish leaders to come to him (Acts 28:17). In speaking to them, Paul summarises what happened during his imprisonment and trials in Jerusalem and Caesarea. Primary emphasis falls on Paul's claim that he has done nothing against the Israelite people or against their customs (Acts 28:17). We know that he had been accused of that (see Acts 21:21, 28; 24:5-6) and he has already denied the charges (see Acts 25:8, 10). Paul stresses that he has been loyal to Israel and its way of life. Indeed, the ironic fact is that, because of his commitment and faithfulness to the 'hope of Israel', he now finds himself in chains (Acts 28:20). This theme of Israel's hope and its fulfilment in the resurrection has been one of the major themes of Paul's defence speeches (see Acts 23:6; 24:15; 26:6-7). He assures the Jewish leaders that he has no charge to bring against those he refers to as '*my* nation' (Acts 28:19). He comes to Rome as a defendant, not as a plaintiff. He felt compelled to appeal to Caesar because of the way things were turning out.

In Acts 28:17-18 Paul says a couple of things that are not quite in line with how things had happened. He was not 'arrested and handed over to the Romans'. The Romans rescued him from an angry Jewish mob in the Temple area (see Acts 21:31-33). As in Acts 21:11, Luke makes this change to bring out more clearly a parallel between Paul and Jesus who was arrested and handed over to the Romans (see Lk 18:32). The same thing is happening in Acts 28:18 where it is said that the Romans wanted to release Paul. In the story of Acts, Roman officials did not state any intention to release Paul, but only recognised his innocence, especially after Paul had appealed to Rome (see Acts 25:18-19, 25; 26:31-32). Again, the wording of Acts 28:18 is meant to recall the trial of Jesus when Pilate found 'nothing worthy of death' in Jesus' case and announced his intention to release him (Lk 23:15-16), to which the Jews objected (Lk 23:18; see Acts 28:19). In Luke's mind, Paul is reliving the passion of Jesus, so details of Jesus' passion flow into the narration of Paul's passion. The Jewish leaders in Rome reply that they have received no instructions or unfavourable reports from Judea concerning Paul himself (Acts 28:21). But they have heard many negative reports about the Christian 'sect' (*hairesis*) and they would like to hear Paul's views on this (Acts 28:22). The focus is shifting away from the bearer of the message to the message itself.

Second Meeting with Jews in Rome (Acts 28:23-28)

Acts 28:23-28 tells of the second meeting between Paul and the Jewish leaders in Rome. This time a greater number turned up at Paul's lodgings on a fixed day (Acts 28:23). From morning till evening Paul witnesses to the kingdom of God and to Jesus, arguing from Israel's scriptures (the law of Moses and the prophets) (Acts 28:23; see also 28:31 which forms an inclusion with 28:23). The kingdom of God was also the central theme of Jesus' message (see, for instance, Lk 4:43-44; 8:1). The parallelism with Jesus continues. One is reminded of the way Jesus interpreted the Scriptures about himself, beginning with Moses and all the prophets (see Lk 24:27). The preaching about the kingdom of God and the preaching about Jesus go hand in hand (as in Acts 8:12 and 28:31). God's reign is breaking through most powerfully in the Christ event. In Acts 28:24 we get the divided response to Paul's preaching, which is a common occurrence in Acts (see Acts 2:12-13; 4:1-4; 5:12-17; 6:8-14; 9:21-25; 13:42-45; 14:1-2; 17:1-5; 18:4, 12-17; 19:8-10). Some show an initial openness to the message, while others refuse to believe. The Jews are disagreeing among themselves (Acts 28:25). Paul has one last statement for the departing Jews (Acts 28:25-28). Notice how Paul, like Stephen (see Acts 7:52), distances himself from unbelieving Israel by speaking of '*your* ancestors' (Acts 28:25); contrast Acts 28:17 ('*our* ancestors'). Paul quotes Is 6:9-10 (which he takes as the words of the Holy Spirit) in Acts 28:26-27.[17] When God called the prophet Isaiah he told him that the people will not listen to his message. This text was used widely in Christian apologetics in dealing with the Jewish rejection of the Good News (see Rm 11:8; Mk 4:12; Mt 13:14-15; Jn 12:40). Luke briefly refers to it in Lk 8:10, but saves the full quotation for the end of his work.

So this text from Isaiah helped the Christian community understand and cope with the disappointing fact that the Jewish people, for the most part, did not respond positively to the Good News. That was something foreseen by God and consequently will not frustrate God's plan of salvation. God has been faithful to Israel, but they have hindered God's desire to heal them by closing their ears, eyes and heart to God. It is now Paul's unpleasant task to make a disobedient people aware of that. In contrast to the unbelieving Jews who do not listen, Paul in Acts 28:28 refers to Gentiles who will listen.[18] 'To the Gentiles has been sent this salvation of God' also represents a certain shift from what Paul said when speaking to Jews in the synagogue at Antioch of Pisidia: 'to us the message of this salvation has been sent' (Acts 13:26). We are left with the question: Where does this leave the Jews in Luke's understanding of God's unfolding plan of salvation?

Paul's Witness to All Comers in Rome (Acts 28:30-31)

In Acts 28:30-31 we have the picture of Paul in his (rented) lodgings, welcoming *all* over a period of two years and proclaiming the kingdom of God and the teaching about Jesus with all *boldness* (*parrēsia*), which is the hallmark of missionary preaching in Acts, and *without hindrance* (*akōlytōs*). The focus of Paul's preaching is more or less the same as that which was mentioned in Acts 28:23 when Paul was preaching to the Roman Jews – 'proclaiming the kingdom of God and teaching about the Lord Jesus Christ'. Despite Paul's imprisonment, the preaching is 'without hindrance' (*akōlytōs* is the last word in the Greek text of Acts). We are reminded of what is said in 2 Tm 2:9: 'the word of God is not chained'. Nothing can stop the spread of the Good News! The last picture we have of Paul in Acts is that of a missionary continuing to respond faithfully to his God-given vocation of preaching the Good News of Jesus Christ to all.

Let's return to the question of the future of the Jewish mission. Acts 28:28 is the third occasion on which Paul solemnly turns from the Jews to the Gentiles in the story of Acts (see Acts 13:46-47; 18:6). Some detect a note of finality and permanence this time in the sense that Paul is giving up on mission to the unresponsive Jews, after so many rejections on their part, and turning to the Gentiles who will listen. Yet, we should keep in mind that after Paul turned from unresponsive Jews on the two previous occasions he did not give up reaching out to Jews in his mission. Furthermore, there were individuals in the Jewish community in Rome who showed some openness to the message (Acts 28:24). In

Acts 28:30 we are told that Paul welcomed *all* who came to him in his quarters and there is no reason to think that Jews were not among those to whom he preached during his two years under house arrest in Rome. We have seen that Paul, having spoken about turning to the Gentiles in Acts 28:28, continues to preach the message he had been preaching to Jews in Rome. If Paul were preaching only to Gentiles in Acts 28:30-31, we would expect that the content of his preaching would be something like what we find in Acts 14:15-17 (Lystra) and Acts 17:22-31 (Athens). So, to the very end Paul remains faithful to the Lord's calling to bear witness to both Jews and Gentiles (Acts 9:15; 22:15; 26:16-18, 23).

Some comment on what they see as an abrupt ending of the narrative of Acts. We are not told of the outcome of Paul's trial before the imperial court. Was he acquitted after two years in Rome, making it possible for him to continue his missionary career in new places? Or was he found guilty and sentenced to death at this time? We can only speculate without arriving at any degree of certainty. It is better to focus, not on historical questions, but on the message that Luke wants to convey at the end of his narrative. In ending his story, Luke's main interest is not the fate and destiny of Paul but the fate and destiny of the word of God. It has been the story about the progress of the dynamic word of God offering salvation to all people. God's plan of universal salvation is now strikingly demonstrated by having Paul, the servant of God's word, preach the Good News boldly and without hindrance at the heart of the known world.

Luke left his story open-ended. He moves our attention away from Paul's personal end to the ongoing story of Christian mission to 'the ends of the earth,' with the expectation that his readers will see it as their story and as a call to play their part in this continuing mission. Luke sees the preaching of the Good News in Rome as a climactic moment in the story of Christian mission, but Rome is not 'the ends of the earth'. The journey to the 'ends of the earth' continues. In summoning his readers to take part in the ongoing story of Christian mission, Luke holds up Paul as the great model of missionary commitment, steadfastness, courage and fidelity to God's call. Remember Luke's original readers were Christian communities which were losing their missionary enthusiasm and nerve, particularly in the face of Jewish resistance. Crowe ends his commentary on Acts with these words: 'His (Paul's) career illustrated the dynamism of the Gospel. It invites Theophilus and others after him to take their part in the continuing action.'[19]

Reflection on Acts 27:1–28:31

As I write this, we are enduring another wave of the deadly Covid-19 virus. The strong message from those helping us deal with the virus is that we must be focused on the safety of all and not just on our own personal safety. We must always think of our own welfare in the context of the welfare of all. That message is quite similar to Luke's emphasis on the salvation of all as he relates the story of the perilous sea voyage in Acts 27. Luke is reminding us in very dramatic fashion of God's plan of universal salvation which means that the salvation of each one is inextricably linked with the salvation of all. We sink or swim together![20] In an older model of mission the focus was often on the salvation of the individual, and indeed on the salvation of the disembodied soul rather than the whole person. In its mission today, the Church must continually stress that God saves us, not just as individuals, but as people in community. We experience salvation in the context of God's plan of all-inclusive salvation. We live in a world where the principle of 'every man for himself' is very much alive and well. In debates about what should be done, group interests often override the common good. Institutions which were set up to promote international cooperation in building a better world are weakening in the face of excessive nationalism which insists that the interests of one's own nation must always be paramount.

Christian mission today means taking a prophetic stance on behalf of the weak and the voiceless who are often forgotten and marginalised in the rush of individuals, groups and nations to focus only on their own interests and concerns. The present Covid-19 pandemic, which respects no borders, nations or races, is showing us our common humanity and interdependence. But we are also seeing once more how the poor are often those most exposed to the disasters that afflict our world. Proclaiming the message of God's all-inclusive salvation in this situation means doing what we can to ensure the poor are not neglected in the economic fallout from the pandemic and in the distribution of a vaccine.

Furthermore, in considering God's all-inclusive salvation, we must not overlook the salvation of the earth. Our human salvation is also inextricably linked with the salvation of all creation. Christian mission cannot ignore the alarming rate of the extinction of species in the natural world due to the exploitation of the earth that is driven by human greed. It has become increasingly clear that natural disasters (famines, droughts, air and water pollution, soil erosion, hurricanes, flooding, wildfires, etc.) are caused in no small measure by this exploitation. Last year, uncontrollable wildfires raged over vast areas in the western regions of the USA, leaving over thirty people dead, dozens missing, and the homes of very many people completely destroyed. All of this is telling us that environmental issues have to be on the agenda of missionaries promoting God's all-inclusive salvation.

Hospitality continues to be highlighted in the closing chapters of Luke's narrative. The centurion allows Paul to avail of the hospitality of fellow Christians at two stops on his way to Rome. And Luke goes out of his way to tell us how Paul was warmly received by the Christian community in Rome. The exceptional hospitality of the inhabitants of Malta for those who were shipwrecked is quite remarkable. In his Gospel, Luke presents Jesus as the one who came into the world seeking hospitality. Those who welcomed him discovered quickly that he is the host offering them an experience of God's boundless, all-inclusive hospitality. To share in the mission of Jesus means inviting people to sit as brothers and sisters at God's table where no one is excluded. Mission entails giving and receiving hospitality. Many missionaries, who have arrived on foreign shores to share the Good News of God's hospitality, can speak of the extraordinary hospitality they received from those to whom they were sent. In reading the story of Paul's shipwreck on the island of Malta and his experience of hospitality there, one thinks of the migrants today who make a dangerous journey in flimsy boats across the same Adriatic Sea seeking welcome and hospitality. Working to make our communities places of welcome, hospitality and refuge for migrants and asylum seekers, who are often fleeing from areas of conflict, persecution and devastating economic hardship and are seeking a life in keeping with their human dignity, is very much part of the Church's mission today.[21]

As I said in the introduction to this book, I went to Pakistan in 1979, not knowing what Christian mission might mean in a predominantly Muslim country. The temptation was to concentrate only on the 'salvation' of the small Christian minority who felt marginalised and insecure. And working with them in their efforts to secure their basic human rights was an essential part of our mission. But we felt our mission in Pakistan should also include some kind of outreach to Muslims. We have seen above that Luke may be presenting the experience of the hazardous sea journey (Acts 27) and Paul's presence in Malta (Acts 28:1-10) as models for good relationships and cooperation between Christians and non-Christians in the Greco-Roman world where Christians were a small minority. The focus is on friendly relationships and working together for the common good.

Mission in places like Pakistan today must include building good relationships with peoples of other religious traditions and seeking ways of cooperation with them in responding to common human needs. The same applies to mission in nominally Christian countries where there is increasing contact with those belonging to other faiths. This kind of mission does not imply that we factor out any reference to our Christian faith which is the ultimate reason why we are committed to working for the common good. In encouraging others on the ship and cooperating with them for the salvation of all, Paul spoke of his vision of 'an angel of the God to whom I belong and whom I worship' (Acts 27:23-26). When he spoke to non-Christians in Athens, he did not hide his belief in Jesus Christ (Acts 17:31). So, in our dialogue with peoples of other religious traditions we should not be shy in speaking about the faith and hope that sustains us, always respecting the faith of others and not imposing our beliefs. 'Always be ready to make your defence to anyone who demands from you an account of the hope that is in you; yet do it with gentleness and reverence' (1 Pt 3:15-16). Often in situations like this, one witnesses through Christ-like deeds rather than words.[22]

What happens next? That question often springs to mind as we read Luke's lively and engaging narrative. We normally find the answer as the story continues to unfold. But at times Luke leaves things open-ended. For instance, at the end of his well-known parable of the Prodigal Son (or the Two Lost Brothers, in Lk 15:11-32), one of the best short stories ever told, Luke portrays the father inviting the elder son to join in the celebrations on the return of his wayward brother. However, we are not told what the elder brother did. Did he accept or refuse his father's invitation? Leaving the story open-ended is Luke's way of saying to his reader: 'You are the one who must decide how the story ends, because it is your story. Are you going to be compassionate as your Father is compassionate (see Lk 6:36)?' Likewise, Luke leaves his whole story of mission open-ended. At the end of Acts we are left wondering what happens next. And, as he told his original readers, Luke is telling us that the story of mission is our story. We are the ones who decide what happens next by engaging in the ongoing mission of Jesus to the nations in the circumstances in which we find ourselves today. That mission of Jesus is the mission of our faithful and hospitable God who continually reaches out, inviting all to sit at his table as brothers and sisters. Luke understands the mission in terms of the journey of the dynamic and saving word of God from Galilee to Jerusalem in the ministry of Jesus, and then from Jerusalem to the ends of the earth in the ministries of Jesus' disciples. The risen Jesus continues on mission in and through his disciples. The Spirit of the risen Jesus guides and empowers his disciples as they continue his mission. Luke has held up the early Christian missionaries, particularly Paul, as models for us who are now called to play our part in the ongoing mission of Jesus to all nations. Having given us assurance that the God who calls us to mission is the faithful God who fulfils his promises, Luke is telling us that it is now over to us. That is the message and relevance of the Acts of the Apostles for us as missionary disciples of Jesus today.[23]

NOTES

1   See, for instance, Dillon, 'Acts of the Apostles' in *The New Jerome Biblical Commentary*, 764; Johnson, *The Acts of the Apostles*, 450-451.
2   See, for instance, Marshall, *Acts*, 401-403.
3   Johnson gives a balanced view on the historicity and literary genre of Acts 27: 'There is no hard and fast line between the narrative conventions of ancient history and fiction. All ancient historians used what contemporaries would regard as "fictional" techniques ... A sound interpretation of this section of Acts, therefore, should avoid the extreme either/or of fiction vs. history. To cling ferociously to the factual character of every detail is not only to ignore the obvious literary motifs, but also to avoid the question most pressing for answer: why does Luke devote so much attention to this voyage? ... On the other hand, to move directly from the presence of literary motifs to the claim that Luke was simply fabricating the entire incident is, as I have suggested, reckless. There is nothing implausible about the basic series of events as they are described, if we leave aside the disproportionate role ascribed to Paul. A sound position recognises the possibility that the narrative is as a whole essentially historical, but also acknowledges its literary (or even "fictional") shaping' (*The Acts of the Apostles*, 451-452).
4   The Augustan Cohort (one thousand soldiers) was stationed in Syria. 'Augustan' (Imperial) was probably an honorific title given to several cohorts.

5 Paul sailed on three different ships during his last journey to Rome. From Caesarea to Myra he was on a ship of Adramyttium (Acts 27:2); from Myra he sailed on an Alexandrian ship which was shipwrecked on Malta (Acts 27:6); the third ship was another Alexandrian ship which travelled from Malta to Italy (Acts 28:11). Egypt was for a long time the granary for the empire and there were regular shipments of grain from there to Rome. There was a special bonus for ships which transported grain in the dangerous winter months.

6 The word used here is *skeuos* and many take this to mean an anchor to slow the ship; Johnson (*The Acts of the Apostles*, 448) thinks it means a sail, perhaps the mainsail.

7 'This announcement (that all will be saved) is a key to understanding the rest of the episode, for it determines what must happen, and the acts of sailors, soldiers, and Paul are to be judged in the light of it. From this point on, no method of escape is acceptable that doesn't include all. Opportunities arise for the sailors to escape, abandoning the rest (v. 30), and for the soldiers to escape after killing their prisoners (v. 42). These plans are thwarted, in spite of the risk involved in trying to get the large ship close to the shore and allowing prisoners to swim for their lives when they might escape. These plans are wrong, not only because they endanger Paul, but also because they offend against the divine plan of saving all' (Tannehill, *The Narrative Unity of Luke-Acts*, vol. 2, 333).

8 Acts 27:37 is an aside to tell us that there were 276 persons on the ship; this is to keep the *all* in view.

9 *The Acts of the Apostles*, 459.

10 *The Narrative Unity of Luke-Acts*, vol. 2, 335-336.

11 See Mullins, *The Acts of the Apostles*, 253-254, for references in the Hebrew Scriptures to God's control over the sea and protection for those threatened by its power (for instance, Pss 77:19; 89:8; 107:23-30).

12 'The possibility of salvation in the social and political sphere depends on Christians and non-Christians being willing to follow the lead of Paul, Julius, and the sailors, when they are acting for the good of all. Perhaps the Christian prophet, like Paul, will have a special role in conveying an understanding of what is possible and promised by God, but non-Christians also have important roles' (Tannehill, *The Narrative Unity of Luke-Acts*, vol. 2, 338-339).

13 *The Acts of the Apostles*, 466-467.

14 *The Narrative Unity of Luke-Acts*, vol. 2, 341.

15 'By this time in the early 60s, Christian communities have been at Rome for about twenty years. But in the flow of the story that has

centred on Peter and Paul, a climax comes with the arrival in the capital of the great missionary' (Brown, *An Introduction to the New Testament*, 314).

[16] Acts 28:29 (footnote in NRSV), which refers to Jews arguing vigorously among themselves, is usually omitted because of weak manuscript evidence.

[17] Acts 28:26-27 is taken from the Greek version (LXX) of Is 6:9-10, which has God predicting that the people will not listen to the prophet's message, rather than the Hebrew version of the same text which speaks of God making the people unresponsive!

[18] 'The function of these concluding words about the Gentiles is not to justify the Gentile mission, which has been done long ago, but to jar the Roman Jews by the contrast between their deafness and the Gentiles' readiness to hear' (Tannehill, *The Narrative Unity of Luke-Acts*, vol. 2, 348).

[19] *The Acts*, 200.

[20] 'True, a worldwide tragedy like the Covid-19 pandemic momentarily revived a sense that we are a global community, all in the same boat, where one person's problems are the problems of all. Once more we realised that no one is saved alone; we can only be saved together' (Pope Francis, *Fratelli Tutti*, no. 32; see also no. 137).

[21] In *Fratelli Tutti* (see nos 37-41 and 129-135), Pope Francis says that the right response to needy migrants and asylum seekers today can be summarised by four words: welcome, protect, promote and integrate. Elsewhere he says that the Church in its mission is 'called to be the house of the Father, with doors always wide open' (*Evangelii Gaudium*, no. 47).

[22] See what we said in Chapter 6 above, when reflecting on Paul's mission in Athens (Acts 17:16-34).

[23] Speaking of the end of Acts, Kurz (*The Acts of the Apostles*, 386) has this to say: 'This open-ended conclusion implies a challenge for us, his readers. The examples of Peter, John, Stephen, Philip, Barnabas and Paul summon us too to be daring witnesses to Jesus. It is now up to us to continue the proclamation of the gospel boldly and without hindrance, no matter what obstacles we may encounter.'

FURTHER READING

Acts of the Apostles

Brown, Raymond E., *An Introduction to the New Testament,* (New York: Doubleday, 1997), 279-332.

Brown, Raymond E., *A Once-and-Coming Spirit at Pentecost* (Collegeville: Liturgical Press, 1994).

Crowe, Jerome, *The Acts*, New Testament Message 8 (Dublin: Veritas, 1979).

Dillon, Richard J., 'Acts of the Apostles,' in *The New Jerome Biblical Commentary,* ed. R.E. Brown et al. (London: Chapman, 1989), 722-767.

Fitzmyer, Joseph A., *The Acts of the Apostles*, The Anchor Bible, vol. 31 (New York: Doubleday, 1998).

Gallagher, Robert L., and Hertig, Paul, eds, *Mission in Acts. Ancient Narratives in Contemporary Context* (New York: Orbis Books, 2004).

Johnson, Luke Timothy, *The Acts of the Apostles,* Sacra Pagina series, vol. 5 (Collegeville: Glazier, 1992).

Kurz, William S., *Acts of the Apostles*, Catholic Commentary on Sacred Scripture Series (Grand Rapids, Michigan: Baker Academic, 2013).

Marshall, I. Howard, *Acts*, Tyndale NT Commentaries (Grand Rapids: Eerdmans 1980).

Marshall, I. H., *The Acts of the Apostles*, New Testament Guides (Sheffield: JSOT Press, 1992).

Mullins, Michael, *The Acts of the Apostles* (Dublin: Columba Press, 2013).

Senior, Donald and Stuhlmueller, Carroll, *The Biblical Foundations for Mission* (New York: Orbis Books, 1983), 255-279.

Tannehill, Robert C., *The Narrative Unity of Luke-Acts*, vol. 2 (Philadelphia: Fortress Press, 1990).

Mission Today

Bevans, Stephen, ed., *A Century of Catholic Mission*, Regnum Edinburgh Centenary Series, vol. 15 (Oxford: Regnum Books International, 2013).

Bevans, Stephen B. and Schroeder, P., *Prophetic Dialogue. Reflections on Christian Mission Today* (New York: Orbis Books, 2011).

Bosch, David J., *Transforming Mission. Paradigm Shifts in the Theology of Mission* (New York: Orbis Books, 1991).

Pope Francis, *Evangelii Gaudium. The Joy of the Gospel* (translated and published by the Catholic Truth Society, London, 2013).

Pope Francis, *Gaudete et Exsultate. On the Call to Holiness in Today's World* (translated and published by the Catholic Truth Society, London, 2018).

Pope Francis, *Laudato Si'. On Care for our Common Home* (translated and published by the Catholic Truth Society, London, 2015).

Pope John Paul II, *Mission of the Redeemer (Redemptoris Missio). On the Permanent Validity of the Church's Missionary Mandate* (published by St Paul Books and Media, Boston, 1991).

Ross, Cathy and Bevans, Stephen B., eds, *Mission on the Road to Emmaus. Constants, Context and Prophetic Dialogue* (London: SCM Press, 2015).